Jiffy
Phrasebook
FRENCH

Langenscheidt
NEW YORK

Phonetic Transcriptions: Walter Glanze Word Books
(The Glanze Intersound System)

Jiffy Phrasebooks are also available for many other languages.

*Jiffy Travel Packs combine the Jiffy Phrasebooks with a
travel-oriented 60-minute cassette. Each can be used independently
of the other.
(Jiffy Travel Pack French ISBN 0-88729-976-8)*

*For detailed information please contact
Langenscheidt Publishers, Inc.
46-35 54th Road, Maspeth, NY 11378
(718) 784-0055*

INFORMATION

GUIDE TO THE USE OF THE PHRASEBOOK

This French phrasebook offers you all the important words and phrases you may need on a visit to France. The phonetic transcriptions which follow the French expressions are designed as an aid to correct pronunciation, and the systematic arrangement of the phrasebook will help you to find what you are looking for in the shortest possible time.

Structure of the phrasebook

The phrasebook is divided into 20 chapters. It begins with general words and phrases, followed by sections on transportation, accommodations, food and drink, and many other important aspects of travel abroad. There are chapters on shopping, health, cultural activities, and entertainment; the appendix gives you lists of common signs and abbreviations, weights and measures, and colors. For easy reference, English words and phrases are printed in heavy black type, while the French translations are in blue. Following these are the phonetic transcriptions of the French phrases in normal black type.

Occasionally two or more phrases have been combined and the interchangeable elements given in italics. For example, the sentence "Is it going to *rain (snow)?*" corresponds to the "Va-t-il *pleuvoir (neiger)*?" Thus "Is it going to rain?" is translated "Va-t-il pleuvoir?" and "Is it going to snow?" becomes "Va-t-il neiger?"

In the boxes you will find help on certain language difficulties, tips on general etiquette, and information on travel, eating out, using the telephone, etc., which will help you get by in everyday situations you may encounter while traveling abroad.

An asterisk at the beginning of a sentence indicates that this is something someone else might say to you.

French pronunciation

On pp. 8–11 you will find a detailed guide to French pronunciation. Most of the symbols used in the phonetic system are taken from the Latin alphabet, so you should have no difficulty getting accustomed to the transcriptions.

French grammar

If you would like to get to know some important aspects of French grammar, the brief survey on pp. 195–202 will give you a basic grounding. Apart from offering you an insight into the structure of the French language and helping you to understand the expressions in the phrasebook, this grammatical survey will also enable you to form simple sentences of your own.

Traveler's Dictionary and Index

The glossary at the end of the book is 53 pages long and is for quick reference to words and phrases. The translations are followed by phonetic transcriptions and page references, so that this glossary serves as an index as well.

Carry this phrasebook with you all the time to make the most of your stay.

CONTENTS

FRENCH PRONUNCIATION

The sounds of a foreign language have to be learned by hearing and imitating a native or near-native speaker of that language. No amount of written information will teach you the true pronunciation of a foreign word or phrase. Many transcription systems have been devised toward this purpose; but all of them use either unfamiliar combinations of letters or odd-looking new characters-combinations or characters that have to be learned in addition to learning the foreign language.

The pronunciation system that was developed for the Langenscheidt Language Guides*) is entirely different: The symbols you find here are the ones you are likely to be familiar with from your use of high-school, college, or desk dictionaries of the **English** language. (That is, the symbols are the same ordinary letters of the alphabet with the same markings, such as [ē] for the vowel sound in he.)

This new pronunciation system is meant to be **an approximation, serving practical needs**, as encountered by the traveler. But, then, even those complicated systems remain an approximation. The true sounds, as we have said, must be learned by listening.

The basic symbols you see in the table are the same that you will find in other Langenscheidt Language Guides for speakers of English. Therefore, when using these Guides in traveling from country to country, you don't have to shift from one set of symbols to another.

For French, the basic symbols of the table are supplemented by two symbols for sounds that have no equivalent in English. These two symbols are set in italic type – with the understanding that you may use the sound of the regular (the preceding nonitalicized) symbol until you have learned the special sound (using [ä] for [*ä*] and [ē] for *ē*]). This is one of the **backup** features that are unique to this system.

The syllables of a French word are usually stressed evenly, with perhaps a slightly greater emphasis on the last syllable. Therefore, no accent marks are shown (except for the two combinations mentioned beneath the table).

To avoid ambiguity, two neighboring vowel symbols (and occasionally two consonant symbols) are separated by a raised dot [·]. This separation is meant to be a convenience to the eye and usually does not mean a break in pronunciation: *réalité* [rä·älētā].

The transcription is that of individual words, even in a sentence (except for some "liaisons"; see also the comment beneath the table). The rhythm of a sentence or phrase has to be learned by ear.

---

*) The Glanze Intersound System

Vowels

Symbol	Approximate Sound	Examples
[ä]	The a of father; the o of mother.	*madame* [mädäm] *garage* [gäräzh] *gâteau* [gätō] *tasse* [täs]
[ā]	The a of fate (but without the "upglide").	*été* [ātā]
[ā̄]	A French sound that has to be learned by listening. (Round the lips for the o of nose; then, without moving the lips, try to pronounce the a of fate.) Until you have learned this sound, use the a of fate, which will be understood.	*deux* [dā̄] *chanteuse* [shäNtā̄z] *oeuf* [ā̄f] *fleur* [flā̄r]
[e]	The e of met.	*adresse* [ädres]
[ē]	The e of he.	*midi* [mēdē] *dire* [dēr]
[ē̄]	A French sound that has to be learned by listening. (Round the lips for the o of nose; then, without the lips, try ro pronounce the e of he.) Until you have learned this sound, use the e of he, which will be understood.	*fumer* [fē̄mā] *déjà vu* [dāzhä vē̄]
[ō]	The o of nose (but without the "upglide").	*rideau* [rēdō] *rôle* [rōl]
[ô]	The o of often. (In French, sometimes shorter, as in *moment*; sometimes longer, as in *sport*.)	*moment* [mômäN] *sport* [spôr]
[oo]	The u of rule.	*trou* [troo] *rouge* [roozh]
[ə]	The neutral vowel sound (like e in listen), always unstressed, such as the a in ago or the u in focus.	*je* [zhə] *demi* [dəmē]

[N]	This symbol does not stand for a sound but shows that the preceding vowel is nasal – is pronounced through nose and mouth at the same time. It has to be learned by listening. (Do not use [äng], [ông], or [eng] instead of nasals.)	*temps* [täN] *nom* [nôN] *matin* [mäteN] *parfum* [pärfeN]

Note also these combinations:

[ô·ä] as in *roi* [rô·ä], *voyage* [vô·äyäzh]
[ô·eN] as in *loin* [lô·eN]
[yeN] as in *bien* [byeN]
[ē·ē] as in *nuit* [nē·ē]
[o͞o·ē] as in *weekend* [o͞o·ēkend], *oui* [o͞o·ē]
[o͞o·e] as in *souhaiter* [so͞o·etä]
(Each of these combinations should be pronounced as almost one "gliding" sound – also [ē·ē] and [o͞o·ē] below.)

Consonants

Here are the most important pronunciation rules: Although the pronunciation of most consonants in French is usually quite similar to English, French consonants are lighter and clearer. The initial *t* and *d* are subtler and pronounced next to the teeth. The initial *p* is softer. The final *s* is never pronounced except when in *liaison* (i.e. when preceding a word beginning with a vowel or a mute h, *pas à pas* [päzäpä]).

Vowel combinations with the letters *c* and *g* deserve special attention. You must distinguish between those which are followed by a, o, u, and consonants and those which are followed by e and i. The pronunciation of *c* and *g* depends on the letters which follow them:

c before a, o, u and consonants is like k [k]: *carte*.

c before e, i and y is an unvoiced s [s]: *cent*.

When a *c* followed by a, o or u is pronounced like [s] rather than [k], then a cedilla (*cédille*) indicates this: *garçon*.

g before a, o, u and consonants is like the g [g] in good: *gare*.

g before e, i and y is an unvoiced fricative [zh], e.g. the sound of the s in pleasure: *Gérard*.

When a *g* followed by a, o, or u takes the [zh] pronunciation rather than the [g] pronunciation, an e is added: *Georges*.

When a *g* followed by e, i or y takes the [g] pronunciation rather than the [zh] pronunciation, a u is added: *guichet*.

ch before vowels is usually pronounced like the sh [sh] in ship: *chapeau*; before consonants and at the end of the word like k [k]: *chronique*.

h is silent.

j is soft, pronounced like the s in pleasure [zh], never like the j in judge: *journal* [zho͞ornäl].

l combined with i is soft: *soleil* [sôlä·ē]

qu is pronounced like k [k], the u is silent: *quarante* [käräNt].

r is a "fricative" r, resembling the j of Spanish Juan: *rire* [rēr].

s at the beginning of a word and after consonants is unvoiced [s], pronounced like the s in safe: *salle* [säl].

s between vowels is voiced s, pronounced like the s in rose: *rosé* [rōzā].

y as a consonant is pronounced [y], like the y in yes: *payer* [pāyā]. A frequent combination ist [ny] as in *agneau* [änyō].

z is always a soft, voiced s [z] as in rose: *douze* [do͞oz].

There are four exceptional cases in which the last syllable of a combination has no stress. This absence of stress is shown through a **preceding accent mark**:

[fē′ē] and [o͞o′ē] as in *fille* [fē′ē] and *bouteille* [bo͞otä′ē]

[b′əl] *as in table* [täb′əl]

or through **parentheses**:

[(ər)] as in *libre* [lēb(ər)]

[n(yə)] as in *ligne* [lēn(yə)]

(The [ə] in the last three examples should be pronounced as faintly as possible.)

French accent marks do not indicate stress but pronunciation. The *accent aigu* ′ (acute accent) over e indicates a closed sound: *é* = [ā]. The *accent grave* ` (grave accent) indicates an open sound: *è* = [ā], and is also used to differentiate between words which sound the same: *ou* = or, *où* = where. The *accent circonflexe* ^ (circumflex accent) can be placed over all vowels [â, ê, î, ô, û] and indicates a drawing-out of the sound. The *cédille* (cedilla) is placed under the letter c to indicate the pronunciation [s]: *français* [fräNsä].

Among other aspects of French that may be learned through listening is "liaison", namely, the linking of the final sound of a word with the initial sound of the next (e.g. *à* [ä] *quelle* [kel] *heure* [ār] = [ä ke lär]) – and silent letters often becoming pronounced (e.g. *ils* [ēl] + *ont* [ôN] = [ēl zôN]) – or pronounced letters sometimes becoming changed (e.g. *en* [äN] + *avion* [ävyôN] = [änävyôN]).

GENERAL WORDS AND PHRASES

Greetings

Good morning!	**Good afternoon!**	**Good evening!**
Bonjour!	Bonjour!	Bonsoir!
bôNzhōōr	bôNzhōōr	bôNsô·är

Hello!	**Hello!** *(on answering phone)*	**Hi!**
Salut!	Allô	Salut!
sälē	älō	sälē

In French it is considered impolite if you don't address someone with monsieur, madame or mademoiselle at the end of a greeting, when addressing someone, or after a short answer (like oui, non, si etc).

---

*Welcome! (Glad to see you!)
Soyez le bienvenu (la bienvenue, les bienvenus).
sô·äyä lə byeNvenē (lä byeNvenē, lā byeNvenē)

How are you?
Ça va?
sä vä

*Did you have a good trip?
Avez- vous fait bon voyage?
ävä-vōō fā bôN vô·äyäzh

I'm delighted to see you.
Très heureux de vous (te) voir!
trāzārā də vōō (tə) vô·är

How're you doing?
Comment allez-vous (vas-tu)?
kômäNtälā-vōō (vä-tē)

How's the family?
Comment va votre famille?
kômäN vä vôt(ər) fämē'ē

My ... is sick.
Mon (Ma) ... est malade.
môN (mä) ... ā mäläd

Did you sleep well?
Avez-vous bien dormi?
ävä-vōō byeN dôrmē

And you?
Et vous?
ā vōō

Thanks, just fine.
Bien (Assez bien), merci!
byeN (äsä byeN), mersē

We're feeling fine.
Nous nous sentons bien (très bien).
nōō nōō säNtôN byeN (trā byeN)

Thanks for your cordial welcome.
Je vous remercie (Nous vous remercions) de l'accueil cordial.
zhə vōō remersē (nōō vōō remersē·ôN) də läkā'ē kôrdyäl

Forms of Address

Mr. *(name)*	Monsieur *(nom)*	məsyā
Mrs. *(name)*	Madame *(nom)*	mädäm
Sir, Madam	Monsieur, Madame ...	məsyā, mädäm
Miss	Mademoiselle	mädəmô·äzel
Ladies and Gentle-	Mesdames et Messieurs	mädämzä mesyā
men!		
Your wife/husband ..	Votre femme/mari	vôt(ər) fäm/märē
Doctor/Professor	Monsieur le Docteur,	məsyā lə dôktār
(when addressing him)	Monsieur le Professeur	məsyā lə prôfesār

> *When using the* "Monsieur le Docteur" *or* "Monsieur le Professeur" *form of address, the proper name is usually omitted.*

Letters

Mr. Jean Duval	Monsieur Jean Duval ..	məsyā zhäN dēväl
Mrs. Marie Duval ...	Madame Marie Duval .	mädäm märē dēväl

> *In France, a married woman does not take her husband's first name.*

Dear Mr. Duval	Cher Monsieur, ...	shär məsyā
Dear Mrs. Duval	Chère Madame, ...	shär mädäm
Dear Miss Duval	Chère Mademoiselle, ..	shär mädəmô·äzel
Dear Peter	Cher Pierre, ...	shär pyär
Dear Michèle, ...	Chère Michèle, ...	shär mēshel
Gentlemen	Messieurs, ...	mesyā
Dear Mr. Martin, *(to a*	Monsieur, ...	məsyā
respected friend) ...		
Dear Mrs. Martin, ...	Madame, ...	mädäm
Yours respectfully,	Veuillez agréer, *Mon-*	vãyā ägrā·ā, məsyā
(old-fashioned form)	*sieur (Madame, Made-*	(mädäm, mädə-
	moiselle), l'expression de	mô·äzel), lekspre-
	mes sentiments distin-	syôN də mä säNtē-
	gués.	mäN dēsteNgā
Yours sincerely,		
Cordially yours, ...	Amitiés, ...	ämētyā
Kindest regards,		
All the best, (Love,) ..	affectueusement, ...	äfektē·āzəmäN

Introductions

My name is . . .
Je m'appelle . . .
zhə mäpel

my son	mon fils	môN fēs
my daughter	ma fille	mä fē'ē
my friend *(male)*	mon ami	mônämē
my friend *(female)* . .	mon amie	mônämē
my friends	mes amis	mäzämē

> *In French, a man speaking of his girlfriend will say* ma petite amie *and a woman speaking of her boyfriend will say* mon petit ami. *Other friends are referred to as* mon ami(e) *or* un(e) ami(e) à moi.

my fiancé	mon fiançe	môN fē·äNsä
my fiancée	ma fiançée	mä fē·äNsä

Glad to meet you. (How do you do?)
Très heureux de faire votre connaissance.
träsārā də fär vôt(ər) kônesäNs

Haven't we seen one another before?
Ne nous connaissons-nous pas déjà de vue?
nə nōō kônesôN-nōō pä dāzhä də vē

Do you live here?	**Are you** *Mr. (Mrs.)* **Duval?**
Vous habitez ici?	Êtes-vous *Monsieur (Madame)* Duval?
vōōzäbētä ēsē	āt-vōō məsyä (mädäm) dēväl

What is your name, please?
Quel est votre nom, s'il vous plaît?
kel ā vôt(ər) nôN, sēl vōō plä

Where are you from?	**We've been here for a week.**
D'où venez-vous?	Nous sommes ici depuis une semaine.
dōō venā-vōō	nōō sômzēsē depē·ē ēn smen

Do you like it here?	***Are*** *you* **here alone?**
Ça vous plaît ici?	*Êtes-vous* seul(e)s (*Es-tu* seul[e]) ici?
sä vōō plä ēsē	āt-vōō säl (ā-tē säl) ēsē

Where *do you work?*
Où est-ce que *vous travaillez (tu travailles)?*
ōō eske vōō träväyā (tē trävä'ē)

What do you do for a living?
Quelle est votre profession?
kel ā vôt(ər) prôfesyôN

What are you studying?
(What's your major?)
Qu'est-ce que *vous étudiez?*
keske vōōzātēdyā

---

*The word élève is a general term for pupils up to the age of 18,
whereas lycéen denotes those in a lycée (beginning at age 11), and
étudiant generally means students at an institute of higher learning. A
professeur is a teacher in a lycée or at an institute of higher learning.*

Got some time?
Avez-vous un peu de temps?
ävä-vōōzeN pə də täN

What time shall we meet?
Quand nous retrouvons-nous?
käN nōō rətrōōvóvóN-nōō

Shall we go *to the* . . .?
On va *au (à la)* . . .?
ôN vä ō (älä) . . .

Please leave me alone!
Laissez-moi tranquille, s'il vous plaît.
lāsā-mô·ä träNkēl, sēl vōō plā

A Visit

Is *Mr. (Mrs., Miss)* . . . at home?
Monsieur (Madame, Mademoiselle) . . . est-il chez lui (est-elle chez elle)?
məsyā (mädäm, mädəmô·äzel) . . . etēl shä lē·ē (etel shäzel)

Could I speak to *Mr. (Mrs., Miss)* . . .?
Je peux parler à *Monsieur (Madame, Mademoiselle)* . . .?
zhə pä pärlä ä məsyā (mädäm, mädəmô·äzel) . . .

Does *Mr. (Mrs., Miss)* live here?
Est-ce que *Monsieur (Madame, Mademoiselle)* . . . habite ici?
eske məsyā (mädäm, mädəmô·äzel) . . . äbēt ēsē

I'm looking for . . .
Je cherche . . .
zhə shärsh . . .

When will *he (she)* be home?
Quand rentre-t-il *(elle)?*
käN räNtrətēl (-el)

I'll drop by again later.
Je reviendrai plus tard.
zhə revyeNdrā plē tär

When *can I (shall we)* come?
Quand est-ce *que je peux (qu'il nous faut)* venir?
käNdeske zhə pä (kēl nōō fō) venēr

I'd (We'd) love to come.
Je viendrai (Nous viendrons) très volontiers.
zhə vyeNdrä (nōō vyeNdrôN) trä vōlôNtyä

*Come in!	*Please have a seat!	*Come right in.
Entrez!	Prenez place, s'il vous plaît!	Entrez!
äNträ	prenä pläs, sēl vōō plä	äNträ

*Just a minute, please.	Thanks so much for the invitation.
Une minute, s'il vous plaît!	Merci beaucoup pour votre invitation!
ēn mēnēt, sēl vōō plä	mersē bōkōō pōōr vôtreNvētäsyôN

Am I bothering you?	Please don't go to a lot of trouble.
Je vous dérange?	Ne vous dérangez pas!
zhə vōō däräNzh	nə vōō däräNzhä pä

*What'll you have? (What may I offer you?)/*Would you like . . .?*
Qu'est-ce que je peux vous offrir?/Est-ce que vous voulez . . .?
keske zhə pā vōōzôfrēr/eske vōō vōōlä . . .

Mr. (Mrs.) Duval sends you his (her) regards (love).
Monsieur (Madame) Duval vous transmet son bon souvenir.
məsyā (mädäm) dēväl vōō träNsmä sôN bôN sōōvnēr

I'm afraid I've got to go now.
Je regrette, mais il faut que je m'en aille maintenant.
zhə regret, mä ēl fō ke zhə mäNä'ē meNt·näN

Thanks so much for *a lovely evening (coming)*.
Merci infiniment pour *cette charmante soirée (votre visite)*.
mersē eNfēnēmäN pōōr set shärmäNt sô·ärä (vôt[ər] vēzēt)

Please give *Mr. (Mrs.)* . . . my best regards.
Saluez *Monsieur (Madame)* . . . de ma part, s'il vous plaît!
sälē·ā məsyā (mädäm) . . . də mä pär, sēl vōō plä

I hope we'll meet again soon!
J'espère que nous nous reverrons bientôt!
zhespär ke nōō nōō reverôN byeNtō

---

*Your French may not be perfect, but the French, like anyone, are
more receptive to foreigners who at least make the effort to speak
their language. Try to use polite expressions such as* s'il vous plaît,
merci beaucoup, pardon *etc. wherever appropriate.*

Farewells

The French say À bientôt! *when they mean that they will be seeing you soon (but not necessarily). It's a more casual way of saying goodbye than* au revoir. *The greeting* Salut! *is a familiar term and depending on when it is said, it means Hi! or Bye!*

Good-bye!
Au revoir!
ō revô·är

See you soon!
À bientôt!
ä byeNtō

Good night!
Bonne nuit!
bônē·ē

See you tomorrow!
À demain!
ä demeN

All the best!
Bonne chance!
bôn shäNs

***Have a good trip!**
Bon voyage!
bôN vô·äyäzh

I'd like to say good-bye!
Je vais *vous (te)* dire au revoir.
zhə vä vōō (tə) dēr ō-revô·är

I'm afraid we have to go.
Malheureusement nous devons partir.
mäl*ā*r*ā*z·mäN nōō devôN pärtēr

Thanks so much for coming.
Je vous remercie de votre visite.
zhə vōō remersē də vôt(ər) vēzēt

Come again soon!
Au plaisir de vous revoir!
ō plāzēr də vōō revô·är

When can we get together again?
Quand nous reverrons-nous?
käN nōō reverôN-nōō

I'll give you a call tomorrow.
Je téléphonerai demain.
zhə tālāfōnərā dəmeN

Can I give you a lift home?
Vous permettez que je vous raccompagne chez vous?
vōō permetä ke zhə vōō räkôNpän(yə) shä vōō

It's pretty late.
Il est déjà tard.
ēl ā dāzhä tär

Give ... my best!
Saluez ...!
sälē·ā

Thanks very much.
Merci beaucoup!
mersē bōkōō

I enjoyed myself very much.
Ça m' a beaucoup plu.
sä mä bōkōō plē

I'll *take you to (give you a lift to)* the ...
Je *vous accompagne (t'accompagne)* encore *jusqu'au (jusqu'à la)* ...
zhə vōōzäkôNpän(yə) (täkôNpän[yə]) äNkôr zhēskō (zhēskä lä)

General Questions

When?	**Why?**	**What?**	**Which? What kind of . . .?**
Quand?	Pourquoi!	Quoi?	*Quel (Quelle?)* . . .
käN	pōōrkô·ä	kô·ä	kel (kel)

If you don't understand what someone has just said, you can say Comment? *or* Pardon? *Using* Quoi? *in this situation is not appropriate.*

Who?	**To whom?**	**With whom?**	**Whom?**
Qui?	À qui?	Avec qui?	Qui?
kē	ä kē	ävekē	kē

How?	**How long?**	**How *much (many)*?**
Comment?	Combien de temps?	Combien de . . .?
kômäN	kôNbyeN də täN	kôNbyeN də

Where?	**Where from?**	**Where to?**	**What for?**
Où?	D'où?	Où?	Pourquoi?
ōō	dōō	ōō	pōōrkô·ä

Is . . . allowed here?	**Can I . . .?**	**Do you need . . .?**
Peut-on . . . ici?	Est-ce que je peux?	Avez-vous besoin de . . .
pətôN . . . ēsē	eske zhə pä	ävä-vōō bezô·eN də

Have you (got) . . .?	**What's that?**	**When can I get . . .?**
Avez-vous . . .?	Qu'est-ce que c'est?	Je peux avoir . . . quand?
ävä-vōō	keske sä	zhə pä ävô·är . . . käN

What time do you open (close)?	**What would you like? (What can I do for you?) / May I help you?)**
À quelle heure vous *ouvrez (fermez)*?	Que désirez-vous?
äkelär vōōzōōvrä (fermä)	ke dāzērā-vōō

What happened?	**What does that mean?**	***Whom do you wish to see?**
Qu'est-ce qui s'est passé?	Qu'est-ce que cela veut dire?	Qui cherchez-vous?
keskē sä päsä	keske sələ vä dēr	kē sharshā-vōō

How much does that cost?	**What are you looking for?**
Combien ça coûte?	Que *cherchez-vous (cherches-tu)*?
kôNbyeN sä kōōt	ke shārshā-vōō (shārsh-tē)

Who's there?   *Who can (Could you) ...?)*   **Whose is that?**
Qui est là?   *Qui peut* (Vous pourriez) ...?   À qui est-ce?
kē ā lä   kē p*ä* (vōo pōorē·ā)   ä kē es

What's *your* name?   **What do you call ...?**
Quel est *votre (ton)* nom?   Comment s'appelle ...?
kel ā vôt(ər) (tôN) nôN   kômäN säpel ...

How do I get *to* ...?
Pour aller *à (au)* ..., s'il vous plaît?
pōor älä ä (ō) ..., sēl vōo plä

How does that work?   **How long does it take?**
Comment est-ce que cela marche?   Combien de temps faut-il?
kômäN eske sǝlä märsh   kôNbyeN dǝ täN fōtēl

How much do I get?   **How much is it?**
Je touche combien?   Ça fait combien?
zhǝ tōosh kôNbyeN   sä fä kôNbyeN

Where *can I find* ... *(is ... located)*?   **Where *is (are)* ...?**
Où se trouve ...?   Où *est (sont)* ...?
ōo sǝ trōov ...   ōo ā (sôN) ...

Where's *the nearest* ...?   **Where can I ...?**
Où est *le prochain (la*   Je peux ... où?
prochaine) ...?   zhǝ p*ä* ... ōo
ōo ā lǝ prôsheN (lä prôshen) ...

Where can I *get (find)* ...?   **Where *is (are)* there ...?**
Je peux *avoir (trouver)* ... où?   Où y a-t-il ...?
zhǝ p*ä*zävô·är (trōovä) ... ōo   ōo yätēl ...

Where *do you live?*   **Where are we?**
Où *habitez-vous (habites-tu)?*   Où sommes-nous?
ōo äbētä-vōo (äbēt-t*ē*)   ōo sôm-nōo

Where do you come from?   **Where are you going?**
D'où *venez-vous (viens-tu)?*   Où *allez-vous (vas-tu)?*
dōo venä-vōo (vyeN-t*ē*)   ōo älä-vōo (vä-t*ē*)

Where does this *road (path)* lead?
Où va *ce chemin (cette route)?*
ōo vä se shmeN (set rōot)

Wishes, Requests

Would you please *bring (give, show)* **me** ....?
Apportez (donnez, montrez) -moi ..., s'il vous plaît.
äpôrtā (dônā, môNtrā) -mô·ä ... sēl vōō plä

Would you please tell me ...?   **Would you please** *get (fetch)* ...?
Dites-moi ..., s'il vous plaît.   Allez me *chercher* ..., s'il vous plaît.
dēt-mô·ä ..., sēl vōō plä   älā mə shārshā ..., sēl vōō plä

Beg your pardon? (Say again?)   *What can I do for you? (May I help*
Pardon?   *you?)*
pärdôN   Que désirez-vous?
   ke dāzērā-vōō

I'd (We'd) like ...   **I need** ...
J'aimerais (Nous aimerions) ...   J'ai besoin de ...
zhāmerā (nōōzāmeryôN) ...   zhā bezô·eN də ...

I'd rather have ...   **Could I** *have (get)* ...?
J'aimerais mieux ...   Je peux *avoir* ...?
zhāmerā my*a* ...   zhə p*a*zävô·är ...

Please help me!   **Certainly!**
Aidez-moi, s'il vous plaît.   Bien entendu.
ādā-mô·ä, sēl vōō plä   byeNäNtäNd*ē*

Allow me? (Excuse me?)   **Get well soon!**
Vous permettez?   Bon rétablissement!
vōō permetā   bôN rātäblēs·mäN

All the best!   **Have** *a good time (fun)!*   **I wish** *you* ...
Bonne chance!   Amusez-vous bien!   Je *vous (te)* souhaite ...
bôn shäNs   äm*ē*zā-vōō byeN   zhə vōō (tə) sōō·et ...

Thanks

Thanks (Thank you) very much!
Merci (Merci bien)!
mersē (byeN)

Thanks a lot!
Merci beaucoup!
mersē bōkōō

No, thanks.
Non, merci.
nôN, mersē

Thank you too!
Merci à *vous (toi)* aussi!
mersē ä vōō (tô·ä) ôsē

I'm very grateful to you.
Je *vous (te)* suis très reconnaissant.
zhə vōō (tə) sē·ē trä rekônäsäN

Thanks very much for *your help (all your trouble)*!
Merci beaucoup pour *votre aide (vos efforts)*!
mersē bōkōō pōōr vôträd (vōzefôr)

You're welcome.
Je vous en prie.
zhə vōōzäN prē

I (We) thank you so much for …
Je vous remercie (Nous vous remercions) infiniment pour …
zhə vōō remersē (nōō vōō remersyôN) eNfēnēmäN pōōr …

Thanks a million!
Mille mercis!
mēl mersē

Don't mention it.
Il n' y a pas de quoi.
ēlnyä pä də kô·ä

Glad to do it.
À votre service.
ä vôt(ər) servēs

Yes and no

Yes.
Oui.
ōō·ē

Certainly.
Certainement.
särten·mäN

Of course.
Cela va sans dire.
sələ vä säN dēr

I'd be glad to.
Très volontiers.
trä vôlôNtyä

Good! (Fine!)
Bien! (Très bien!)
byeN (trä byeN)

Right!
C'est ça!
sä sä

Terrific!
Extra!
eksträ

With pleasure!
Avec plaisir!
ävek plāzēr

No.
Non.
nôN

Never.
Jamais.
zhämä

Nothing.
Rien.
rē·eN

Certainly not! (No way!)
En aucun cas!
äNōkeN kä

Out of the question!
Pas question!
pä kestyôN

I'd rather not!
Il vaut mieux pas.
ēl vō myä pä

I *don't want to (can't)*.
Je ne *veux (peux)* pas.
zhə nə vä (pā) pä

Perhaps (Maybe).
Peut-être.
pātät(ər)

Probably.
Probablement.
prôbäbləmäN

Pardon

Excuse me!	**I beg your pardon!**	**Please excuse me!**
Excusez-moi!	Pardon!	Excusez-moi, s'il vous plaît.
ekskēzä-mô·ä	pärdôN	ekskēzä-mô·ä, sēl vōō plä

I'm very sorry.	**Please forgive me!**	**I'm extremely sorry.**
Je suis désolé.	Pardonnez-moi!	Je regrette infiniment.
zhə sē·ē dāzōlā	pärdônā-mô·ä	zhə rəgret eNfēnēmäN

I must apologize to *you.*	**Please don't be angry!**
Je *vous (te)* prie de m'excuser.	Ne m'en veuillez pas!
zhə vōō (tə) prē də mekskēzā	nə mäN vāyā pä

> Excusez-moi *and* Pardon *are ways of excusing yourself, but they are also used to catch someone's attention. For example:* "Pardon, monsieur. Où se trouve le Grand Hôtel?" *(Excuse me, sir. Where is the Grand Hotel?)*

Regrets

What a pity! (Too bad!)	**To my (great) regret …**	**What a shame that …**
(Quel) dommage!	À mon (grand) regret …	Quel dommage, que …
(kel) dômäzh	ä môN (gräN) rəgrā	kel dômäzh ke

I'm so very sorry about that.	**I'm afraid that isn't possible.**
J'en suis désolé.	Malheureusement c'est impossible.
zhäN sē·ē dāzōlā	mälərāzəmäN seteNpôsēb'əl

I'm afraid that can't be done.
Je crois bien que ce n'est pas possible.
zhə krô·ä byeN ke sə nā pä pôsēb'əl

Congratulations and Condolences

Congratulations!

I congratulate you …	Mes félicitations!	mā fālēsētäsyôN
on *your* **birthday**	Bon anniversaire!	bônänēversär
on *your* **engagement** .	pour *vos (tes)* fiançailles	pōōr vō (tā) fē·äNsä'ē
on *your* **marriage**	pour *votre (ton)* mariage	pōōr vôt(ər) (tôN) märē·äzh

All the best! (Best wishes!)
Toutes mes félicitations!
tōot mā fālēsētäsyôN

Happy birthday!
Bon anniversaire!
bônänēversär

Merry Christmas!
Joyeux Noël!
zhô·äyä nō·el

Happy New Year!
Bonne année!
bônänä

I (We) wish you ...
Je vous souhaite (Nôus vous souhaitons) ...
zhə vōō sōō·et (nōō vōō sōō·etôN) ...

All the best!
Bonne chance!
bôn shäNs

Good luck!
Bonne chance!
bôn shäNs

Our warmest sympathy.
Nous vous assurons de notre sympathie.
nōō vōōzäsērôN də nôt(ər) seNpätē

My sincerest condolences.
Mes sincères condoléances.
mā seNsār kôNdōlā·äNs

Complaints

I'd like to register a complaint.
Je désire faire une réclamation.
zhə dāzēr fār en räklämäsyôN

I'd like to speak to the manager.
Je voudrais parler au gérant.
zhə vōōdrā pärlā ō zhäräN

I'm afraid I'll have to make a complaint about ...
Il faut que je fasse une réclamation au sujet de ...
ēl fō ke zhə fäs ēn räklämäsyôN ō sēzhä də ...

That's very annoying.	*... is (are) missing.*	**I haven't got any ...**
C'est très fâcheux.	*Il n'y a pas de ...*	Je n'ai pas de ...
sä trä fäshä	ēlnyä pä də ...	zhə nā pä də ...

... doesn't work.	*... is not in order.*	*... is out of order.*
... ne marche pas.	... ne marche pas.	... ne fonctionne pas.
... nə märsh pä	... nə märsh pä	... nə fôNksyôn pä

... is (are) broken.	*... is (are) torn.*
... est cassé (sont cassés).	*... s'est déchiré (se sont déchirés).*
... ä käsä (sôN käsä)	... sä dāshērä (sə sôN dāshērä)

Communication

Do you speak English?	**German?**	**French?**
Parlez-vous anglais?	allemand?	français?
pärlā-vōōzäNglä	älmäN	fräNsä

Can you understand me?	**I understand.**	**I can't understand a thing.**
Vous comprenez?	Je comprends.	Je ne comprends rien.
vōō kôNprenä	zhə kôNpräN	zhə nə kôNpräN rē·eN

Would you please speak a little slower?
Parlez un peu plus lentement, s'il vous plaît!
pärlā eN pä plē läNtəmäN, sēl vōō plä

What do you call . . . in French?	**How do you say that in French?**
Comment dit-on en français . . .?	Comment dit-on ça en français?
kômäN dētôN äN fräNsä	kômäN dēt-ôN sä äN fräNsä

What does that mean?	*I beg your pardon? (Say again?)*
Qu'est-ce que ça veut dire?	Pardon?
keske sä vä dēr	pärdôN

How do you pronounce this word?
Comment prononce-t-on ce mot?
kômäN prônôNstôN sə mō

Would you please translate this for me?
Pourriez-vous le traduire pour moi, s'il vous plaît.
pōōrē·ä-vōō lə trädē·ēr pōōr mô·ä, sēl vōō plä

Would you please write that down for me?
Écrivez(-le), s'il vous plaît.
äkrēvä(-lə), sēl vōō plä

Would you spell that please?
Épelez, s'il vous plaît.
äpəlā, sēl vōō plä

Weather

How's the weather going to be?
Quel temps fera-t-il?
kel täN ferätēl

What's the weather report?
Qu'annonce la météo?
känôNs lä mātā·ō

The barometer's *rising (falling)*.
Le baromètre *monte (descend)*.
lə bärōmät(ər) môNt (desäN)

We're going to have . . .
Nous aurons . . .
nōōzôrôN

fine weather	du beau temps	dē bō täN
bad weather	du mauvais temps	dē mōvā täN
changeable weather	un temps instable	eN täN eNstäb'əl

It's going to stay nice.
Il continue à faire beau.
ēl kôNtēnē ä fär bō

It looks like rain.
On dirait qu'il va pleuvoir.
ôN dērā kēl vä plāvô·är

Is it going to *rain (snow)*?
Va-t-il *pleuvoir (neiger)*?
vätēl plāvô·är (nāzhā)

Is the weather going to stay nice?
Continuera-t-il à faire beau?
kôNtēnē·ərätēl ä fär bō

How are the road conditions between here and . . .?
Quel est l'état des routes pour . . .?
kel ā lātä dā rōōt pōōr

It's very slippery.
Il y a du verglas.
ēlyä dē verglä

– very hot.
Il fait très chaud.
ēl fā trä shō

– foggy (misty).
Il y a du brouillard.
ēlyä dē brōōyär

– very muggy.
Il fait très lourd.
ēl fā trä lōōr

– very windy.
– du vent.
– dē väN

– stormy.
– une tempête.
– ēn täNpāt

It's *cold (hot)*.
Il fait *froid (chaud)*.
ēl fā frô·ä (shō)

I'm *cold (hot)*.
J'ai *froid (chaud)*.
zhā frô·ä (shō)

What's the temperature?
Quelle température fait-il?
kel täNpārätēr fātēl

It's . . . *above (below)* zero.
Le thermomètre marque . . . *au-dessus (au-dessous)* de zéro.
lə termōmät(ər) märk . . . ōdəsē (ōdəsōō) də zārō

The weather's going to change.
Le temps va changer.
lə täN vä shäNzhä

It'll be nice again.
Le temps se remet au beau.
lə täN sə remetō bō

The wind has dropped.
Le vent est tombé.
lə väN ä tôNbä

The wind has changed.
Le vent a tourné.
lə väN ä toๅornä

We're going to have a thunderstorm.
Nous aurons un orage.
noๅozôrôN eNôräzh

There's going to be a storm.
Il y aura de la tempête.
ēlyôrä dəlä täNpät

Is the fog going to lift?
Est-ce que le brouillard se dissipera?
eske lə broๅoyär sə dēsēperä

It's stopped raining.
Il a cessé de pleuvoir.
ēl ä sesä də plävô·är

It's clearing up.
Le temps s'éclaircit.
lə täN säklärsē

The sun is shining.
Il fait du soleil.
ēl fä dē sôlä'ē

The sun is burning hot.
Le soleil est brûlant.
lə sôlä'ē ä brēläN

The sky is clear.
Le ciel est dégagé.
lə syel ä dägäzhä

European temperatures are always measured in degrees Celsius.
Here's a handy conversion table:
Fahrenheit to Celsius = (x—32) 5/9 = °C
Celsius to Fahrenheit = 32 + 9/5x = °F

---

air	air *m*	är
atmospheric pressure	pression *f* atmosphérique	presyôN ätmôsfärēk
barometer	baromètre *m*	bärōmät(ər)
climate	climat *m*	klēmä
cloud	nuage *m*	nē·äzh
cloudburst	pluie *f* torrentielle	plē·ē tôräNsyel
cloud cover, cloudy skies	nuages *m/pl.*	nē·äzh
cloudy	couvert	koๅovär
dawn	aube *f*	ôb
dew	rosée *f*	rōzā
draft	courant *m* d'air	koๅoräN där

dusk	crépuscule *m*	krāpₑskₑl
fog	brouillard *m*	brōōyär
frost	gelée *f*	zhelā
hail	grêle *f*	grāl
heat	canicule *f*	känēkₑl
high pressure (system)	anticyclone *m*	äNtēsēklón
ice	glace *f*	gläs
icy road	verglas *m*	verglä
it's freezing	il gèle	ēl zhāl
it's hailing	il grêle	ēl grāl
it's raining	il pleut	ēl pla
it's snowing	il neige	ēl nāzh
it's thawing	il dégèle	ēl dāzhāl
it's windy	il fait du vent	ēl fā de väN
lightning	éclair *m*	āklār
low pressure (system)	basses pressions *f/pl.*	bäs presyôN
mist	brouillard *m*	brōōyär
moon	lune *f*	lēn
north (east) wind	vent *m* du nord	väN de nôr
	(d'est)	(dest)
precipitation	chute *f* de pluie	shet de plē·ē
road conditions	état *m* des routes	ātä dā rōōt
shower	averse *f*	ävers
snow	neige *f*	nāzh
snow flurries	tourbillons *m/pl.* de neige	tōōrbēyôN de nāzh
south (west) wind	vent *m* du sud	väN de sēd
	(d'ouest)	(dōō·est)
star	étoile *f*	ātô·äl
storm	tempête *f*	täNpāt
sun	soleil *m*	sôlā′ē
sunrise	lever *m* du soleil	levā de sôlā′ē
sunset	coucher *m* du soleil	kōōshā de sôlā′ē
temperature	température *f*	täNpārāter
thaw	dégel *m*	dāzhāl
thunder	tonnerre *m*	tônār
thunderstorm	orage *m*	ôräzh
weather	temps *m*	täN
weather prediction	prévisions *f/pl.* météo-rologiques	prāvēzyôN mātā·ô-rōlōzhēk
weather report	météo(rologie) *f*	mātā·ō(rōlōzhē)
wind	vent *m*	väN

Numbers

CARDINAL NUMBERS

0	zéro	zārō	5	cinq	seNk
1	un	eN	6	six	sēs
2	deux	dā	7	sept	set
3	trois	trô·ä	8	huit	ē·ēt
4	quatre	kät(ər)	9	neuf	nāf

10	dix	dēs
11	onze	ôNz
12	douze	dōoz
13	treize	trāz
14	quatorze	kätôrz
15	quinze	keNz
16	seize	sāz
17	dix-sept	dēset
18	dix-huit	dēzē·ēt
19	dix-neuf	dēznāf
20	vingt	veN
21	vingt et un	veNtā·eN
22	vingt-deux	veNdā
23	vingt-trois	veNtrô·ä
30	trente	träNt
40	quarante	käräNt
50	cinquante	seNkäNt
60	soixante	sô·äsäNt
70	soixante-dix	sô·äsäNdēs
80	quatre-vingts	kätrəveN
90	quatre-vingt-dix	kätrəveNdēs
100	cent	säN
200	deux cents	dāsäN
1.000	mille	mēl

When writing numbers in French, the function of periods and commas is reversed from the English function. Commas are used in decimals, and periods in numbers of four or more digits. Thus 1,000 – one thousand – becomes 1.000 – mille (mēl) in French, and 1.5 – one point five – is translated as 1,5 – un virgule cinq (eN vērgəl seNk).

2.000	deux mille	d*a* mēl
10.000	dix mille	dē mēl
1.000.000 ...	un million	eN mēlyôN
1.000.000.000 ...	un milliard.............	eN mēlyär

ORDINAL NUMBERS

*When speaking about days of the month, the French do not use
ordinal numbers. Thus the fourteenth of July is* le quatorze juillet (lə
kätôrz zh*ē*·ēyä). *The same applies to Roman numerals: Louis XVI is
spoken of as* Louis Seize (loo'ē sāz). *(see page 34).*

1.	premier ...	prəmyā	**6.**	sixième ...	sēzyām
2.	deuxième;	d*a*zyām;	**7.**	septième ..	setyām
	second ...	səgôN	**8.**	huitième ..	*ē*·ētyām
3.	troisième ..	trô·äzyām	**9.**	neuvième..	n*a*vyām
4.	quatrième .	kätrēyām	**10.**	dixième ...	dēzyām
5.	cinquième :	seNkyām	**11.**	onzième...	ôNzyām

12.	douzième	doōzyām
13.	treizième	trāzyām
14.	quatorzième	kätôrzyām
15.	quinzième	keNzyām
16.	seizième	sāzyām
17.	dix-septième	dēsetyām
20.	vingtième	veNtyām
21.	vingt et unième	veNt-ā-*ē*nyām
22.	vingt-deuxième	veN-d*a*zyām
23.	vingt-troisième	veNtrô·äzyām
30.	trentième	träNtyām
40.	quarantième	käräNtyām
50.	cinquantième..........	seNkäNtyām
60.	soixantième	sô·äsäNtyām
70.	soixante-dixième	sô·äsäNt-dēzyām
80.	quatre-vingtième	kätrə-veNtyām
90.	quatre-vingt-dixième	kätrə-veN-dēzyām
100.	centième...............	säNtyām
200.	deux centième	d*a* säNtyām
1.000.	millième	mēlyām
10.000.	dix millième...........	dē(s) mēlyām
1.000.000.	millionième	mēlyônyām

Time

What time is it?
Quelle heure est-il?
kelār etēl

It's one o'clock.
Il est une heure.
ēl ätēnār

It's exactly three o'clock.
Il est exactement trois heures.
ēl ätägzäktəmäN trô·äzār

It's half past seven.
Il est sept heures et demie.
ēl ā setār ā dəmē

It's five (minutes) past four.
Il est quatre heures cinq.
ēl ā kätrār seNk

Have you got the exact time?
Avez-vous l'heure exacte?
ävā-voo lār egzäkt

It's about two o'clock.
Il est environ deux heures.
ēl ätäNvērôN dāzār

It's quarter past five.
Il est cinq heures et quart.
ēl ā seNkār ā kär

It's quarter to nine.
Il est neuf heures moins le quart.
ēl ā nāvār mô·eN lə kär

It's ten (minutes) to eight.
Il est huit heures moins dix.
ēl ā ē·ētār mô·eN dēs

> *The 24 hour clock is used on timetables, signs, announcements, TV schedules and in written French in general. In spoken French, however, you can use the 12 hour clock, adding du matin, de l'après-midi or du soir to the time if there is any doubt.*

When?
À quelle heure?
ä kelār

At half-past nine (nine-thirty).
À neuf heures et demie (trente).
ä nāvār ā dəmē (träNt)

From eight to nine A.M.
De huit à neuf du matin.
də ē·ēt ä nāf dē mäteN

At five P.M.
À cinq heures de l'après-midi.
ä seNkār də läprä-mēdē

At ten o'clock (10:00).
À dix heures.
ä dēzār

At eight-fifteen P.M.
À huit heures et quart du soir.
ä ē·ētār ā kär dē sô·är

Between ten and twelve A.M.
Entre dix et onze du matin.
äNt(ər) dēsä ôNz dē mäteN

At eleven sharp.
À onze heures précises.
ä ôNzār präsēz

At seven P.M.
À sept heures du soir.
ä setār dē sô·är

In half an hour.
Dans une demi-heure.
däNze͞n dəmē-ār

In two hours.
Dans deux heures.
däN dāzār

Not before seven.
Pas avant sept heures.
päzäväN setār

Shortly after eight.
Peu après huit heures.
pā äprä ē̃-ētār

It's (too) late.
Il est (trop) tard.
ēl ā (trō) tär

It's still too early.
Il est encore trop tôt.
ēl ätäNkôr trō tō

Is this clock right?
Cette montre est à l'heure?
set môNträtä lār

It's too fast (slow).
Elle avance (retarde).
el äväNs (retärd)

Times of the Day

During the day.
Pendant la journée.
päNdäN lä zho͞ornä

In the morning.
Le matin.
lə mäteN

During the morning.
Dans la matinée.
däN lä mätēnä

This morning (afternoon, evening).
Ce matin (Cet après-midi. Ce soir).
sə mäteN (setäprä-mēdē, sə sô·är)

At noon.
À midi.
ä mēdē

Around noon.
Vers midi.
vär mēdē

In the afternoon.
L' après-midi.
läprä-mēdē

In the evening.
Le soir.
lə sô·är

At night.
La nuit.
lä nē·ē

Tonight.
Cette nuit.
set nē·ē

At midnight.
À minuit.
ä mēnē·ē

Daily (Every day).
Tous les jours.
to͞o lä zho͞or

Hourly (Every hour).
Toutes les heures.
to͞ot läzār

The day before yesterday.
Avant-hier.
äväNtē-ār

Yesterday.
Hier.
ē-ār

Today.
Aujourd'hui.
ōzho͞ordē·ē

Tomorrow.
Demain.
dəmeN

Tomorrow morning.
Demain matin.
dəmeN mäteN

The day after tomorrow.
Après-demain.
äprä-dəmeN

A week from now.
Dans une semaine.
däNze͞n smen

A week from Wednesday.
Mercredi en huit.
märkrədi äN ē-ēt

Two weeks from now.
Dans quinze jours.
däN keNz zho͞or

This noon.	**A month ago.**	**At the moment.**
Ce midi.	Il y a un mois.	Actuellement.
sə mēdē	ēlyä eN mô·ä	äktē·ēləmäN

For the last ten days.	**Within a week.**	**This coming weekend.**
Depuis dix jours.	Dans les huit jours.	Le week-end prochain.
depē·ē dē zhoor	däN lā ē·ē zhoor	lə oo·ēkend prôsheN

Last (Next) year.	*Every year (Annually).*
L'année *dernière (prochaine)*.	Tous les ans.
länä dernyär (prôshen)	too läzäN

Every week (Weekly).	**From time to time.**	**Now and then.**
Toutes les semaines.	De temps en temps.	De temps à autre.
toot lā smen	də täNzäN täN	də täNzä ôt(ər)

About this time.	*During this time (Meanwhile).*
À cette *heure (date)*.	*Pendant ce temps (Entre-temps).*
ä set är (dät)	päNdäN sə täN (äNtrətäN)

a little while ago	récemment	räsämäN
any time	à tout moment	ä too mômäN
earlier	plus tôt	plē tō
later	plus tard	plē tär
now	maintenant	meNtənäN
on time	à temps	ä täN
previously (before)	avant	äväN
recently	l'autre jour	lōt(ər) zhoor
since	depuis	depē·ē
sometimes	quelquefois	kelkefô·ä
soon	bientôt	byeNtō
temporarily (for the time being)	en ce moment	äN sə mômäN
until	jusqu'à	zhēskä
second	seconde *f*	səgôNd
minute	minute *f*	mēnēt
hour	heure *f.*	är
day	jour *m*	zhoor
week	semaine *f*	smen
month	mois *m*	mô·ä
year	année *f*, an *m*	änä, äN
half year	six mois	sē mô·ä
quarter, three months	trois mois	trô·ä mô·ä

Days of the Week

Monday	lundi *m*	leNdē
Tuesday	mardi *m*	märdē
Wednesday	mercredi *m*	märkrədē
Thursday	jeudi *m*	zhādē
Friday	vendredi *m*	väNdrədē
Saturday	samedi *m*	sämdē
Sunday	dimanche *m*	dēmäNsh

Months

January	janvier *m*	zhäNvyä
February	février *m*	fävrē·ā
March	mars *m*	märs
April	avril *m*	ävrēl
May	mai *m*	mā
June	juin *m*	zhē·eN
July	juillet *m*	zhē·ēyä
August	août *m*	o͞o(t)
September	septembre *m*	septäNb(ər)
October	octobre *m*	ōktōb(ər)
November	novembre *m*	nôväNb(ər)
December	décembre *m*	dāsäNb(ər)

Seasons, Holidays

Spring	printemps *m*	preNtäN
Summer	été *m*	ātā
Fall/Autumn	automne *m*	ôtôn
Winter	hiver *m*	ēvār
New Year's Eve	(la) Saint-Sylvestre	(lä) seN sēlvest(ər)
New Year's Day	jour *m* de l'an	zho͞or də läN
Good Friday	vendredi *m* saint	väNdrədē seN
Easter; Christmas	Pâques *m*; Noël *m*	päk; nō·el

Public Holidays in France: New Year's Day, Easter Sunday and Monday, May Day (May 1), Ascension Day, Whitsunday and Whitmonday, France's National Day (July 14), The Assumption (August 15), All Saints' Day (November 1), Armistice Day (November 11), Christmas Day.
Recently, another holiday has been added: Armistice Day *(May 8 – commemorating the end of World War II).*

The Date

What's the date today?
Nous sommes le combien
aujourd'hui?
nōō sôm lə kôNbyeN ōzhōōrdē·ē

It's the second of July.
Aujourd'hui, c'est le deux juillet.
ōzhōōrdē·ē, se lə dā zhē·ēyā

On the *fifteenth of May (May fifteenth)*, 19 ...
Le quinze mai dix-neuf cent ...
lə keNz mā dēz-nāf säN ...

On the fifth of *this (next)* month.
Le cinq *de ce mois (du mois prochain)*.
lə seNk də sə mô·ä (dē mô·ä prôsheN)

Until the 10th of March.
Jusqu'au dix mars.
zhēskō dē märs

On April first of *this (last)* year.
Le premier avril *de cette année (de l'année passée)*.
lə prəmyā ävrēl də cetänā (də länā päsā)

We leave on *the twentieth of September (September 20th)*.
Nous partirons le vingt septembre.
nōō pärtērôN lə veN septäNb(ər)

We arrived on *the twelfth of August (August 12th)*.
Nous sommes arrivés le douze août.
nōō sômzärēvā lə dōōz ōō

Thank you for your letter of February 2nd.
Je vous remercie (Nous vous remercions) de votre lettre du deux février.
zhə vōō remersē (nōō vōō remersyôN) də vôt(ər) let(ər) dē dā fāvrē·ā

Age

I'm twenty years old.
J'ai vingt ans.
zhā veNtäN

I'm over 18.
J'ai plus de dix-huit ans.
zhā plē də dēzē·ēt äN

Children under 14.
Enfants au-dessous de quatorze ans.
äNfäN ō-dəsōō də kätôrzäN

I was born on the ...
Je suis né le ...
zhə sē·ē nā lə ...

He's *younger (older)*.
Il est *plus jeune (plus âgé)*.
ēl ā plē zhän (plēzäzhā)

– under age.
– mineur.
mēnār

– grown up.
– adulte.
ädēlt

At the age of ...
À l'âge de ... ans.
äläzh də ... äN

At my age.
À mon âge.
ä môNäzh

Family

aunt	tante *f*	täNt
boy	garçon *m*	gärsôN
brother	frère *m*	frär
brother-in-law	beau-frère *m*	bō-frär
cousin *(female)*	cousine *f*	kōōzēn
cousin *(male)*	cousin *m*	kōōzeN
daughter; girl	fille *f*	fē'ē
daughter-in-law	belle-fille *f*	belfē'e
family	famille *f*	fàmē'ē
father	père *m*	pär
father-in-law	beau-père *m*	bō-pär
grandchild	petit-fils *m*	pətē-fēs
granddaughter	petite-fille *f*	pətēt-fē'ē
grandfather	grand-père *m*	gräN-pär
grandmother	grand-mère *f*	gräN-mär
grandparents	grands-parents *m/pl.*	gräN-päräN
grandson	petit-fils *m*	pətē-fēs
husband	mari *m*	märē
mother	mère *f*	mär
mother-in-law	belle-mère *f*	bel-mär
nephew	neveu *m*	nevā
niece	nièce *f*	nē-äs
parents	parents *m/pl.*	päräN
sister	sœur *f*	sär
sister-in-law	belle-sœur *f*	bel-sär
son; son-in-law	fils *m*; gendre *m*	fēs; zhäNdrə
uncle	oncle *m*	ôNk'əl
wife	femme *f*; épouse *f*	fàm; āpōōz

The terms époux *and* épouse *(husband and wife) are more formal than the common reference to one's spouse as* mon mari *(my husband) and* ma femme *(my wife).*

Occupations

apprentice	apprenti *m*	äpräNtē
artist	artiste *m*	ärtēst
auto mechanic	mécanicien *m*	mäkänēsyeN
baker	boulanger *m*	bōōläNzhä
bank teller	employé *m* de banque	äNplô·äyä də bäNk
bookkeeper	comptable *m*	kôNtäb'əl
bookseller	libraire *m*	lēbrär
bricklayer	maçon *m*	mäsôN
butcher	boucher *m*	bōōshā
cabinetmaker	ébéniste *m*	äbänēst
carpenter	menuisier *m*	menē·ēzyä
chef	chef cuisinier *m*	shef kē·ēzēnyä
civil servant	fonctionnaire *m*	fôNksyônär
clergyman	prêtre *m*	prät(ər)
cobbler	cordonnier *m*	kôrdónyä
computer programmer	programmeur *m*	prógrämär
confectioner	pâtissier *m*	pätēsyä
cook	cuisinier *m*	kē·ēzēnyä
dentist	dentiste *m, f*	däNtēst
doctor	médecin *m*	mädəseN
dressmaker	tailleur *m*	täyär
driver	chauffeur *m*	shôfär
driving instructor	moniteur *m* d'auto-école	mônētär dôtō-äkôl
druggist *(pharmacist)*	pharmacien *m*	färmäsyeN
druggist *(drugstore owner)*	droguiste *m*	drôgēst
electrician	électricien *m*	älektrēsyeN
engineer *(scientific)*	ingénieur *m*	eNzhänyär
engineer *(railroad)*	mécanicien *m* (de train)	mäkänēsyeN (də treN)
farmer	agriculteur *m*	ägrēkēltär
fisherman	pêcheur *m*	pāshär
forester	garde *m* forestier	gärd fôrestyä
gardener	jardinier *m*	zhärdēnyä

glazier	vitrier *m*	vētrēyä
interpreter	interprète *m*	eNterprät
journalist	journaliste *m*	zhōōrnälēst
judge	juge *m*	zhēzh
kindergarten teacher	jardinière *f* d'enfants	zhärdēnyär däNfäN
lawyer	avocat *m*	ävōkä
librarian	bibliothécaire *m*	bēblē·ōtäkär
locksmith	serrurier *m*	serēryä
mailman	facteur *m*	fäktär
mechanic	mécanicien *m*	mäkänēsyeN
metalworker	métallurgiste *m*	mätälērzhēst
midwife	sage-femme *f*	säzh-fäm
miner	mineur *m*	mēnär
musician	musicien *m*	mēzēsyeN
notary	notaire *m*	nôtär
nurse *(female)*	infirmière *f*	eNfērmyär
nurse *(male)*	infirmier *m*	eNfērmyä
optician	opticien *m*	ôptēsyeN
painter	peintre *m*	peNt(ər)
pastry chef	pâtissier *m*	pätēsyä
pharmacist	pharmacien *m*	färmäsyeN
plumber	plombier *m*	plôNbyä
postal clerk	employé *m* de postes	äNplô·äyä də pôst
pupil	élève *m, f;* lycéen *m*	ālāv; lēsä·eN
railroad man	cheminot *m*	shəmēnō
retailer	commerçant *m*	kômersäN
retiree	retraité *m*	reträtä
salesperson	vendeur *m*	väNdär
scholar	savant *m*	säväN
scientist	scientifique *m*	syäNtēfēk
sculptor	sculpteur *m*	skēlptär
secretary	secrétaire *m, f*	sekrätär
shoemaker	cordonnier *m*	kôrdônyä
storekeeper	propriétaire *m* d'un magasin	prôprē·ätär deN mägäzeN
student	étudiant *m*	ētēdyäN
tailor	tailleur *m*	täyär
teacher	instituteur *m*, professeur *m*	eNstētētär, prôfesär

technician	technicien *m*	teknēsyeN
trainee	apprenti *m*	äpräNtē
translator	traducteur *m*	trädēktär
truck driver	camionneur *m*	kämyônär
veterinarian	vétérinaire *m*	vātārēnär
waiter	serveur *m*	servär
waitress	serveuse *f*	servāz
watchmaker	horloger *m*	ôrlōzhā
wholesaler	grossiste *m*	grōsēst
worker	ouvrier *m*	ōōvrēyā
writer	écrivain *m*	ākrēveN

There is no simple rule for forming the feminine of occupations (and other nouns). There is un artiste *and* une artiste *for example, as well as* tailleur *and* tailleuse. *Nouns ending in* -er *and* -ier *change the ending to* -ère *and* ière *respectively:* boucher *and* bouchère, ouvrier *and* ouvrière. *Nouns ending in* -teur *usually change the ending to* -teuse *and* -trice: facteur *and* factrice. *But there is no feminine form for* auteur, docteur, médecin *and* professeur. *The word* femme *generally precedes these nouns:* une femme médecin.

Education

Where are you studying?
Où étudiez-vous?
ōō ātēdyā-vōō

What college or university do you attend?
À quelle université étudiez-vous?
ä kel ēnēversētā ātēdyā-vōō

I'm at ... *college (university).*
Je vais à l'université *de (des)* ...
zhə vāzä lēnēverzētā də [dā]

I'm *studying (majoring in)* ...
J'étudie ... (comme matière principale).
zhātēdē ... [kôm mätyār preNsēpäl]

lecture	cours *m*	kōōr
major	matière *f* principale	mätyār preNsēpäl
school	école *f*	ākôl
– boarding school	internat *m*	eNternä
– business school	école *f* de commerce	ākôl də kômers
– grammar school	école *f* primaire	ākôl prēmār
– high school *(acad.)*	académie *f*	äkädāmē
– *(general)*	lycée *m*; collège *m*	lēsā; kôläzh

– vocational school ..	centre *m* de formation professionnelle	säNt(ər) də fôrmäsyôn prófesyónel
subject	matière *f*.	mätyär
– American studies ..	langue *f* et littérature *f* américaines	läNgä lētärätẽr ämärēken
– archaeology	archéologie *f*	ärkä·ōlōzhē
– architecture	architecture *f*.	ärkētektẽr
– art history	histoire *f* de l'art	ēstô·är də lär
– biology	biologie *f*	bē·ōlōzhē
– business admin.	gestion *f*.	zhestyóN
– chemistry	chimie *f*.	shēmē
– computer science ..	informatique *f*.	eNfôrmätēk
– dentistry	études *f/pl.* dentaires ..	ātẽd däNtär
– economics	économie *f*.	ākónōmē
– education	pédagogie *f*	pādägōzhē
– English	langue *f* et littérature *f* anglaises...........	läNgä lētärätẽr äNglāz
– geology	géologie *f*.	zhā·ōlōzhē
– history	histoire *f*.	ēstô·är
– journalism	journalisme *m*	zhōornälēsm
– law	droit *m*	drô·ä
– mathematics	mathématiques *f/pl.* ...	mätāmätēk
– mechanical engineering	construction *f* mécanique	kôNstrẽksyôN mäkänēk
– medicine	médecine *f*.	mādəsēn
– painting	peinture *f*.	peNtẽr
– pharmacy	pharmacie *f*.	färmäsē
– physics	physique *f*.	fēzēk
– political science ...	sciences *f/pl.* politiques	sē·äNs pôlētēk
– psychology	psychologie *f*.	sēkōlōzhē
– Romance languages	langues *f/pl.* romanes..	länNg rômän
– sociology	sociologie *f*.	sōsē·ōlōzhē
– veterinary medicine	médecine *f* vétérinaire .	mādəsēn vätärēnär
– zoology	zoologie *f*.	zō·ōlōzhē
technical college	école *f* supérieure technique	äkôl sẽpäryẽr teknēk
university	université *f*.	ēnēversētā

La Sorbonne *is the familiar name for one of the many branches of the Université de Paris.*

ON THE ROAD

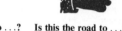

Asking the Way

Where is (are) ...?	**How do I get to ...?**	**Is this the road to ...?**
Où est (sont) ...?	Pour aller à ...?	Est-ce la route de ...?
ōō·ā (sôN) ...	pōōr älä ä ...	es lä rōōt də ...

How many kilometers is it to the next town?
Combien de kilomètres y a-t-il jusqu'à la prochaine ville?
köNbyeN də kēlōmāt(ər) yätēl zhěskä lä prōshen vēl

8 kilomètres = 5 miles

Is this the right way to ...?	**Do I have to go ...?**
Est-ce la bonne direction pour ...?	Dois-je aller ...?
es lä bôn dēreksyôN pōōr ...	dô·äzhälä ...

Right.	**Left.**	**Straight ahead.**	**Back.**
À droite.	À gauche.	Tout droit.	En arrière.
ä drô·ät	ä gōsh	tōō drô·ä	äNäryär

Here.	**There.**	**This way.**	**As far as ...**
Ici.	Là.	Dans cette direction.	Jusqu'à ...
ēsē	lä	däN set dēreksyôN	zhěskä ...

How long?	**Where (to)?**	**How far is it to ...?**
Combien de temps?	Où?	C'est loin d'ici (à) ...?
kôNbyeN də täN	ōō	se lô·eN dēsē (ä) ...

Would you please show me that on the map?
Indiquez-le-moi sur la carte, s'il vous plaît.
eNdēkā-lə mó·ä sēr lä kärt, sēl vōō plä

Vehicles

camping trailer	..... caravane f	.... kärävän
car	.... voiture f	.... vô·ätēr
– delivery truck	..... camionnette f	.... kämyōnet
– passenger car	..... voiture f	.... vô·ätēr
	particulière	.... pärtēkēlyär

– *ranch (station)*

wagon	voiture *f* familiale	vô·ät*ē*r fämēlyäl
– **truck**	camion *m*	kämyôN
bicycle	bicyclette *f*	bēsēklet
horse cart	roulotte *f*	rōōlôt
moped	cyclomoteur *m*	sēklōmôtär
motorcycle	moto *f*	môtō
motor scooter	scooter *m*	skōōtär
trailer	remorque *f*	remôrk
vehicle	véhicule *m*	vā·ēk*ē*l

Renting a Car

Where can I rent a car?
Je peux louer une voiture où?
zhə pā lōō·ā *ē*n vô·ät*ē*r ōō

I'd like to rent a car.
J'aimerais louer une voiture.
zhämerā lōō·ā *ē*n vô·ät*ē*r

... with chauffeur.
... avec chauffeur.
... ävek shōfär

... for 2 (6) people.
... pour *deux (six)* personnes.
... pōōr dä (sē) persôn

... for one day (one week, two weeks).
... pour *un jour (une semaine, deux semaines).*
... pōōr eN zhōōr (*ē*n smen, dä smen)

How much will it cost?
Ça coûte combien?
sä kōōt kôNbyeN

... including full coverage insurance?
... l'assurance tous risques inclus?
... läs*ē*räNs tōō rēsk eNkl*ē*

Will I have to pay for the gasoline myself?
Dois-je payer l'essence moi-même?
dô·äzh pāyā lesäNs mô·ä mäm

How much will I have to deposit?
Je dois vous verser une caution de combien?
zhə dô·ä vōō versā *ē*n kôsyóN də kôNbyeN

When (Where) can I pick up the car?
Quand (Où) puis-je venir chercher la voiture?
käN (ōō) pē·ēzh vənēr shershā lä vô·ät*ē*r

Will somebody be there when I bring the car back?
Est-ce qu'il y aura quelqu'un quand je ramènerai la voiture?
es kēlyôrä kelkeN käN zhə rämānərā lä vô·ät*ē*r

On a Drive

I'm *going (driving)* to ...
Je vais à ...
zhə vāzä ...

Are you going to ...?
Allez-vous à ...?
älävōōzä ...

To go by *car (motorcycle, bicycle)*.
Aller *en voiture (en moto, à bicyclette)*.
älä äN vô·ätēr (äN môtō, ä bēsēklet)

		Fast.	Slow.
		Vite.	Lentement.
		vēt	läNtmäN

access road	route *f* d'accès	rōōt däksā
automobile club	automobile club *m*	ôtōmōbēl klĕb
bike lane	piste *f* cyclable........	pēst sēkläb'əl
bridge	pont *m*	pôN
center strip	bande *f* médiane	bäNd mādē·än
city limits	panneau *m* de	pänō də
sign	localité	lōkälētā
curve	virage *m*	vērazh
detour	déviation *f*	dāvē·äsyôN
direction sign	panneau *m* indicateur .	pänō eNdēkät*ā*r
driver's license	permis *m* de conduire .	permē də kôNd*ē*·ēr
driveway	entrée *f*	äNtrā
exit	sortie *f*	sôrtē
falling rocks	chute *f* de pierres	sh*ĕ*t də pyär
highway	auto-route *f*	ôtōrōōt
highway patrol	police *f* routière......	pôlēs rōōtyär
intersection	croisement *m*	krô·äzmäN
lane	chaussée *f*...........	shôsā
limited parking zone .	zone bleue *f*	zōn bl*ā*
maximum speed	vitesse *f* maximum	vētes mäksēmôm
(mountain) pass	col *m*	kôl
no parking	stationnement *m*	stäsyônmäN
	interdit	eNterdē
no passing	interdiction *f*	eNterdēksyôN
	de dépasser	də däpäsā
no stopping	arrêt *m* interdit	ärä eNterdē
parking disc	disque *m* bleu	dēsk bl*ā*
parking lot	parking *m*...........	pärkēng
parking meter	parcomètre *m*	pärkōmāt(ər)
path	chemin *m*	shəmeN
– footpath	trottoir *m*	trôtô·är
railroad crossing	passage *m* à niveau ...	päsäzh ä nēvō

registration	immatriculation f	ēmätrēkēläsyôN
right of way	priorité f	prē·ôrētä
road	route f	root
– coastal road	route f côtière	root kôtyär
– country road	route f de campagne	root də käNpän(yə)
– cross road	route f secondaire	root səgóNdär
– main *road* *(street)*	route f (rue f) principale	root (rē) preNsēpäl
road sign	panneau m de signalisation	pänō də sēnyälēzäsyôN
road under construction	route en travaux	root äN trävō
route	route f	root
sidewalk	trottoir m	trótó·är
side wind	vent m latéral	väN lätäräl
slippery road *(literally: danger of sliding)*	(attention) route glissante	(ätäNsyôN) root glēsäNt
speed limit	limitation f de vitesse	lēmētäsyôN də vētes
steep downgrade	pente f	päNt
steep upgrade	côte f	kōt
traffic	circulation f	sērkēläsyôN
traffic circle	sens m giratoire	säNs zhērätô·är
traffic light	feux m/pl.	fä
traffic regulations	code m de la route	kôd də lä root
trip (journey)	voyage m en voiture	vô·äyäzh äN vô·ätēr
– brake	freiner	frānā
– drive	conduire	kôNdē·ēr
– get in lane	se ranger	sə räNzhā
– get out *(of the car)*	descendre	desäNd(ər)
– hitch-hike	faire de l'auto-stop	fär də lôtōstôp
– park	stationner	stäsyônā
– pass *(on the road)*	dépasser; doubler	dāpäsā; dōōblā
– stop	arrêter	ärātā
– turn *(the car)*	faire demi-tour	fär dəmē-tōor
– turn *(into a road)*	tourner	tōornā
– turn off *(a road)*	bifurquer	bēfērkā
winding road	route f en lacets	root äN läsā
zebra crossing	passage m clouté	päsäzh klōōtā

Garage, Parking Lot

Where can I leave my car *(for safekeeping)*?
Je peux garer ma voiture où?
zhə pä gärä mä vô·ätĕr oo

Is there a garage near here?
Il y a un garage dans le coin?
ēlyä eN gäräzh däN lə kô·eN

Have you still got a vacant *garage (parking space)*?
Avez-vous encore *un garage (un box)* de libre?
ävävoozäNkôr eN gäräzh (eN bôks) də lēb(ər)

Where can I leave the car?
Je peux laisser la voiture où?
zhə pä läsä lä vô·ätĕr oo

Can I leave it here?
Je peux la laisser ici?
zhə pä lä läsā ēsē

Can I park here?
Je peux me garer ici?
zhə pä mə gärä ēsē

Is this parking lot guarded?
Le parking est gardé?
lə pärkēng ā gärdā

Is there a space free?
Y a-t-il encore une place libre?
ēyätēl äNkôr ēn pläs lēb(ər)

How long can I park here?
Combien de temps je peux stationner ici?
kôNbyeN də täN zhə pä stäsyônä ēsē

How much does it cost to park here *overnight (until ...)*?
Combien coûte le garage *une nuit (jusqu'à ...)*?
kôNbyeN koot lə gäräzh ēn nē·ē (zhēskä ...)

Is the garage open all night?
Le garage est-t-il ouvert toute la nuit?
lə gäräzh etēl oovär toot lä nē·ē

When do you close?
Quand fermez-vous?
käN fermä voo

I'll be leaving *this evening (tomorrow morning at eight)*.
Je partirai *ce soir (demain à huit heures)*.
zhə pärtērä sə sô·är (dəmeN ä ē·ētär)

I'd like to take my car out of the garage.
Je voudrais sortir ma voiture du garage.
zhə voodrä sôrtĕr mä vô·ätĕr dē gäräzh

Gas Station, Car Repair

Where's the nearest gas station?

Où est la station d'essence la plus proche?
ōō ā lä stäsyóN desäNs lä plē prōsh

How far is it?

C'est à quelle distance?
sätä kel dēstäNs

Fifteen liters of *regular (high test)*, please.

Donnez-moi quinze litres *d'essence ordinaire (de super)*, s'il vous plaît.
dônä mô·ä keNz lēt(ər) desäNs ôrdēnār (də sēpār), sēl vōō plä

> *1 gallon = approx.* 4 litres

I'd like 20 liters of diesel, please.

Je voudrais vingt litres de diesel.
zhə vōōdrä veN lēt(ər) də dyezel

Fill her up, please.

Faites le plein, s'il vous plaît.
fāt lə pleN, sēl vōō plä

I need *water (coolant)*.

J'ai besoin d'eau (du radiateur).
zhā bəzô·eN dō (dē rädē·ätār)

A road map, please.

Une carte routière, s'il vous plaît.
ēn kärt rōōtyār, sēl vōō plä

Would you please fill up the radiator?

Faites le plein d'eau du radiateur, s'il vous plaît.
fāt lə pleN dō dē rädē·ätār, sēl vōō plä

Would you please check the brake fluid?

Vérifiez le liquide de freins, s'il vous plaît.
vārēfē·ä lə lēkēd də freN, sēl vōō plä

anti-freeze	antigel *m*	äNtēzhel
attendant	pompiste *m*	pôNpēst
brake fluid	liquide *m* de freins	lēkēd də freN
car repair service	service-entretien *m*	servēs äNtrətyeN
coolant	fluide *m* réfrigérant ...	flē·ēd räfrēzhäräN
(cooling) water	eau *f* du radiateur	ō dē rädē·ätār
gasoline	essence *f*	esäNs
gasoline can	jerrycan *m*	zherēkän
gas station	station *f* d'essence	stäsyóN desäNs
gas tank	réservoir *m* d'essence ..	rāzervō·är desäNs
oil	huile *f*	ē·ēl
reserve tank	bidon *m* de réserve ...	bēdôN də rāzärv
spark plug	bougie *f* d'allumage ...	bōōzhē dälēmäzh
water	eau *f*	ō
– distilled water	eau *f* distillée	ō dēstēlā

Oil

Please check the oil.
Vérifiez le niveau d'huile, s'il vous plaît.
vārēfē·ä lə nēvō dē·ēl, sēl vōō plä

Have I got enough oil?
Y a-t-il encore assez d'huile?
ēyätēl äNkôr äsä dē·ēl

I need *motor oil (gear oil)*.
Il me faut d'huile *de moteur (de graissage)*.
ēl mə fō dē·ēl də môtār (də gresäzh)

. . . liters of oil please.
. . . litres d'huile, s'il vous plaît.
. . . lēt(ər) dē·ēl, sēl vōō plä

> *1 liter = approx.* 2 pints

Please fill up the oil tank.
Faites le plein d'huile, s'il vous plaît.
fāt lə pleN dē·ēl, sēl vōō plä

Please change the oil.
Changez l'huile, s'il vous plaît.
shäNzhā lē·ēl, sēl vōō plä

gear oil	huile *f* de graissage	ē·ēl də gresäzh
lubrication	lubrification *f*	lēbrēfēkäsyóN
motor oil	huile *f* de moteur	ē·ēl də môtār
oil	l'huile *f*	lē·ēl
– special/standard . . .	spéciale/normale	spesyäl/nôrmäl
oil can	burette *f*	bēret
oil change	vidange *f* d'huile	vēdäNzh dē·ēl
oil level	niveau *m* d'huile	nēvō dē·ēl

Tires

Can you *repair (retread)* this tire?
Pouvez-vous *réparer (rechaper)* ce pneu?
pōōvā-vōō rāpärä (reshäpā) sə pnä

One of the tires had a blow-out.
Un pneu a crevé.
eN pnä ä krəvä

Please change this tire.
Changez ce pneu, s. v. p.
shäNzhā sə pnä, sēl vōō plä

A new inner tube, please.
Une nouvelle chambre à air, s'il vous plaît.
ēn nōōvel shäNb(ər) ä ār, sēl vōō plä

Would you please pump up the spare tire?
Gonflez le pneu de rechange, s'il vous plaît.
gôNflā lə pnä də rəshäNzh, sēl vōō plä

Would you please check the tire pressure?
Vérifiez la pression des pneus, s'il vous plaît.
värēfē·ā lä presyôN dä pn*a*, sēl v$\overline{oo}$ plä

The front tires are 22.7, and the rear ones are 28.4.
À l'avant 1,6, à l'arrière 2,0 kg.
äläväN eN vērg*e*l sēs, äläryär d*a* kēlōgräm

> *Since tire pressure varies from car to car, it's a good idea to write down the pressure needed for your car and keep it handy for reference.*

blow-up	crevaison *f*	kreväzôN
inner tube	chambre *f* à air	shäNb(ər) ä är
jack	cric *m*	krēk
puncture	trou *m*	tr$\overline{oo}$
tires *(in general)* ...	pneus *m/pl.*	pn*a*
– tubeless tire	pneu *m* plein	pn*a* pleN
tire change	changement *m* de pneu	shäNzh·mäN də pn*a*
tire pressure	pression *f* des pneus ...	presyôN dä pn*a*
valve	soupape *f*	s$\overline{oo}$päp
wheel	roue *f*	r$\overline{oo}$
– back wheel	roue *f* arrière	r$\overline{oo}$ äryär
– front wheel	roue *f* avant	r$\overline{oo}$ äväN
– reserve wheel	roue *f* de secours	r$\overline{oo}$ də sək$\overline{oo}$r
– wheels	roues *f/pl.*	r$\overline{oo}$

Car Wash

Please wash the *windshield (the windows)*.
Nettoyez *le pare-brise (les vitres)*, s'il vous plaît.
netô·äyä lə pärbrēz/lä vēt(ər), sēl v$\overline{oo}$ plä

I'd like my car washed, please.
Lavez la voiture, s'il vous plaît.
lävä lä vô·ät*e*r, sēl v$\overline{oo}$ plä

Please clean out the inside too.
Nettoyez aussi l'intérieur de la voiture, s'il vous plaît.
netô·äyä ôsē leNtārē·*a*r dəlä vô·ät*e*r, sēl v$\overline{oo}$ plä

Breakdown, Accident

I've (We've) had a breakdown.

Je suis (Nous sommes) en panne.
zhə sē·ē (noo sôm) äN pän

I've had an accident.

J'ai eu un accident.
zhā ē eNäksēdäN

Would you please call the police?

Appelez la police, s'il vous plaît.
äplā lä pôlēs, sēl voo plä

Call an ambulance quickly.

Faites venir une ambulance immédiatement!
fāt vənēr ēn äNbēläNs ēmādē·ätmäN

Please help me!

Aidez-moi, s'il vous plaît.
ādā-mô·ä, sēl voo plä

Could you lend me . . . ?

Pouvez-vous me prêter . . . ?
poovā-voo mə prātā . . .

– give me a ride?

– m'emmener un bout de chemin?
– mämnā eN boo də shəmeN

– get me a *mechanic (a tow truck)*?

– m'envoyer *un mécanicien (une dépanneuse)*?
– mäNvô·äyā eN mākänēsyeN (ēn dāpänāz)

– look after the injured?

– prendre soin des blessés?
– präNd(ər) sô·eN dā blesā

. . . is *busted (not working)*.

. . . ne marche pas.
. . . nə märsh pä

May I use your phone?

Je peux téléphoner de chez vous?
zhə pā tālāfônā də shā voo

Get a doctor!

Faites venir un médecin!
fāt vənēr eN mādəseN

I need bandages.

J'ai besoin de pansement.
zhā bezô·eN də päNs·mäN

Could you . . . ?

Pourriez-vous . . . ?
poorē·ā voo . . .

– tow my car?

– remorquer ma voiture?
– remôrkä mä vô·ätēr

Where is there a *service station (repair shop)*?

Où y a-t-il *une station-service (un garage)*?
oo yätēl ēn stäsyôN servēs (eN gäräzh)

Would you please give me your name and address?

Donnez-moi vos nom et adresse, s'il vous plaît.
dônā-mô·ä vō nôN ā ädres, sēl voo plä

It's your fault.
C'est de votre faute.
sä də vôt(ər) fōt

I had the right of way.
J'avais la priorité.
zhävä lä prē·ôrētä

Nobody's hurt.
Personne n'est blessé.
persôn nä blesä

Will you be my witness?
Pouvez-vous être mon témoin?
pōovä-vōo ät(ər) môN tāmô·eN

You've damaged . . .
Vous avez abîmé . . .
vōozävā äbēmä . . .

. . . is (badly) injured.
. . . est (grièvement) blessé.
. . . ä grē·äv·mäN blesä

Thanks very much for your help.
Merci beaucoup pour votre aide!
mersē bōkōo pōor vôträd

Where is your car insured?
Où est assurée votre voiture?
ōo ätäsērä vôt(ər) vô·ätēr

accident	accident *m*	äksēdäN
bandages	pansement *m*	päNs·mäN
body and fender damage	dégâts *m/pl.* matériels	dägä mätärē·el
breakdown	panne *f*	pän
careful!	Attention!	ätäNsyôN
collision	collision *f*	kôlēzyôN
damage	dommages *m/pl.*	dômäzh
dealership garage	garage *m* concessionnaire	gäräzh kôNsesyônär
emergency ward	poste *m* de secours	pôst də səkōor
fire department	pompiers *m/pl.*	pôNpyä
first aid station	poste *m* de secours	pôst də səkōor
head-on collision	collision *f* de face	kôlēzyôN də fäs
help	aide *f*, secours *m*	äd, səkōor
injury	blessure *f*	blesēr
insurance	assurance *f*	äsēräNs
mechanic	mécanicien *m*	mäkänēsyeN
rear-end collision	télescopage *m*	tāläskôpäzh
repair shop	atelier *m* de réparation	ätelyä də räpäräsyôN
service station	station-service *f*	stäsyôN servēs
towing service	service *m* de dépannage	servēs də dāpänäzh
tow line	câble *m* de remorquage	käb'əl də remôrkäzh
tow truck	dépanneuse *f*	dāpänäz

Repair Workshop

Where's the nearest garage (Volkswagen garage)?
Où est le garage (i.e. Volkswagen) le plus proche?
ōō ä lə gäräzh (fōlksvägän ...) lə plē prôsh

... isn't working right.
... n'est pas en bon état.
... näpä äN bônätä

... is out of order (isn't working).
... ne marche pas.
... nə märsh pä

Can you fix it?
Pouvez-vous faire cela?
pōōvä-vōō fär səlä

Where can I have this fixed?
Qui peut faire cela?
kē pə fär səlä

Would you please check the ...
Vérifiez ..., s'il vous plaît.
vārēfē·ä ..., sēl vōō plä

Would you please give me ...
Donnez-moi, s'il vous plaît ...
dônä-mô·ä, sēl vōō plä ...

Would you please fix this.
Réparez cela, s'il vous plaît.
rāpärä səlä, sēl vōō plä

Have you got manufacturer's spare parts for ...?
Avez-vous des pièces de rechange d'origine pour ...?
ävä-vōō dā pyäs də reshäNzh dôrēzhēn pōōr ...

How soon can you get the spare parts?
Quand aurez-vous les pièces de rechange?
käNdôrā-vōō lā pyäs də reshäNzh

I need a new ...
J'ai besoin d'une nouvelle (d'un nouveau) ...
zhā bezô·eN dēn nōōvel (deN nōōvō) ...

Can I still drive it?
Puis-je encore rouler ainsi?
pē·ēzhäNkôr rōōlä eNsē

Just do the essentials, please.
Ne faites que les réparations strictement nécessaires.
nə fāt ke lā rāpäräsyôN strēkt·mäN nāsesär

When will it be ready?
Quand la voiture sera-t-elle prête?
käN lä vô·ätēr serätel prät

How much does (will) it cost?
Ça coûte (coûtera) combien?
sä kōōt (kōōterä) kôNbyeN

Car Parts, Repairs

accelerator	accélérateur *m*	äkselärätär
– accelerate	accélérer	äkselärä
– slow down	ralentir	räläNtēr
air filter	filtre *m* d'air	fēlt(ər) dār
air pump	pompe *f* à air	pôNp ä ār
anti-freeze	antigel *m*	äNtēzhäl
automatic transmission	changement *m* de vitesse automatique	shäNzh·mäN də vētes ôtōmätēk
axle	essieu *m*	esyā
backfire	raté *m*	rätā
ball bearings	roulement *m* à billes	rōōlmäN ä bē'ē
battery	batterie *f*	bätərē
bearing	coussinet *m*	kōōsēnā
blinker	clignotant *m*	klēnyôtäN
body	carrosserie *f*	kärôsrē
bolt; nut	vis *f*; écrou *m*	vēs; äkrōō
brake drum	tambour *m* de frein	täNbōōr də freN
brake fluid	liquide *m* de freinage	lēkēd də frenäzh
brake lights	feux *m/pl.* de stop	fā də stôp
brake lining	garniture *f* de frein	gärnētẽr də freN
brakes	freins *m/pl.*	freN
– disc brake	frein *m* à disques	freN ä dēsk
– foot brake	frein *m* à pied	freN ä pyā
– hand brake	frein *m* à main	freN ä meN
bulb	ampoule *f*	äNpōōl
– change the bulb	changer l'ampoule	shäNzhä läNpōōl
bumper	pare-chocs *m*	pär-shôk
cable	câble *m*	käb'əl
camshaft	arbre *m* à cames	ärbrä käm

The battery *has run down (needs charging)*.
La batterie *est vide (Il faut recharger la batterie)*.
lä bätərē ä vēd (ēl fō reshärzhä lä bätərē)

The brakes aren't working right.   They're *slack (too tight)*.
Les freins ne sont pas en bon état.   Ils sont *peu (trop)* serrés.
lä freN nə sôN päzäN bônätä   ēl sôN pā (trō) serä

The brake drums are getting too hot.
Les tambours de frein chauffent.
lä täNbōōr də freN shōf

carburetor	carburateur *m*	kärbē̲rätär
carburetor jet	gicleur *m*	zhēklär
car door	portière *f*	pôrtyär
car keys	clé *f* de la voiture	klä də lä vô·ätēr
chain	chaîne *f*	shän
– snow chains	chaînes *f/pl.*	shän
	antidérapantes	äNtēdäräpäNt
chassis	chassis *m*	
	de la voiture	shäsē̲ də lä vô·ätēr
clutch	embrayage *m*	äNbräyäzh
– clutch pedal	pédale *f* d'embrayage.	pädäl däNbräyäzh
compression	compression *f*	kôNpresyôN
condenser	condensateur *m*	kôNdäNsätär
connecting rod	bielle *f*	byel
– connecting rod	coussinet *m*	kōōsēnā̲
bearing	de tête de bielle	də tāt də byel
contact	contact *m*	kôNtäkt
crankshaft	vilebrequin *m*	vēlbrekeN
cylinder	cylindre *m*	sēleNd(ər)
– cylinder head	culasse *f*	kē̲läs
– cylinder head		
gasket	joint *m* de culasse	zhô·eN də kē̲läs
diesel nozzle	gicleur *m* diesel	zhēklär dyezel
differential	différentiel *m*	dēfäräNsyel
dip stick	réglette-jauge *f*	rāglet-zhōzh
distributor	distributeur *m*	dēstrēbē̲tär
door lock	serrure *f* de la	serēr də lä
	portière	pôrtyär
drive shaft	arbre *m moteur*	ärb(ər) môtär
	(de couche)	(də kōōsh)

The dynamo isn't charging.
La dynamo ne fonctionne pas.
lä dēnämō nə fôNksyôN pä

It won't stay in ... gear.
La ... vitesse est mal enclenchée.
lä ... vētes ā mäl äNkläNshā

The gearshift needs to be checked over.
Il faut contrôler la boîte à vitesses.
ēl fō kôNtrōlā lä bô·ät ä vētes

There's oil leaking out of the gear-box.
Il y a de l'huile qui goutte de la boîte à vitesses.
ēlyä də lē̲·ēl kē gōōt də lä bô·ät ä vētes

dynamo	dynamo *f*	dēnämō
exhaust	échappement *m*	äshäp·mäN
fan	ventilateur *m*	väNtēlätär
fan belt	courroie *f* trapézoidale	kōōrô·ä träpäzō·ēdäl
fender	garde-boue *m*	gärd-bōō
fire extinguisher	extincteur *m*	eksteNktär
float	flotteur *m*	flôtär
free wheel (hub)	moyeu *m* à roue libre	mô·äyä ä rōō lēb(ər)
fuel injector	pompe *f* à injection	pôNp ä eNyeksyôN
fuel lines	conduite *f* d'essence	kôNdē·ēt desäNs
fuel pump	pompe *f* à essence	pôNp ä esäNs
fuse	fusible *m*	fēsēb'əl
gas	accélérateur *m*	äkselärätär
gasket	joint *m*	zhô·eN
gear	vitesse *f*	vētes
– neutral	point *m* mort	pô·eN môr
– reverse	marche *f* arrière	märsh äryär
– to put it in gear	passer en ... vitesse	päsä äN ... vētes
gear box	boîte *f* de vitesses	bô·ät də vētes
gear lever	levier *m* de changement de vitesse	levyä də shäNzh-mäN də vētes
gearshift	changement *m* de vitesse	shäNzh·mäN də vētes
grease	graisse *f*	gres
handle	poignée *f*	pô·änyä
headlight	phare *m*	fär
– dimmed headlights	feux *m/pl.* de croisement	fä də crô·äz·mäN

The heating doesn't work.
Le chauffage ne fonctionne pas.
lə shôfäzh nə fôNksyôn pä

The radiator has sprung a leak.
Il y a de l'eau qui goutte du radiateur.
ēlyä də lō kē gōōt dē rädē·ätär

The clutch *slips (won't disengage).*
L'embrayage *glisse (ne débraie pas).*
läNbrāyäzh glēs (nə dābrā pä)

– high beam	feux *m/pl.* de route	fā də rōot
– parking lights	feux *m/pl.* de position	fā də pôzēsyôN
– rear lights	feux *m/pl.* arrières	fā äryär
heating system	chauffage *m*	shôfäzh
hood	capot *m*	käpō
horn	avertisseur *m* sonore	ävertēsär sônôr
– flashing signal	avertisseur *m* lumineux	ävertēsär lēmēnā
hub	moyeu *m*	mô·äyā
hub cap	enjoliveur *m*	äNzhôlēvär
ignition	allumage *m*	älēmäzh
– ignition cable	fil *m* d'allumage	fēl dälēmäzh
– ignition key	clé *f* de contact	klä də kôNtäkt
– ignition lock	serrure *f* de contact	serēr də kôNtäkt
– ignition system	installation *f*	eNstäläsyôN
	de l'allumage	də lälēmäzh
indicator light	lampe-témoin *f*	läNp-tämô·eN
insulation	isolement *m*	ēzôlmäN
interrupter	interrupteur *m*	eNterēptär
lamp	lampe *f*	läNp
license plate	plaque *f*	pläk
	d'immatriculation	dēmätrēkēläsyôN
lighting system	éclairage *m*	äkläräzh
lubricant	lubrifiant *m*; graisse *f*	lēbrēfē·äN; gres
mileage indicator	compteur *m*	kôNtär
	kilométrique	kēlōmätrēk
motor	moteur *m*	môtär
– diesel motor	moteur *m* diésel	môtär dyezel
– rear motor	moteur *m* à l'arrière	môtär äläryär
– two-stroke motor	moteur *m*	môtär
	(à) deux temps	(ä) dā täN

The motor lacks power.   – is overheating.
Le moteur ne tire pas.   – chauffe.
lə môtär nə tēr pä   – shôf

– knocks.	– suddenly stalls.	– misses.
– cogne.	– cale.	– a des ratés.
– kôn(yə)	– käl	– ä dā rätä

nationality plate	plaque *f* de nationalité	pläk də näsyônälētä
oil filter	filtre *m* à huile	fēlt(ər) ä *ē*·ēl
oil pump	pompe *f* à huile	pôNp ä *ē*·ēl
paint job	laque *m, f*	läk
pedal	pédale *f*	pädäl
piston	piston *m*	pēstôN
– piston ring	segment *m* de piston ..	segmäN də pēstôN
pipe	chambre *f* à air	shäNb(ər) ä ār
radiator	radiateur *m*	rädē·ätär
– radiator grill	volet *m* du radiateur...	vôlä d*ē* rädē·ätär
rear view mirror	rétroviseur *m*	rätrōvēzär
repair	réparation *f*	räpäräsyôN
reserve fuel can	bidon *m* de réserve	bēdôN də räzärv
roof	capote *f*	käpôt
screw	vis *f*	vēs
seat belt	ceinture *f* de sécurité	seNt*ēr* də säk*ē*rētä
shock absorber	amortisseur *m*	ämôrtēsär
short circuit	court-circuit *m*	kōōr-sērk*ē*·ē
sliding (sun) **roof**	toit *m* ouvrant	tô·ä ōōvräN
solder	souder	sōōdä
speedometer	tachymètre *m*	täkēmät(ər)
spoke	rayon *m*	räyôN
seat	siège *m*	syäzh
– back seat	siège *m* arrière	syäzh äryär
– driver's seat	siège *m* du conducteur	syäzh d*ē* kôNd*e*ktär
– front seat	siège *m* avant	syäzh äväN
– front passenger seat	siège *m* avant droit	syäzh äväN drô·ä
spare part	pièce *f* de rechange	pyäs də reshäNzh
spare wheel	roue *f* de secours	rōō də səkōōr

The windshield wiper *smears (is broken off)*.
L'essuie-glace *nettoie mal (est cassé)*.
les*ē*·ē-gläs netô·ä mäl (ä käsā)

This screw needs *tightening (loosening)*.
Cette vis doit être *serrée (desserrée)*.
set vēs dô·ätät(ər) serä (deserä)

The fuse has blown.
Le fusible est fondu.
lə f*ē*zēblä fôNd*ē*

spark	étincelle *f*	āteNsel
spark plug	bougie *f* d'allumage	bōōzhē dälēmäzh
spring	ressort *m*	resôr
starter	démarreur *m*	dāmärār
steering	conduite *f*	kôNdē·ēt
– steering wheel	volant *m*	vôläN
switch	commutateur *m*	kômētätār
thermostat	thermostat *m*	termôstä
(screw) thread	filet *m*	fēlā
top	capote *f*	käpôt
transmission	boîte *f* de vitesses	bô·ät də vētes
trunk	coffre *m*	kôf(ər)
tube	chambre *f* à air	shäNbrä är
valve	soupape *f*	sōōpäp
warning triangle	triangle *m* avertisseur	trē·äNgl ävertēsār
washer	produit *m*	prôdē·ē
	du lave-vitre	dē läv-vēt(ər)
wheel	roue *f*	rōō
windshield	pare-brise *m*	pär-brēz
windshield washer	lave-vitre *m*	läv-vēt(ər)
windshield wiper	essuie-glace *m*	esē·ē-gläs

Would you please straighten out my bumper?
Redressez le pare-chocs, s'il vous plaît.
redresā lə pär-shôk, sēl vōō plä

Would you please *check (clean)* the carburetor?
Voudriez-vous *vérifier (nettoyer)* le carburateur?
vōōdrē·ā·-vōō vārēfē·ā (netô·äyä) lə kärbērätār

Would you please change the spark plugs?
Changez les bougies, s'il vous plaît.
shäNzhā lā bōōzhē, sēl vōō plä

Tools

Can you loan me . . .?
Pourriez-vous me prêter . . .?
po͞orē·ā-vo͞o mə prātā

I need . . .
J'ai besoin de . . .
zhā bezô·eN də

air pump	pompe *f* à air	pôNpä är
bolt	vis *f*	vēs
– **nut**	écrou *m*	ākro͞o
cable	câble *m*	käb'əl
chisel	ciseau *m*	sēzō
cloth	chiffon *m*	shēfôN
drill	foret *m*	fôrā
file	lime *f*	lēm
funnel	entonnoir *m*	äNtônô·är
hammer	marteau *m*	märtō
inspection light	lampe-témoin *f*	läNp-tāmô·eN
jack	cric *m*	krēk
pincers	tenailles *f/pl.*	tenä′ē
pliers	pinces *f/pl.*	peNs
rag	chiffon *m*	shēfôN
sandpaper	papier *m* verré	päpyā verā
screw	vis *f*	vēs
screwdriver	tournevis *m*	to͞orn·vēs
socket wrench	clé *f* à douille	klā ä do͞o′ē
string	ficelle *f*	fēsel
tool	outil *m*	o͞otē
– **tool** *box (kit)*	coffre *m* à outils	kôfrä o͞otē
wire	fil *m* métallique	fēl mātälēk
– **a piece of wire**	un bout de fil métallique	eN bo͞o də fēl mātälēk
wrench	clé *f* anglaise	klā äNglāz

TRAFFIC SIGNS

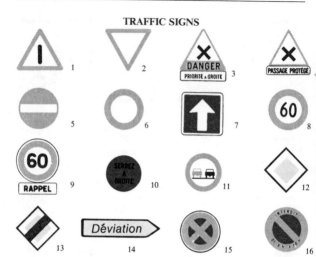

1 DANGER Danger · 2 YIELD RIGHT OF WAY Cédez le passage ·
3 DANGER – GIVE WAY TO TRAFFIC FROM RIGHT Priorité à
droite · 4 PRIORITY CROSSING *(for you)* Intersection de priorité ·
5 DO NOT ENTER Sens interdit · 6 NO VEHICLES ALLOWED
Circulation interdite à tout véhicule dans les deux sens · 7 ONE WAY
STREET Sens unique · 8 SPEED LIMIT *(kilometers)* Limitation de
vitesse · 9 SPEED LIMIT CONTINUED Rappel de vitesse limitée · 11
NO PASSING Interdiction de dépasser · 10 KEEP RIGHT Serrez à
droite · 12 PRIORITY ROAD Route à priorité · 13 END OF
PRIORITY ROAD Fin de route à priorité · 14 DETOUR Déviation ·
15 NO STOPPING Arrêt interdit · 16 NO PARKING *between 8 and 10
a.m.* Stationnement interdit (entre 8 et 10 h)

Road signs are color and shape-coded. Triangular signs with a red
rim are *warning signs*; round blue signs are *regulatory signs*; round
signs with a red rim are *prohibit movement signs*; rectangular
yellow signs with a black rim are *destination signs*; rectangular
blue signs with white letters are *destination signs* on highways.

ON THE BUS

Where is the next bus stop?
Où est l'arrêt d'autobus le plus proche?
ōō ā lärā dôtōbēs lə plē prôsh

Where do the buses to . . . stop?
Où s'arrêtent les autobus pour . . .?
ōō särät lāzôtōbēs pōor . . .

Is that far?
Est-ce loin?
es lô•eN

When does a (the first/last) bus leave for . . .?
Quand part un (le premier/dernier) autobus pour . . .?
käN pär eNôtōbēs (lə prəmyā / dernyā ôtōbēs) pōor

Which bus goes to . . .?
Quel autobus va à . . .?
kel ôtōbēs vä ä . . .

Where does the bus go?
Où va l'autobus?
ōō vä lôtōbēs

Is there a bus (Does this bus go) to . . .?
Y a-t-il un autobus pour . . . (Cet autobus va-t-il à . . .)?
ēyätēl eNôtōbēs pōor . . . (set ôtōbēs vätēl ä . . . .)

When do we get to . . .?
Quand arrivons-nous à . . .?
käNdärēvôN-nōo ä . . .

Do I have to change buses for . . .?
Faut-il changer d'autobus pour . . .?
fōt-ēl shäNzhā dôtōbēs pōor . . .

Where do I have to change?
Où faut-il changer?
ōō fōt-ēl shäNzhā

One (Two) round-trip ticket(s), please.
Un ticket (Deux tickets) aller et retour
pour . . .
eN tēkā (dā tēkā) älā ā retōor pōor

One full-fare and one half-fare to . . . please.
Un ticket et une demi-place pour . . ., s'il vous plaît.
eN tēkā ā ēn dəmē-pläs pōor . . ., sēl vōo plā

bus	autobus *m*	ôtōbēs
bus terminal	terminus *m*	termēnēs
direction	direction *f*	dēreksyôN
driver	conducteur *m*	kôNdĕktār
luggage	bagages *m/pl.*	bägäzh
route	ligne *f*	lēn(yə)
stop	arrêt *m*	ärä
ticket	ticket *m*, billet *m*	tēkā, bēyā
transfer	ticket *m*	tēkā
	de correspondance	də kôrespôNdäNs

At the Station   BY TRAIN

Where is the *station (main station)*?
Où est la gare (centrale)?
о͞о ā lä gär (säNträl)

Where *is (are)* ...?
Où *est (sont)* ... ?
о͞о ā (sôN)

baggage check area ..	l'enregistrement *m* des bagages	läNrezhēstrəmäN dä bägäzh
baggage claim area ..	la consigne	lä kôNsēn(yə)
first aid station	l'infirmerie *f*	leNfērmərē
information office ...	le bureau de renseignements	lə bēr̄o də räNsen(yə)mäN
Platform 2	le quai deux	lə kā dā
rest room	les toilettes *f/pl.*, les lavabos *m/pl.*	lā tô·älet, lā läväbō
room referral office .	la réservation de chambres	lä räzerväsyóN də shäNb(ər)
ticket window	le guichet	lə gēshä
a time table	l'horaire *m.*	lôrär
waiting room	la salle d'attente	lä säl dätäNt

Time Table

arrival/departure	arrivée *f*/départ *m*	ärēvā/dāpär
connection	correspondance *f*	kôrespôNdäNs
couchette sleeper	voiture-couchettes *f* ...	vô·ätēr-ko͞oshet
dining car	wagon-restaurant *m* ...	vägôN-restôräN
express train	train *m* direct; express *m*	treN dērekt; ekspres
fast train	rapide *m*	räpēd
motorail service	train *m* auto-couchettes	treN ôtō-ko͞oshet
platform	voie *f*; quai *m*	vô·ä; kā
rail car	automotrice *f*	ôtōmôtrēs
sleeper/sleeping car ..	wagon-lit *m*	vägôN-lē
suburban train	train *m* de banlieue....	treN də bäNlēyā

A couchette *car provides overnight travelers with a simple bench and blanket to stretch out during the night. A sleeping car* (wagon-lit) *contains little bedrooms complete with private washing facilities.*

system time table ...	indicateur *m*, Chaix *m*	eNdēkätär, shäks
through car	voiture *f* directe	vô·ätēr dērekt
track	voie *f*	vô·ä

Information

When is there a *local (express)* train to ...?
Quand part un *train omnibus (express)* pour ...?
käN pär eN treN ômnēbēs (ekspres) pōōr ...

Where is the train to ...?
Où est le train pour ...?
ōō ā lə treN pōōr ...

Is this the train to ...?
Est-ce le train pour ...?
es lə treN pōōr ...

Does this train go by way of ....?
Ce train passe par ...?
sə treN päs pär ...

Does this train stop in ...?
Ce train s'arrête à ...?
sə treN särāt ä ...

Is the train from ... late? **How late?** **When does it get to ...?**
Le train de ... a du retard? Combien? Quand arrive-t-il à ...?
lə treN də ... ä dē retär kôNbyeN käNdärēvtēl ä ...

Can we make a connection to...?
Avons-nous une correspondance pour ...?
ävôN-nōō ēn kôrespôNdäNs pōōr ...

Do we have to change trains? **Where?**
Faut-il changer de train? Où?
fōtēl shäNzhā də treN ōō

Is there a dining car (Are there sleepers) on the train?
Le train a un *wagon-restaurant (wagon-lit)?*
lə treN ä eN vägôN-restôräN (vägôN-lē)

Can I interrupt the trip in ...?
Je peux interrompre mon voyage à ...?
zhə pāzeNterôNp(ər) môN vô·äyäzh ä ...

What platform does the train from ... come in on?
Sur quel quai arrive le train de ...?
sēr kel kā ärēv lə treN də ...

What platform does the train for ... leave from?
De quel quai part le train pour ...?
də kel kā pär lə treN pōōr ...

Tickets

– round trip.	– one way.	– first class.	– second class.
– aller et retour.	– aller.	– de première.	– de seconde.
– älä ā retōor	– älä	– də prəmyär	– də səgôNd

I'd like to reserve a seat on the twelve o'clock train to ...
Je voudrais réserver une place pour le train de douze heures pour ...
zhə vōodrā rāzervä ēn pläs pōor lə treN də dōozār pōor ...

How long is the ticket valid?
Jusqu'à quand ce billet est-il valable?
zhēskä käN sə bēyā etēl väläb'əl

I'd like to interrupt the trip in ...
J'aimerais interrompre le voyage à ...
zhämerä eNterôNp(ər) lə vô·äyäzh ä ...

I'd like to reserve ...	**Please reserve two seats.**
Je voudrais réserver ...	Réservez deux places, sil vous plaît.
zhə vōodrā rāzervā ...	rāzervā dā pläs, sēl vōo plä

How much is the fare to ...?
Le billet pour ... coûte combien?
lə bēyā pōor ... kōot kôNbyeN

fare	prix *m* du billet	prē dē bēyā
group fare ticket	billet *m* de groupe	bēyā də grōop
half fare	demi-place *f*	dəmē-pläs
one-day round-trip	aller et retour valable vingt-quatre heures	älä ā retōor väläb'əl veN-käträr
round-trip ticket	billet *m* circulaire	bēyā sērkelär
seat reservation	réservation *f* de place assise	rāzervāsyóN də pläs äsēz
sleeper reservation	réservation *f* de wagon-lit	rāzervāsyóN də vägôN-lē
supplemental fare ticket	supplément *m*	sēplämäN
ticket	ticket *m*; billet *m*	tēkā; bēyā
– one-way ticket	billet *m* aller	bēyā älä
– reduced fare ticket	billet *m* à tarif réduit	bēyā ä tärēf rādē·ē

Baggage

> In European countries, you can check your bag with the railroad, just
> as you do with an airline, and then pick it up at your destination. If you
> are checking your baggage to be forwarded, you should go to the
> Enregistrement des bagages (äNrezhēstrəmäN dā bägäzh). If you
> are simply checking your luggage within the station, go to the
> Consigne (automatique), (kôNsēnyə ōtōmätēk).

I'd like to ...
Je voudrais ...
zhə vōōdrā ...

– send this luggage on to ...
– faire enregistrer ces bagages pour ...
– fār äNrezhēstrā sā bägäzh pōor ...

– leave this luggage here.
– laisser ces bagages ici.
– lesā sā bägäzh ēsē

– insure (claim) my luggage.
– faire assurer (retirer) mes bagages.
– fār äsērā (retērā) mā bägäzh

Here's my claim check.
Voici le bulletin d'enregistrement.
vô·äsē lə bēlteN däNrezhēstrəmäN

There are two suitcases and a traveling bag.
Il y a deux valises et un sac de voyage.
ēlyä dā välēz ā eN säk də vô·äyäzh

Will my baggage be on the same train?
Mes bagages partent par le même train?
mā bägäzh pärt pär lə mām treN

When does it get to ...?
Quand arriveront-ils à ...
käNdärēvəróNt-ēlzä ...

These aren't mine.
Ce ne sont pas mes bagages.
se nə sôN pä mā bägäzh

One suitcase is missing.
Il manque une valise.
ēl mäNk ēn välēz

baggage, luggage	bagages *m/pl.*	bägäzh
baggage check area/ forwarding office ..	enregistrement *m* des bagages	äNrezhēstrəmäN dā bägäzh
baggage claim/(deposit)area	consigne *f*	kôNsēn(yə)
claim check	bulletin *m* d'enregistrement	bēlteN däNrezhēstrəmäN
hand luggage	bagage *m* à main	bägäzh ä meN

luggage locker	......	consigne *f*	....	kôNsēn(yə)
		automatique	....	ôtōmätēk
suitcase	....	valise *f*	....	välēz
traveling bag	....	sac *m* de voyage	......	säk də vô·äyäzh

Porter

| **porter** | .... | porteur *m* | .... | pôrtœr |

Please bring this *luggage (suitcase)* ...
Ces bagages (Cette valise), s'il vous plaît,
sā bägäzh (set välēz), sēl voo plä

– **to the ... train.**
– au train pour ...
– ō treN poor

– **to the baggage check area.**
– à la consigne (à l'enregistrement des bagages).
– älä kôNsēn(yə) (ä läNrezhēstrəmäN dā bägäzh)

– **to the exit.**
– à la sortie.
– älä sôrtē

– **to a taxi.**	– **to the ... bus.**	**How much does that cost?**
– au taxi.	– à l'autobus pour ...	Ça coûte combien?
– ō täksē	– ä lôtōbēs poor ...	sä koot kôNbyeN

On the Platform

Is this the train *to (from)* ...?
Est-ce le train *pour (venant de)* ...?
es lə treN poor (venäN də) ...

Where is ...?
Où est ...?
oo ā ...

– **first class?**	– **the through car to ...?**
– la première classe?	– la voiture directe pour ...?
– lä prəmyär kläs	– lä vô·ätœr dērekt poor ...

> *European express trains frequently get reassembled at major stations*
> *with different cars going to different destinations. Make sure before*
> *you get aboard that your car will take you where you want to go.*

– **the luggage car?**	– **car number ...?**
– le fourgon?	– la voiture numéro ...?
– lə foorgôN	– lä vô·ätœr nēmārō ...

– **the couchette car?**	– **the sleeping car?**	– **the dining car?**
– la voiture-couchettes?	– le wagon-lit?	– le wagon-restaurant?
– lä vô·ätœr-kooshet	– lə vägôN-lē	– lə vägôN-restôräN

There.	**Up front.**	**In the middle.**
Là (Là-bas).	À l'avant.	Au milieu.
lä (läbä)	äläväN	ō mēlēy*a*

At the rear.	**What time does the train arrive?**
À l'arrière (En queue).	À quelle heure arrive le train?
äläryär (äN k*a*)	ä kel*a*r ärēv lə treN

CHEF DE GARE	SORTIE	RENSEIGNEMENTS
shef də gär	sôrtē	räNsen(yə)mäN
Station Master	**Exit**	**Information**

ACCÈS AU QUAIS	ENREGISTREMENT DES BAGAGES	VOIE
äksä ō kä	äNrezhēstrəmäN dā bägäzh	vô·ä
To Trains	**Luggage Checking**	***Platform (Track)***

POSTE DE SECOURS	EAU POTABLE	LAVABOS
pôst də səkoor	ō pôtäb'əl	läväbō
First Aid	**Drinking Water**	**Rest Rooms**

MESSIEURS	DAMES	PONT
mesy*a*	däm	pôN
Gentlemen	**Ladies**	**Overpass**

SALLE D'ATTENTE	PASSAGE SOUTERRAIN
säl dätäNt	päsäzh sootereN
Waiting Room	**Underpass**

On the Train

Is this seat taken?
Cette place est libre, s'il vous plaît?
set pläs ā lēb(ər), sēl voo plä

That's my seat.
C'est ma place.
sā mä pläs

Mind if I *open (close)* the window?
Vous permettez que *j'ouvre (je ferme)* la fenêtre?
voo permetä kə *zhoov(ər) (zhə färm)* lä fenät(ər)

Could you please help me?

Pourriez-vous m'aider, s'il vous plaît?

po͞ore̅·ā·vo͞o mādā, sēl vo͞o plä

Would you mind changing places?

Pourrions-nous changer de place?

po͞ore̅·óN-no͞o shäNzhā də pläs

I don't like riding backwards.

Je n'aime pas rouler dans le sens contraire de la marche.

zhə näm pä ro͞olä däN lə säNs kôNträr dəlä märsh

*Tickets, please.

Les billets, s'il vous plaît.

lā bēyā, sēl vo͞o plä

How many stations before . . .?

Combien d'arrêts y a-t-il encore jusqu'à . . .?

kôNbyeN därā yätēl äNkôr zhe̅skä . . .

Will we get to . . . on time?

Arrivons-nous à l'heure à . . .?

ärēvôN-no͞o älār ä . . .

Where are we now?

Où sommes-nous maintenant?

o͞o sôm-no͞o meNtənäN

How long do we stop here?

Combien de temps le train s'arrête ici?

kôNbyeN də täN lə treN säret ēse̅

*All change, please!

Tout le monde descend!

to͞o lə môNd·desäN

Will I make it on time to change trains for . . .?

Est-ce que j'aurai la correspondance pour . . .?

eske zhôrā lä kôrespóNdäNs po͞or . . .

*Passengers for . . . change at . . .

Messieurs les voyageurs pour . . . changez à . . .

mesyā lā vô·äyäzhār po͞or . . . shäNzhā ä . . .

*Passengers for . . . get on the *front (rear)* of the train!

Messieurs les voyageurs pour . . ., montez en voiture *à l'avant (à l'arrière)* du train!

mesyā lā vô·äyäzhār po͞or . . . môNtā äN vô·ätēr ä lävaN (äläryär) de̅ treN

NON-FUMEURS	FUMEURS	LIBRE	OCCUPÉ
No smoking	Smoking	Vacant	Occupied

WAGON-RESTAURANT	WAGON-LIT
Dining Car	Sleeping Car

*all aboard!	en voiture,	äN vô·ätēr,
	s'il vous plaît!	sēl vōō plä
arrival	arrivée f	ärēvā
arrive	arriver	ärēvā
baggage, luggage	bagages m/pl.	bägäzh
baggage car	fourgon m	fōōrgôN
barrier	barrière f	bäryär
car	voiture f	vô·ätēr
car door	portière f	pôrtyär
change trains	changer de train	shäNzhā də treN
compartment	compartiment m	kôNpärtēmäN
conductor	contrôleur m	kôNtrôlär
connection	correspondance f	kôrespôNdäNs
depart	partir	pärtēr
departure	départ m	dāpär
engine, locomotive	locomotive f	lōkōmōtēv
entrance	entrée f	äNtrā
exit	sortie f	sôrtē
fare	prix m du billet	prē dē bēyā
– discount	tarif m réduit	tärēf rādē·ē
get in (aboard)	monter (en voiture)	môNtā (äN vô·ätēr)
get off	descendre	desäNd(ər)
heating	chauffage m	shôfäzh
– cold	froid	frô·ä
– warm	chaud	shō
information	renseignement m	räNsen(yə)mäN
luggage rack	filet m	fēlā
passenger	voyageur m	vô·äyäzhär
platform	quai m	kā
railroad	chemin m de fer	shəmeN də fär
route	ligne f	lēn(yə)
station	gare f	gär
station master	chef m de gare	shef də gär
stop	arrêt m	ärā
system time table	indicateur m, Chaix m	eNdēkätär, shäks
ticket	billet m, ticket m	bēyā, tēkā
track	voie f	vô·ä
train	train m	treN
window seat	coin-fenêtre m	kô·eN-fnät(ər)

BY AIR

Information and Reservations

Is there a (direct) flight to ...?
Y a-t-il un vol (direct) pour ...?
ēyätēl eN vôl (dērekt) p͞oͅor

Is there a connection to ...?
J'ai une correspondance pour ...?
zhā ēn kôrespóNdäNs p͞oͅor

When is there a plane *today (tomorrow)* to ...?
À quelle heure part *aujourd'hui (demain)* un avion pour ...?
äkelär pär ōzh͞oͅordē·ē (demeN) eNävyôN p͞oͅor

When is the next plane to ...?
Quand part le prochain appareil pour ...?
käN pär lə prôshenäpärä'ē p͞oͅor

Does the plane make a stopover in ...?
L'appareil fait escale à ...?
läpärä'ē fäteskäl ä

When do we get to ...?
À quelle heure serons-nous à ...?
äkelär serôN-n͞oͅozä

Are there still seats available?
Il y a encore des places libres?
ēlyä äNkôr dā pläs lēb(ər)

How much is a (round-trip) flight to ...?
Combien coûte un vol (aller et retour) à ...?
kôNbyeN k͞oͅot eN vôl (älä ā ret͞oͅor) ä

What's the luggage allowance?
À combien de bagages a-t-on droit?
ä kôNbyeN də bägäzh ätôN drô·ä

How much does excess baggage cost?
Les bagages en excédent, c'est combien?
lā bägäzh äNeksädäN, sā kôNbyeN

How much is the airport service charge?
La taxe d'aéroport, c'est combien?
lä täks dä·ārôpôr, sā kôNbyeN

How do I get to the airport?
Pour aller à l'aéroport?
p͞oͅor älä älä·ārōpôr

When is check-in time?
Je dois me présenter au guichet à quelle heure?
zhə dô·ä mə präzäNtā ō gēshä äkelär

I'd like to reserve a seat on the Friday flight to . . .
Je voudrais faire une réservation pour un vol pour . . ., vendredi, s. v. p.
zhə voodrä fār eN räzerväsyôN poor eN vôl poor . . ., väNdrədē, sēl voo plä

I'd like to reserve a round-trip ticket to . . . on the 8th of May.
Réservez un vol aller et retour pour le huit mai pour . . ., s'il vous plaît.
räzervä eN vôl älä ā rətoor poor lə e·ē mä poor . . ., sēl voo plä

– First Class.	– Economy Class.	**How much does it cost?**
– première classe.	– classe économique.	Combien dois-je payer?
– prəmyār kläs	– kläs ākônōmēk	kôNbyeN dó·äzh päyā

How long is the ticket valid?
Quelle est la durée de validité du billet d'avion?
kel ā lä derä də välēdētä de bēyä dävyôN

I have to *cancel (change)* my reservation.
Il me faut *annuler (changer)* la réservation.
ēl mə fōtänēlä (shäNzhā) lä räzerväsyôN

What is the cancellation fee?
La taxe d'annulation, c'est combien?
lä täks dänēläsyôN, sä kôNbyeN

At the Airport

Can I take this along as hand luggage?
Puis-je prendre cela comme bagage à main?
pe·ēzh präNd(ər) səlä kôm bägäzh ä meN

Where is *the waiting room (Exit B, Gate B)*?
Où est *la salle d'attente (la sortie B)*?
oo ā lä säl dätäNt (lä sôrtē bä)

Where is the information counter?
Où sont les renseignements?
oo sôN lā räNsen(yə)mäN

Where's the duty-free shop?
Où peut-on acheter des marchandises hors-taxe?
oo pətôN äshtä dā märshäNdēz ôr-täks

Is the plane to . . . late?	**Has the plane from . . . already landed?**
L'appareil pour . . . a du retard?	L'avion venant de . . . a-t-il déjà atterri?
läpärā·ē poor . . . ä de retär	lävyôN vənäN də . . . ätēl dāzhä äterē

On the Plane

*Kindly refrain from smoking.
Éteignez vos cigarettes!
ätenyā vō sēgäret

*Please fasten your seat belts.
Attachez vos ceintures!
ätäshā vō seNtĕr

How high are we flying?
À quelle altitude sommes-nous?
ä kel ältētĕd sôm-nōō

Where are we now?
Où sommes-nous maintenant?
ōō sôm-nōō meNt·näN

What *mountains are those (river is that)*?
Quelle montagne (Quel fleuve) est-ce?
kel môNtän(yə) (kel flāv) es

Can I have ...?
Je peux avoir ...?
zhə pāzävô·är

I feel sick.
J'ai mal au cœur.
zhä mäl ō kăr

Have you got an air-sickness remedy?
Avez-vous un remède contre le mal de l'air?
ävā-vōō eN rəmād kôNt(ər) lə mäl dəlār

When do we land?
Quand atterrissons-nous?
käNdäterēsôN-nōō

How's the weather in ...?
Quel temps fait-il à ...?
kel täN fātēl ä ...

aircraft	avion *m*	ävyôN
air jet		
(over the seat)	buse *f* d'aération *f*	bēz dä·är äsyôN
airline	compagnie *f* aérienne . .	kôNpänyē ä·ärē·en
air passenger	passager *m*	päsäzhā
airport	aéroport *m*	ä·ärōpôr
airport		
service charge	taxe *f* d'aéroport	täks dä·ärōpôr
air sickness	mal *m* de l'air	mäl də lār
approach	approche *f*	äprôsh
arrival	arrivée *f*	ärēvā
charter plane	charter *m*	shärtär
climb	s'élever	säləvā
crew	équipage *m*	ākēpäzh
destination	destination *f*	destēnäsyôN
duty-free goods	marchandises *f/pl.*	märshäNdēz
	hors-taxe	ôr-täks
emergency chute	glissoire *f* de secours . . .	glēsô·är də səkōōr
emergency exit	sortie *f* de secours	sôrtē də səkōōr
emergency landing . .	atterrissage *m* forcé . . .	äterēsäzh fôrsā

engine	réacteur *m*	rā·äkt*ēr*
excess baggage	excédent *m* de bagages	eksādäN də bägäzh
exit	sortie *f*	sôrtē
flight	vol *m*	vôl
flight attendant	hôtesse *f* de l'air	ôtes də lār
fly	voler	vôlā
flying time	durée *f* de vol	dērā də vôl
fog	brouillard *m*	brōōyär
fuselage	fuselage *m*	fēzəläzh
gate	pont *m* d'embarquement	pôN däNbärkmäN
hand luggage	bagage *m* à main	bägäzh ä meN
helicopter	hélicoptère *m*	ālēkôptär
information	information *f*	eNfôrmäsyôN
information counter	guichet *m*	gēshā
	d'information	deNfôrmäsyôN
intermediate landing	escale *f*	eskäl
jet	turbo-réacteur *m*	tērbō-rā·äkt*ēr*
jet plane	avion *m* à réaction	ävyôN ä rääksyôN
land	atterrir	äterēr
landing	atterrissage *m*	äterēsäzh
landing gear	train *m* d'atterrissage	treN däterēsäzh
life jacket	gilet *m* de sauvetage	zhēlā də sōvtäzh
pilot	commandant *m* de bord	kômäNdäN də bôr
plane	avion *m*	ävyôN
reservation	réservation *f*	rāzervāsyôN
return flight	vol *m* de retour	vôl də retōōr
route	ligne *f* aérienne	lēn(yə) ä·ārē·en
scheduled flight	vol *m* régulier	vôl rägēlyā
seat belt	ceinture *f*	seNt*ēr*
– fasten seat belts	attachez vos ceintures	ätäshā vō seNt*ēr*
stopover	escale *f*	eskäl
system timetable	indicateur *m* des liaisons aériennes	eNdēkät*ēr* dā lē·äzôN ä·ārē·en
take-off	départ *m*	dāpär
thunderstorm	orage *m*	ôräzh
ticket	billet *m* d'avion	bēyā dävyôN
waiting room	salle *f* d'attente	säl dätäNt
weather	temps *m*	täN
wing	aile *f*	āl

ON BOARD SHIP

Information, Ship Tickets

When does *a ship (the ferry)* leave for ...?   **Where?**
Quand part *un bateau (le ferry-boat)* pour ...?   Où?
käN pär eN bätō (lə ferē-bōt) po͞or ...   o͞o

How often does the car ferry go to ...?
Combien de fois *(par jour/par semaine)* le ferry-boat va à ...?
kôNbyeN də fô·ä (pär zho͞or/pär smen) lə ferē-bōt vä ä ...
or: Est-ce que le ferry-boat va *souvent* à ...?
eske lə ferē-bōt vä so͞ovä Nt ä ...

How long does the crossing (from ...) to ... take?
Quelle est la durée de la traversée (de ...) à ...?
kel ā lä dĕrā də lä träversä (də ...) ä ...

How far is the railroad station from the harbour?
Quelle est la distance entre la gare et le port?
kel ā lä dēstäNs äNt(ər) lä gär ä lə pôr

What are the ports of call?
Dans quels ports fait-on escale?
däN kel pôr fätôN eskäl

When do we *dock (land)* at ...?   **Can I get a connection to ...?**
Quand faisons-nous escale à ...?   J'ai une correspondance pour ...?
käN fāzôN-no͞o eskäl ä ...   zhā ĕn kôrespôNdäNs po͞or ...

Can we go ashore at ...?   **For how long?**
Peut-on descendre à terre à ...?   Combien de temps?
pȧtôN desäNdrä tär ä ...   kôNbyeN də täN

Will there be any land excursions?   **Where can we get tickets?**
A-t-on organisé des excursions?   On prend les billets où?
ätôN ôrgänēzä dāzekskĕrsyôN   ôN präN lā bēyä o͞o

When do we have to be back on board?
À quelle heure faut-il être à bord?
äkelᵃr fōtēl āträbôr

I'd like ...	– to book passage to ...
Je voudrais ...	– un billet pour ...
zhə vōōdrā ...	– eN bēyā pōor ...

– two tickets on the ... to ... tomorrow.
– deux billets sur le ... qui part pour ... demain.
– dā bēyā sĕr lə ... kē pär pōor ... dəmeN

– a round-trip ticket from ... to ... and back.
– un billet circulaire de ... à ... et retour.
– eN bēyā sĕrkēlär də ... ā ... ā retōōr

– a ticket for a car (motorcycle, bicycle).
– un billet pour une auto (motocyclette, bicyclette).
– eN bēyā pōor ēn ôtō (môtōsēklet, bēsēklet)

– a single cabin.	**– an outside (inside) cabin.**
– une cabine individuelle.	– une cabine extérieure (intérieure).
– ēn käbēn eNdēvēdē·el	– ēn käbēn ekstārē·är (eNtārē·är)

– a double cabin.	**First Class.**	**Tourist Class.**
– une cabine à deux personnes.	Première classe.	Classe touriste.
– ēn käbēn ä dā persôn	prəmyär kläs	kläs tōōrēst

In the Harbor

Where is the „ ..." lying?	**Where does the „ ..." dock?**
Où a accosté le „ ...."?	Où accoste le „ ...."?
ōō ä äkôstā lə ...	ōō äkôst lə ...

Does this ship sail to ...?	**When does she sail?**
Est-ce que ce bateau va à ...?	À quelle heure part-il?
eske se bätō vä ä ...	äkelär pärtēl

Where is the shipping company's office (harbor police station, customs office)?
Où est la compagnie de navigation (la police du port, l`administration des douanes)?
ōō ā lä kôNpänyē də nävēgäsyôN (lä pôlēs dē pôr, lädmēnēsträsyôN dä dōō·än)

Where can I pick up my luggage?	**I come from the „ ...".**
Où est-ce que je reprends mes bagages?	Je viens du „ ....".
ōō eske zhə repräN mā bägäzh	zhə vyeN dē ...

On Board

I'm looking for cabin no. ...	Where's my baggage?
Je cherche la cabine numéro ...	Où sont mes bagages?
zhə shärsh lä käbēn nēmärō ...	ōō sôN mā bägäzh

Have you got ... on board?	Please, where is ...?
Avez-vous ... à bord?	Où est ..., s'il vous plaît?
ävä-vōō ... ä bôr	ōō ā ..., sēl vōō plä

the bar	le bar	lə bär
the *barber shop*	*le salon de coiffure*	lə sälôN də kô·äfēr
(beauty parlor)	*(le salon de beauté)*	(lə sälôN də bōtā)
the dining room	la salle à manger	lä säl ä mäNzhā
the lounge	la salle de séjour	lä säl də sāzhōōr
the purser's office	le bureau du commis-	lə bērō dē kômēsär
	saire	
the radio room	la cabine radio	lä käbēn rädē·ō
the reading room	la salle de lecture	lä säl də lektēr
the ship's photogra-		
pher	le photographe de bord	lə fōtōgräf də bôr
the sick bay	l'hôpital	lôpētäl
the swimming pool	la piscine	lä pēsēn
the tour guide's office	le guide	lə gēd

I'd like to speak to the ...
J'aimerais parler au ...
zhāmrā pärlā ō

– captain	capitaine	käpēten
– chief steward	maître-d'hôtel	mātrə dôtel
– deck officer	premier officier	prəmyā ôfēsyā
– luggage master	responsable des bagages	respôNsäb'əl dā bägäzh
– purser	commissaire	kômēsär
– ship's doctor	médecin de bord	mādəseN də bôr
– tour guide	guide	gēd

Steward, please bring me ...	What is the voltage here?
Garçon, apportez-moi ..., s'il vous plaît.	Quel est le voltage?
gärsôN, äpôrtā-mô·ä ..., sēl vōō plä	kel ā lə vôltäzh

Please call the ship's doctor!
Appelez le médecin de bord, s'il vous plaît.
äplā lə mādəseN də bôr, sēl voo plä

Have you got anything for seasickness?
Avez-vous un remède contre le mal de mer?
ävä-voo eN remäd kôNt(ər) lə mäl də mār

air conditioning	climatisation *f*	klēmätēzäsyôN
anchor	ancre *f*	äNk(ər)
bank	rivage *m*	rēväzh
barge	chaland *m*	shäläN
bay	baie *f*	bā
blanket	couverture *f*	kōōvertēr
board	bord *m*	bôr
– on board	à bord	ä bôr
boat	bateau *m*	bätō
– fishing trawler	bateau *m* de pêche	bätō də pāsh
– launch	barcasse *f*	bärkäs
– lifeboat	canot *m* de sauvetage	känō də sōvtäzh
– motorboat	bateau *m* à moteur	bätō ä môtēr
– sailboat	bateau *m* à voiles	bätō ä vô·äl
bow	proue *f*	prōō
breeze	brise *f*	brēz
bridge	passerelle *f* de manœuvre	päserel də mänēv(ər)
buoy	bouée *f*	bōō·ā
cabin	cabine *f*	käbēn
cable	câble *m*	käb'əl
call *(at port)*	cordage *m*	kôrdäzh
canal	canal *m*	känäl
captain	capitaine *m*	käpēten
captain's table	table *f* du commandant	täb(əl) dē kômäNdäN
coast	côte *f*	kōt
course	route *f*	rōōt
crew	équipage *m*	äkēpäzh
crossing	traversée *f*	träversā
cruise	croisière *f*	krô·äzyēr
deck	pont *m*	pôN
– boat deck	pont *m* des embarcations	pôN däzäNbärkäsyôN

– foredeck	plage *f* avant	pläzh äväN
– main deck	pont *m* principal	pôN preNsēpäl
– poop deck	plage *f* arrière	pläzh äryär
– promenade deck	pont-promenade *m*	pôN-prômenäd
– saloon deck	pont *m* de première classe	pôN də prəmyär kläs
– steerage	entrepont *m*	äNtrəpôN
– sun deck	sundeck *m*	sändek
– upper deck	pont *m* supérieur	pôN sēpārē·*ar*
deck chair	chaise *f* longue	shäz-lôNg
disembark	débarquer	dābärkā
dock *(noun)*	débarcadère *f*	dābärkädär
dock *(verb)*	aborder	äbôrdā
excursion	excursion *f* (à terre)	ekskĕrsyôN (ä tär)
excursion program	programme *m* d'excursion	prôgräm dekskĕrsyôN
farewell dinner	dîner *m* d'adieux	dēnā dädy*a*
ferry	ferry-boat *m*	ferē-bōt
– car ferry	ferry-boat *m*	ferē-bōt
– train ferry	ferry-boat *m*	ferē-bōt
first officer	premier officier *m*	prəmyā ôfēsyā
gangway	passerelle *f*	päserel
harbor	port *m*	pôr
harbor police	police *f* du port	pôlēs d*ē* pôr
helm	gouvernail *m*	gōovernä'ē
helmsman	pilote *m*	pēlôt
island	île *f*	ēl
jetty	môle *m*	môl
knot	nœud *m*	n*a*
lake	lac *m*	läk
land *(noun)*	terre *f*	tär
land *(verb)*	aborder, accoster	äbôrdā, äkôstā
landing place	endroit *m* de débarquement	äNdrô·ä də dābärkmäN
landing stage	débarcadère *m*	dābärkädär
lap rug	couverture *f* de laine	kōovertĕr də län
life belt	bouée *f* de sauvetage	bōo·ā də sōvtäzh
life jacket	gilet *m* de sauvetage	zhēlā də sōvtäzh
lighthouse	phare *m*	fär
mast	mât *m*	mä
mole	môle *m*	môl

ocean	océan *m*	ōsä·äN
passenger	passager *m*	päsäzhā
pier	jetée *f*	zhetā
place on deck	place *f* de pont	pläs də pôN
playroom	nurserie *f*	nārsrē
port *(land)*	port *m*	pôr
port *(side)*	bâbord *m*	bäbôr
port fees	taxe *f* portuaire	täks pôrtē·är
quay	quai *m*	kā
railing	bastingage *m*	bästeNgäzh
river	fleuve *m*	flāv
rope	cordage *m*	kôrdäzh
rough seas	mer *f* agitée	mär äzhētā
rudder	rame *f*	räm
sail	voile *f*	vô·äl
sailor	matelot *m*	mätlō
sea	mer *f*	mär
– on the high seas	en haute mer	äN ōt mär
seasickness	mal *m* de mer	mäl də mār
ship	bateau *m*	bätō
– freighter	cargo *m*	kärgō
– passenger ship	transatlantique *m*	träNsätläNtēk
– warship	bâtiment *m* de guerre	bätēmäN də gär
ship's doctor	médecin *m* de bord	mādəseN də bôr
shipboard party	fête *f* à bord	fāt ä bôr
shipping agency	agence *f* maritime	äzhäNs märētēm
shipping company	compagnie *f* de navigation	kôNpänyē də nävēgäsyôN
shore	rivage *m*	rēväzh
starboard	tribord *m*	trēbôr
steamer	paquebot *m*	päkbō
stern	poupe *f*	pōōp
steward	steward *m*	stōō·ärt
strait	détroit *m*	dātrô·ä
tourist class	classe *f* touriste	kläs tōōrēst
trug	remorqueur *m*	remôrkär
voyage	voyage *m* en bateau	vô·äyäzh äN bätō
wave	vague *f*	väg
yacht	yacht *m*	yôt (yäk)

AT THE BORDER

Passport Control

When do we get to the border?
Quand arriverons-nous à la frontière?
käNdärēverôN-noo lä lä frôNtyär

*Your passport, please.
Votre passeport, s'il vous plaît.
vôt(ər) päspôr, sēl voo plä

*Your papers, please.
Vos papiers, s'il vous plaît.
vō päpyä, sēl voo plä

Here they are.
Tenez, s'il vous plaît.
tenā, sēl voo plä

I'll be staying *a week (two weeks, until the . . .)*.
Je resterai *une semaine (deux semaines, jusqu'à . . .)*.
zhə resterä ēn smen (dä smen, zhēskä . . .)

I'm here *on business (on vacation)*.
C'est un *voyage d'affaires (voyage touristique)*.
seteN vô·äyäzh däfär (vô·äyäzh toorēstēk)

I'm (We're) visiting . . .
Je visite (Nous visitons) . . .
zhə vēzēt (noo vēzētôN) . . .

I'm traveling with the . . . group.
Je fais partie du groupe de . . .
zhə fä pärtē dē groop də . . .

I haven't got a vaccination certificate.
Je n'ai pas de certificat de vaccination.
zhə nä pä də sertēfēkä də väksēnäsyôN

What should I do?
Qu'est-ce qu'il faut faire?
keskēl fō fär

I *have (haven't)* had a *smallpox (cholera)* vaccination.
Je *(ne) suis (pas)* vacciné contre *la variole (le choléra)*.
zhə (nə) sē·ē (pä) väksēnā kôNt(ər) lä värē·ôl (lə kôlärä)

Do I have to fill in this form?
Dois-je remplir ce formulaire?
dô·äzh räNplēr sə fôrmēlär

The children are entered in my passport.
Les enfants sont inscrits dans mon passeport.
läzäNfäN sôNt eNskrē däN môN päspôr

Can I get my visa here?
Je peux avoir le visa ici?
zhə pāzävô·är lə vēzä ēsē

May I please phone my consulate?
Je peux téléphoner à mon consulat?
zhə pā tālāfônā ä môN kôNsēlä

border	frontière *f*	frôNtyär
color of eyes	couleur *f* des yeux	kōōlär dāzyā
color of hair	couleur *f* des cheveux	kōōlär dā shevā
date of birth	date *f* de naissance	dät də nesäNs
departure	sortie *f*	sórtē
distinguishing marks	signes *m/pl.* particuliers	sēn(yə) pärtēkēlyā
driver's license	permis *m* de conduire	permē də kôNdē·ēr
entry	entrée *f*	äNtrā
entry visa	visa *m* d'entrée	vēzä däNtrā
exit visa	visa *m* de sortie	vēzä də sórtē
extend	prolonger	prōlôNzhā
height	taille *f*	tā'ē
identity card	carte *f* d'identité	kärt dēdäNtētā
insurance certificate	carte *f* d'assurance	kärt däsēräNs
international vaccination certificate	certificat *m* (international) de vaccination	sertēfēkä (eNternäsyônäl) də väksēnäsyôN
maiden name	nom *m* de jeune fille	nôN də zhän fē'ē
marital status	situation *f* de famille	sētē·äsyôN də fämē·ē
– single	célibataire	sälēbätär
– married	marié	märē·ā
– widowed	veuf *m*, veuve *f*	vāf, vāv
– divorced	divorcé	dēvôrsā
name	nom *m* de famille	nôN də fämē'ē
– first name	prénom *m*	prānôN
nationality	nationalité *f*	näsyônälētā
nationality plate	plaque *f* de nationalité	pläk də näsyônälētā
number	numéro *m*	nēmärō
occupation	profession *f*	prôfesyôN
passport	passeport *m*	päspôr
passport control	contrôle *m* des passeports	kôNtrôl dā päspôr
place of birth	lieu *m* de naissance	lēyā də nesäNs
place of residence	domicile *m*	dômēsēl
renew	prolonger; renouveler	prōlôNzhā; renōōvlā
signature	signature *f*	sēnyätēr
valid	valable	väläb'əl

Customs Control

*Do you have anything to declare?
Avez-vous quelque chose à déclarer?
ävā-voo kelke shõz ä dāklärä

I only have articles for my personal use.
Je n'ai que des objets personnels.
zhə nā ke dāzóbzhä persónel

That isn't mine.
Ce n'est pas à moi.
sə nā päzä mô·ä

*Please open ...
Ouvrez ..., s'il vous plaît.
oovrā ..., sēl voo plā

This is a *present (souvenir)*.
C'est un *cadeau (souvenir de voyage)*.
seteN kädō (soovenēr də vô·äyäzh)

I have ... *cigarettes (a bottle of perfume)*.
J'ai ... *cigarettes (du parfum)*.
zhā ... sēgäret (dē pärfeN)

That's my suitcase.
C'est ma valise.
sā mä välēz

*What's in here?
Qu'est-ce qu'il y a là-dedans?
keskēlyä lä dedäN

That's all.
C'est tout.
sā too

*All right!
D'accord.
däkôr

I'd like to declare this.
Je voudrais déclarer ça.
zhə voodrā dāklärā sä

Do I have to pay duty on this?
Dois-je déclarer ça?
dô·äzh dāklärā sä

How much can I bring in duty free?
J'ai droit à combien, en franchise?
zhā drô·ä ä kôNbyeN, äN fräNshēz

What do I have to pay for it?
Combien je dois payer pour ça?
kôNbyeN zhə dô·ä pāyā poor sä

border, frontier	frontière *f*	frôNtyär
border crossing	passage *m* de la frontière	päsäzh də lä frôNtyär
customs	douane *f*	doo·än
customs control	passage *m* de la douane	päsäzh də lä doo·än
customs examination	contrôle *m* de douane .	kôNtrôl də doo·än
customs office	bureau *m* de douane ..	bērō də doo·än
customs officer	douanier *m*	doo·änyā
duty	droits *m/pl.* de douane ·	drô·ä də doo·än
– export duty	droits *m/pl.* de sortie ..	drô·ä də sôrtē
– import duty	droits *m/pl.* d'entrée ...	drô·ä däNtrā

ACCOMMODATION

Checking it out

Where is the ... *hotel (pension)*?
Où est *l'hôtel* ... *(la pension...)*?
o͞o ä lôtel ... (lä päNsyôN...)

Can you recommend a good hotel?
Pourriez-vous me recommander un bon hôtel?
po͞orē·ä-vo͞o mə rekômäNdä eN bônôtel

***Is (Are)* there ... near here?**
Y a-t-il près d'ici ...?
ēyätēl prä dēsē ...

accommodations	un logis	eN lōzhē
apartments	des appartements	dāzäpärtəmäN
a boarding house	une pension	ēn päNsyôN
bungalows	des bungalows	dā beNgälō
a camping site	un terrain	eN tereN
	de camping	də käNpēng
a hotel	un hôtel	eNôtel
an inn	une auberge	ēn ōbärzh
a motel	un motel	eN môtel
a pension	une pension	ēn päNsyôN
rooms in private	des chambres	dā shäNb(ər)
homes	chez l'habitant	shā läbētäN
a youth hostel	une auberge	ēn ōbärzh
	de jeunesse	də zhānes

– near the beach.	**– *in a quiet place (centrally located)*.**
– près de la plage.	– dans un site *tranquille (central)*.
– prä dəlä pläzh	– däNzeN sēt träNkēl (säNträl)

How *are the prices (is the food)* there?
Comment *sont les prix (est la nourriture)*?
kômäN sôN lā prē (ä lä no͞orētēr)

> *Only the most modern European hotels have bathrooms attached to every room, and most rooming houses and pensions will require guests to share a bathroom down the hall with others.*

Checking in

I reserved a room here.	**... six weeks ago.**
J'ai retenu chez vous une chambre.	... il y a six semaines.
zhä retenē shä vōō ēn shäNb(ər)	... ēlyä sē smen

The ... travel agency reserved a room for me (us).
L'agence de voyage ... a fait retenir pour moi (nous) une chambre.
läzhäNs də vô·äyäzh ... ä fä retenēr pōōr mô·ä (nōō) ēn shäNb(ər)

Have you got a *single (double)* room available?
Vous avez une chambre pour une personne (deux personnes)?
vōōzävä ēn shäNb(ər) pōōr ēn persón (pōōr dä persón)

I'd like to have...	Je voudrais ...	zhə vōōdrä ...
– an apartment	un appartement	eNäpärtəmäN
– bungalow	un bungalow	eN beNgälō
– double room	une chambre à	ēn shäNbrä
	deux lits	dä lē
– an efficiency apartment	une location	ēn lôkäsyôN
– a quiet room	une chambre calme	ēn shäNb(ər) kälm
– a room	une chambre	ēn shäNb(ər)
– on the *first (second)* floor	au premier (deuxième) étage	ō prəmyer (dāzyäm) ātäzh
– with balcony	avec balcon	ävek bälkôN
– with *bath (shower)*	avec bain (douche)	ävek beN (dōōsh)
– with hot and cold running water	avec eau courante chaude et froide	ävek ō kōōräNt shôd ā frô·äd
– with terrace	avec terrasse	ävek teräs
– with toilet	avec W.-C.	ävek dōōbləvä-sä

... for *one night (two nights, one week, four weeks).*
... pour une nuit (deux jours, une semaine, quatre semaines).
... pōōr ē·nē·ē (dä zhōōr, ēn smen, kät(ər) smen)

Careful! Buildings in all European countries – including Britain – use a different numbering system for the floors. The bottom floor is called the ground floor (in French le rez-de-chaussée), the second (American) floor is called the first floor (le premier étage), the third floor the second floor (le deuxième étage), and so on.

Can I have a look at the room?
Puis-je voir la chambre?
pē·ēzh vó·är lä shäNb(ər)

I like it.
Elle me plaît.
el mə plä

I'll (We'll) take it.
Je la prends (Nous la prenons).
zhə lä präN (noo lä prenôN)

Could you show me another room?
Pouvez-vous me montrer encore une autre chambre?
poovä-voo mə môNträ äNkôr ēnôt(ər) shäNb(ər)

Could you put in an extra bed (a crib)?
Pouvez-vous mettre *encore un lit (un lit d'enfant)* dans la chambre?
poovä-voo meträNkôr eN lē (eN lē däNfäN) däN lä shäNb(ər)

Price

How much is the room per day (week)?
Quel est le prix de la chambre par *jour (semaine)*?
kel ā lə prē də lä shäNb(ər) pär zhoor (smen)

– with breakfast.	– with two meals a day.	– American plan.
– avec petit déjeuner.	– avec demi-pension.	– avec pension complète.
– ävek pətē dāzhänä	– ävek dəmē-päNsyôN	– avec päNsyôN kôNplet

Is everything (service) included?
Tout (Le service) est compris?
too (lə servēs) ā kôNprē

What's the single room surcharge (seasonal surcharge)?
Pour une *chambre individuelle, le supplément (La taxe saisonnière)* c'est combien?
poor en shäNbreNdēvēdē·el lə sēplämäN (lä täks sāzônyär) sā kôNbyeN

Are there reduced rates for children?
Y a-t-il une réduction pour enfants?
ēyätēl ēn rädēksyôN poor äNfäN

How much is that altogether?
Ça fait combien en tout?
sä fä kôNbyeN äN too

How much deposit do I have to pay?
Quel accompte désirez-vous?
kel äkôNt dāzērä-voo

Registration, Luggage

I'd like to *register (check in)*.
Je voudrais remplir la fiche
(d'hôtel).
zhə voodrä räNplēr lä fēsh dôtel

Do you need our passports?
Est-ce qu'il vous faut nos passeports?
eskēl voo fō nō päspôr

When do you want back the registration form?
On doit vous remettre la fiche d'hôtel quand?
ôN dô·ä voo remet(ər) lä fēsh dôtel käN

What do I have to fill out here?
Qu'est-ce qu'il faut mettre ici?
keskēl fō metrēsē

*I just need your signature.
Votre signature suffit.
vôt(ər) sēnyätēr sēfē

Would you have my luggage picked up?
Pouvez-vous envoyer chercher mes bagages?
poovä-voozäNvô·äyä shärshā mā bägäzh

It's still at the *station (airport)*.
Ils sont encore *a la gare (à l'aéroport)*.
ēl sôNtäNkôr ä lä gär (ä lä·ärōpôr)

Here's the baggage check.
Voici le bulletin d'enregistrement.
vô·äsē lə bēlteN däNrezhēstrəmäN

Where's my luggage?
Où sont mes bagages?
oo sôN mä bägäzh

Is my baggage already up in the room?
Mes bagages sont-ils déjà dans la chambre?
mā bägäzh sôNtēl dāzhä däN lä shäNb(ər)

Can I leave my luggage here?
Puis-je laisser mes bagages ici?
pē·ēzh lāsā mā bägäzh ēsē

Would you put these valuables in the safe?
Pourriez-vous garder ces objets de valeur dans votre coffre-fort?
poorē-ä-voo gärdā sezôbzhā də välār däN vôt(ər) kôf(ər)-fôr

Do you have a *garage (parking lot)*?
Avez-vous *un garage (un parking)*?
ävä-voozeN gäräzh (eN pärkēng)

Reception, Desk Clerk

Where is room 308?
Où est la chambre numéro trois cent huit?
o͞o ā lä shäNb(ər) nēmārō trô·ä säN*e͞*·ēt

The key, please.
La clé, s'il vous plaît!
lä klā, sēl vo͞o plā

Number ..., please.
Numéro ..., s'il vous plaît.
nēmārō ..., sēl vo͞o plā

Has anyone asked for me?
Quelqu' un m'a-t-il demandé?
kelkeN mätēl dəmäNdā

Is there any mail for me?
Y a-t-il du courrier pour moi?
ēyätel d*e͞* ko͞oryä po͞or mô·ä

What time does the mail come?
Quand arrive le courrier?
käNdärēv lə ko͞oryä

Do you have any *stamps (picture postcards)*?
Avez-vous des *timbres-postes (cartes postales)*?
ävä-vo͞o dā teNb(ər)-pôst (kärt pôstäl)

What's the postage on a *letter (postcard)* to the United States?
Combien coûte *une lettre (une carte postale)* pour les États-Unis?
kôNbyeN ko͞ot *e͞*n let(ər) (*e͞*n kärt pôstäl) po͞or lāzätäz*e͞*nē

Where can I *get (rent)* ...?
Je peux *avoir (louer)* ... où?
zhə päzävô·är (p*a͞* lo͞o·ä) ... o͞o

Where do I sign up for the excursion to ...?
Je peux m'inscrire où, pour l'excursion à ...?
zhə p*a͞* meNskrēr o͞o, po͞or leksk*e͞*rsyôN ä ...

Where can I *make a phone call (change some money)*?
Je peux *téléphoner (changer de l'argent)* où?
zhə p*a͞* tālāfōnā (shäNzhā·də lärzhäN) o͞o

I'd like to place a long distance call to ...
Je voudrais une communication pour ...
zhə vo͞odrä *e͞*n kôm*e͞*nēkäsyôN po͞or ...

I'm expecting a long distance call from the United States.
J'attends un appel des États-Unis.
zhätäN eNäpel dāzätäz*e͞*nē

Where can I get an American newspaper?
Où peut-on acheter des journaux américains?
o͞o pătôN äshtā dā zho͞ornō ämārēkeN

Where *is (are)* ...?
Où *est (sont)* ...?
o͞o ā (sôN) ...

Could you get me ...?
Pouvez-vous me procurer ...?
po͞ovā-vo͞o mə prôkērā ...

What's the voltage here?
Le courant, c'est du combien ici?
lə ko͞oräN, sā dē kôNbyeN ēsē

> *Electric current: In general (as in most of Europe) it is 220 volts, but in some places it is still 110 volts. You'll need the European circular two pin adaptor plugs as well as an adaptor if your appliance doesn't have a built-in converter switch.*

I'll be back in *ten minutes (a couple of hours)*.
Je reviendrai dans *dix minutes (deux heures)*.
zhə revyeNdrā däN dē mēnēt (dāzār)

We're going *down to the beach (into town)*.
Nous allons *à la plage (en ville)*.
no͞ozälôN älä pläzh (äN vēl)

I'll be in the *lounge (bar)*.
Je suis *au salon (au bar)*.
zhə sē·ē ō sälôN (ō bär)

I *lost my key (left my key in the room)*.
J'ai *perdu la clé (laissé la clé dans la chambre)*.
zhā perde lä klā (lesā lä klā däN lä shäNb(ər)

What time are meals served?
Quelles sont les heures de repas?
kel sôN lāzār də repä

Where's the dining room?
Où est la salle à manger?
o͞o ā lä säl ä mäNzhā

Can we have breakfast in the room?
Pouvons-nous prendre le petit déjeuner dans la chambre?
po͞ovôN-no͞o präNd(ər) lə pətē dāzhānā däN lä shäNb(ər)

Could we have breakfast at seven tomorrow morning, please?
Pouvons-nous prendre le petit déjeuner demain à sept heures?
po͞ovôN-no͞o präNd(ər) lə pətē dāzhānā dəmeN ä setār

I'd like a box lunch tomorrow morning, please.
Pour demain matin un panier-repas, s'il vous plaît.
po͞or dəmeN mäteN eN pänyā-repä, sēl vo͞o plā

Please wake me at 7:30 tomorrow.
Réveillez-moi demain à sept heures et demie.
rāvāyā-mô·ä dəmeN ä setār ā dəmē

Maid

Come in!	**Just a moment, please!**	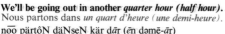
Entrez!	Un instant, s'il vous plaît.	
äNträ	eNeNstäN, sēl voo plä	

Could you wait another *five (ten)* minutes?
Pourriez-vous attendre encore *cinq (dix)* minutes?
poorē·ā·voo ätäNdräNkôr seNk (dē) mēnēt

We'll be going out in another *quarter hour (half hour)*.
Nous partons dans *un quart d'heure (une demi-heure)*.
noo pärtôN däNseN kär dār (ēn dəmē-ār)

Please bring *me (us)* ...
Apportez-*moi (-nous)*, s'il vous plaît ...
äpôrtā-mô·ä (-noo), sēl voo plä ...

another blanket	encore une couverture .	äNkôr ēn koovertēr
another towel	encore une serviette ...	äNkôr ēn servyet
an ash tray	un cendrier	eN säNdrē·ā
a blanket	une couverture de laine ...	ēn koovertēr də lān
breakfast	le petit déjeuner	lə pətē dāzhānā
a bar of soap	un morceau de savon ..	eN môrsō də sä-vôN
a couple of clothes hangers	quelques cintres	kelke seNt(ər)

How does this thing work?	**Is our room ready?**
Comment est-ce que cela fonctionne?	Notre chambre est déjà faite?
kômäNteske səlä fôNksyôn	nôt(ər) shäNbrā dāzhä fāt

Would you have these things laundered for me?
Pouvez-vous faire laver ce linge?
poovā-voo fār lävä sə leNzh

Thanks very much!	**This is for you.**
Merci beaucoup!	C'est pour vous.
mersē bōkoo	sā poor voo

Complaints

I'd like to speak to the manager, please.
Je voudrais parler au gérant, s'il vous plaît.
zhə vōōdrā pärlä ō zhäräN, sēl vōō plä

There's no ...	**There are no ...**	**... doesn't work.**
Il manque ...	Il manque ...	... ne fonctionne pas.
ēl mäNk ...	ēl mäNk ...	... nə fôNksyôn pä

There's no light in my room.
Dans ma chambre il n'y a pas
de lumière.
däN mä shäNbrēlnyä pä də lēmyār

This bulb has burned out.
Cette ampoule est grillée.
set äNpōōl ā grēyā

The socket is broken.
La prise de courant ne marche pas.
lä prēz də kōōräN nə märsh pä

The fuse has blown.
Le plomb a sauté.
lə plôN ä sôtā

The *bell (heating)* doesn't work.
La sonnette (Le chauffage) ne marche pas.
lä sônet (lə shôfäzh) nə märsh pä

The key doesn't fit.
La clé ne va pas.
lä klā nə vä pä

The rain comes in.
La pluie rentre.
lä plē·ē räNt(ər)

This window *won't shut properly (won't open).*
Cette fenêtre *ferme mal (ne s'ouvre pas).*
set fenät(ər) färm·mäl (nə sōōv(ər) pä)

There's no *(hot)* water.
Il n'y a pas d'eau *(chaude).*
ēl nyä pä dō (shōd)

The faucet drips.
Le robinet goutte.
lə rôbēnā gōōt

The toilet won't flush.
La chasse d'eau ne marche pas.
lä shäs dō nə märsh pä

There's a leak in this pipe.
Il y a une fuite.
ēlyä ēn fē·ēt

The drain is stopped up.
Le lavabo est bouché.
lə läväbō ā bōōshā

Checking out

I'll be leaving tomorrow.
Je pars demain.
zhə pär dəmeN

We're continuing on tomorrow.
Nous continuerons notre voyage demain.
nōō kôNtēnē·ərôN nôt(ər) vô·äyäzh dəmeN

Would you please make up my bill?
Préparez la note, s'il vous plaît.
prāpärā lä nôt, sēl vōō plā

Could I please have *my (our)* bill?
Je peux avoir *ma (notre)* note, s'il vous plaît?
zhə pāzävô·är mä (nôtər) nôt, sēl vōō plā

Please wake me tomorrow morning.
Réveillez-moi demain matin, s'il vous plaît.
rāvāyā-mô·ä dəmeN mäteN, sēl vōō plā

Please order a taxi for me tomorrow morning at 8.
Appelez un taxi pour *demain (huit heures)*, s'il vous plaît.
äplā eN täksē pōōr dəmeN (ē·ētär), sēl vōō plā

Would you have my luggage taken to the *station (airport)*?
Pouvez-vous faire porter mes bagages *à la gare (à l'aéroport)*?
pōōvā-vōō fār pôrtā mā bägäzh ä lä gär (ä lä·ārōpôr)

When does the *bus (train)* to ... leave?
Quand part *l'autobus (le train)* pour ...?
käN pär lôtōbēs (lə treN) pōōr ...

Please forward my mail.
Faites-moi suivre mon courrier, s'il vous plaît.
fāt-mô·ä sē·ēv(ər) môN kōōryā, sēl vōō plā

Thanks for everything!
Merci infiniment pour tout!
mersē eNfēnēmäN pōōr tōō

We had a very good *time (rest)* here.
Ça a été très agréable ici.
sä ä ātā trāzägrā·äb'əl ēsē

accommodations	logis *m*	lôzhē
adapter plug	fiche *f* intermédiaire	fēsh eNtermädyär
air conditioning	climatisation *f*	klēmätēzäsyôN
alternating current	courant *m* alternatif	kōōräN älternätēf
American plan	pension *f* complète	päNsyôN kôNplet
apartment	appartement *m*,	äpärtəmäN,
	studio *m*	stēdē·ō
apartment building	immeuble *m* de studios	ēmāb'əl də stēdē·ō
armchair	fauteuil *m*	fōtā'ē
arrival	arrivée *f*	ärēvā
ash tray	cendrier *m*	säNdrē·ā
balcony	balcon *m*	bälkôN
basement	sous-sol *m*	sōō-sôl
bathroom	salle *f* de bains	säl də beN
bed	lit *m*	lē
– blanket	couverture *f*	kōōvertēr
	(de laine)	(də lān)
– crib	lit *m* d'enfant	lē däNfäN
– mattress	matelas *m*	mätlä
– pillow	oreiller *m*	ôrāyā
bed and two meals	demi-pension *f*	dəmēpäNsyôN
bed linen	draps *m/pl.* de lit	drä də lē
– cover	housse *f* d'édredon	hōōs dādredôN
– pillowcase	taie *f* d'oreiller	tā dôrāyā
bed rug	descente *f* de lit	desäNt də lē
bedside table	table *f* de nuit	täb'əl də nē·ē
bell	sonnette *f*	sônet
bill	note *f*	nôt
breakfast	petit déjeuner *m*	pətē dāzhānā
– eat breakfast	prendre son petit	präNd(ər) sôN pətē
	déjeuner	dāzhānā
bucket	seau *m*	sō
carpet	tapis *m*	täpē
category	catégorie *f*	kätāgôrē
ceiling	plafond *m*	pläfôN
cellar	cave *f*	käv
central heating	chauffage *m* central	shôfäzh säNträl
chair	chaise *f*	shāz
check-in	déclaration *f* de	dākläräsyôN də
	séjour	säzhōōr

closet	placard *m*	pläkär
clothes hanger	cintre *m*	seNt(ər)
complaint	réclamation *f*	räklämäsyóN
concierge	concierge *m*;	kôNsyärzh;
	portier *m*	pôrtyä
corridor	corridor *m*; couloir *m* .	kôrēdôr; kŏŏlŏ·är
curtain	rideau *m*	rēdō
day bed	canapé-lit *m*	känäpā-lē
deck chair	chaise *f* longue	shāz-lôNg
departure	départ *m*	dāpär
deposit	acompte *m*; arrhes *f/pl.*	äkóNt; är
dining room	salle *f* à manger	säl ä mäNzhā
dinner	dîner *m*	dēnā
door	porte *f*	pôrt
door handle	poignée *f*	pô·änyā
drapery	rideau *m*	rēdō
drawer	tiroir *m*	tērô·är
elevator	ascenseur *m*	äsäNsär
entrance	entrée *f*	äNtrā
exit	sortie *f*	sôrtē
extension cord	rallonge *f*	rälôNzh
extra week	semaine *f*	smen
	supplémentaire	sēplämäNtär
fan	ventilateur *m*	väNtēlätär
faucet	robinet *m* d'eau	rôbēnā dō
fireplace	cheminée *f*	shemēnā
floor	étage *m*	ātäzh
front desk	réception *f*	rāsepsyóN
front door	porte *f* d'entrée	pôrt däNtrā
fuse	fusible *m*	fēzēb'əl
garden umbrella	parasol *m*	päräsôl
grill room	grill-room *m*	grēl-rŏŏm
guest house	pension *f*	päNsyóN
hall	hall *m* d'hôtel	äl dôtel
head clerk	chef *m* de réception	shef də rāsepsyóN
heating	chauffage *m*	shôfäzh
hotel	hôtel *m*	ôtel
– beach hotel	hôtel *m* de la plage	ôtel dəlä pläzh
hotel restaurant	restaurant *m* d'hôtel	restôräN dôtel
house	maison *f*	māzôN
house key	clé *f* de la maison	klā dəlä māzôN

inquiry	renseignement *m*	räNsen(yə)mäN
key	clé *f*	klā
kitchen	cuisine *f*	kē-ēzēn
kitchenette	coin *m* cuisine	kô•eN kē-ēzēn
lamp	lampe *f*	läNp
laundry	linge *m*	leNzh
– do laundry	laver	lävā
– dry	sécher	sāshā
– iron	repasser	repäsā
light bulb	ampoule *f*	äNpoōl
	(électrique)	älektrēk
lights	éclairage *m*	ākläräzh
lobby	vestibule *m*; hall *m*	vestēbēl; äl
lock	serrure *f*	serēr
– lock up	fermer à clé	fermā ä klā
– unlock	ouvrir (avec une	ōōvrēr (avek ēn
	clé)	klā)
lunch	déjeuner *m*	dāzhānā
maid	femme *f* de chambre	fäm də shäNb(ər)
mirror	miroir *m*, glace *f*	mērô•är, gläs
move	déménager *f*	dāmānäzhā
move in	emménager	äNmānäzhā
move out	déménager	dāmānäzhā
night's lodging	nuitée *f*	nē•ētā
pail	seau *m*	sō
patio	cour *f* intérieure	kōōr eNtārē•ār
pension	pension *f*	päNsyôN
plug	fiche *f*, prise *f*	fēsh, prēz
	(d'électricité)	(dālektrēsētā)
pot	pot *m*	pô
price	prix *m*	prē
private beach	plage *f* privée	pläzh prēvā
radiator	radiateur *m*	rädē•ätär
reading lamp	lampe *f* de chevet	läNp də shevā
reception desk	réception *f*	rāsepsyôN
refrigerator	réfrigérateur *m*	rāfrēzhärätär
registration	déclaration *f*	dāklaräsyôN
	de séjour	də sāzhōōr
rent *(noun)*	loyer *m*	lô•äyā
rent *(verb)*	louer	lōō•ā

rest room	toilettes *f/pl.*	tô·älet
– ladies' room	toilettes *f/pl.*	tô·älet
	pour dames	poōr däm
– men's room	toilettes *f/pl.*	tô·älet
	pour messieurs	poōr mesyā
room	pièce *f*	pyās
– bedroom	chambre *f* à coucher . .	shäNbrä koōshā
– living room	séjour *m*	sāzhoōr
– nursery	chambre *f* d'enfants . . .	shäNb(ər) däNfäN
season	saison *f*	sāzòN
service (charge)	service *m*	servēs
shower	douche *f*	doōsh
sink	lavabo *m*	lävä bō
socket	prise *f*	prēz
staircase	escalier *m*	eskälyā
stairwell	cage *f* d'escalier	käzh deskälyā
stove	fourneau *m*	foōrnō
swimming pool	piscine *f*	pēsēn
switch	interrupteur *m*	eNterēptär
table	table *f*	täb'əl
tablecloth	nappe *f*	näp
telephone	téléphone *m*	tālāfôn
terrace	terrasse *f*	teräs
toilet paper	papier *m* hygiénique . . .	päpyā ēzhē·änēk
tour guide	guide *m*	gēd
travel agency	agence *f* de voyage	äzhäNs də vô·äyäzh
vacate the room	libérer la chambre	lēbārā lä shäNb(ər)
ventilation	aération *f*	ä·āräsyóN
voltage	voltage *m*	vôltäzh
wall	mur *m*	mēr
water	eau *f*	ō
– cold water	eau *f* froide	ō frô·äd
– hot water	eau *f* chaude	ō shōd
water glass	verre *f* à eau	vär ä ō
window	fenêtre *f*	fenāt(ər)
windowpane	vitre *f*	vēt(ər)

Camping, Youth Hostels

Is there a *camping site (youth hostel)* near here?

Y a-t-il *un terrain de camping (une auberge de jeunesse)*?
ēyätēl eN tereN də käNpēng (ēnōbärzh də zhānes)

Can we camp here?

Pouvons-nous camper ici?
pōōvóN-nōō käNpā ēsē

Is the site guarded at night?

Le terrain est-il gardé la nuit?
lə tereN ātēl gärdā lä nē·ē

Do you have room (for another tent)?

Y a-t-il encore de la place (pour une tente)?
ēyätēl äNkôr dəlä pläs (pōōr ēn täNt)

How much does it cost to stay overnight?

Combien coûte une nuit?
kôNbyeN kōōt ēn nē·ē

How much is it for the *car (trailer)*?

Quels sont les frais pour *l'auto (la caravane)*?
kel sôN lā frā pōōr lōtō (lä kärävän)

I'll be staying ... *days (weeks)*.

Je reste ... *jours (semaines)*.
zhə rest ... zhōōr (smen)

Can we ... here?

Peut-on ... ici?
pāt-ôN ... ēsē

Is there a grocery store near here?

Y a-t-il près d'ici un magasin d'alimentation?
ēyätēl prā dēsē eN mägäzeN dälēmäNtäsyôN

Can I *rent bottled gas (exchange gas bottles)* here?

Je peux *emprunter (échanger)* ici des bouteilles de gaz?
zhə pāzäNpreNtā (āshäNzhā) ēsē dā bōōtā'ē də gäz

Where are the *rest rooms (wash rooms)*?

Où sont les *toilettes (lavabos)*?
ōō sôN lā tô·älet (läväbō)

Are there any electrical connections here?

Y a-t-il l'électricité?
ēyätēl lälektrēsētā

Can we drink the water?

L'eau est potable?
lō ā pôtāb'əl

Can I rent ...?

Je peux emprunter ...?
zhə pāzäNpreNtā ...

Where can I ...?

Où peut-on ...?
ōō pātôN ...

advance reservation	réservation *f*	rāzerväsyôN
camp bed	lit *m* pliant	lē plē·äN
camping	camping *m*	käNpēng
camping ID	carte de l'A.C.C.F.	kärt dəlä·sā·sā·ef
camp out	faire du camping	fār dē käNpēng
camp site	terrain *m* de camping	tereN də käNpēng
check-in	déclaration *f* de séjour	dākläräsyôN də sāzhōōr
check-out	déclaration *f* de départ	dākläräsyôN də dāpär
cook	préparer les repas	prāpärā lā repä
cooking utensils	gamelle *f*; ustensiles *m/pl.* de cuisine	gämel; ēstäNsēl də kē·ēzēn
day room	salle *f* commune	säl kômēn
dishes	vaisselle *f*	vāsel
dormitory	dortoir *m*	dôrtô·är
drinking water	eau *f* potable	ō pôtäb'əl
get	avoir	ävô·är
go swimming	se baigner	sə bānyā
hostel parents	parents *m/pl.* aubergistes	päräN ōberzhēst
– hostel mother	mère *f* aubergiste	mār ōbārzhēst
– hostel father	père *m* aubergiste	pār ōbārzhēst
iron	repasser	repäsā
membership card	carte *f* de membre	kärt də mäNb(ər)
park	stationner	stäsyônā
playground	terrain *m* de jeux	tereN də zhā
recreation room	salle *f* commune	säl komēn
rent	prêter	prātā
rental fee	prix *m* de location	prē də lôkäsyôN
sleeping bag	sac *m* de couchage	säk də kōōshäzh
take a bath	prendre un bain	präNdreN beN
tent	tente *f*	täNt
trailer	caravane *f*	käräván
usage fee	frais *m/pl.* d'utilisation	frā dētēlēzäsyôN
wash	laver	lävā
youth group	groupe *m* de jeunes	grōōp də zhān
youth hostel	auberge *f* de jeunesse	ōbārzh də zhānes
youth hostel card	carte *f* d'A.J.	kärt dä·zhē

EATING AND DRINKING

Ordering

Is there a *good (Chinese, seafood)* restaurant here?

Y a-t-il ici un *bon restaurant (restaurant chinois, restaurant de poisson et crustacés)*?

ēyätēl ēsē eN bôN restôräN (restôräN shēnô·ä, restôräN də pô·äsôN ā krēstäsä)

Would you please reserve a table for four at eight P.M.?

Réservez une table de quatre personnes pour 8 heures, s'il vous plaît.

räzervä ēn täb'əl də kät(ər) persôn pōōr ē·ētær, sēl vōō plä

Is this *table (seat)* taken?	**I'd like a meal.**
Cette *table (place)* est-elle réservée?	Je voudrais commander un plat.
set·täb'əl (pläs) ätel räzervä	zhə vōōdrä kômäNdä eN plä

Waiter!	**Waitress!**	**Is this your table?**
Garçon!	Madame!	Faites-vous le service ici?
gärsôN	mädäm	fāt-vōō lə servēs ēsē

We'd like a drink.

Nous voudrions commander des boissons.

nōō vōōdrē·ôN kômäNdä dā bô·äsôN

Could I see the *menu (wine list)*, please?

La *carte (carte des vins/boissons)*, s'il vous plaît.

lä kärt (kärt dä veN/bô·äsôN), sēl vōō plä

What can we have right away?	**Do you have . . .?**
Que pouvez-vous nous servir tout de suite?	Avez-vous . . .
ke pōōvā-vōō nōō servēr tōōtsē·ēt	ävä-vōō

Do you have *vegetarian (diet)* food too?

Avez-vous aussi des menus *végétariens (diététiques)*?

ävä-vōō ôsē dä menē väzhätärē·eN (dē·ātätēk)

Please bring us *one portion (two portions)* of . . . .

Apportez-nous *un(e) . . . (deux . . .)*, s'il vous plaît.

äpôrtā-nōō eN (ēn) . . . (dā . . .), sēl vōō plä

A *cup (pot, glass, bottle)* of . . ., please.

Une tasse (un pot, un verre, une bouteille) de . . ., s'il vous plaît.

ēn täs (eN pô, eN vär, ēn bōōtä'ē) də . . ., sēl vōō plä

Table Service

ash tray	cendrier *m*	säNdrē·ā
bottle	bouteille *f*	bōōtä'ē
bowl	terrine *f*	terēn
bread basket	corbeille *f* à pain	kôrbā'ē ä peN
carafe	carafe *f*	käräf
corkscrew	tire-bouchon *m*	tēr-bōōshôN
cruet stand	huilier *m*	ē·ēlēyā
cup	tasse *f*	täs
– saucer	soucoupe *f*	sōōkōōp
cutlery	couvert *m*	kōōvär
decanter	carafe *f*	käräf
egg cup	coquetier *m*	kôketyā
fork	fourchette *f*	fōōrshet
glass	verre *m*	vär
– water glass	verre *m* à eau	vär ä ō
– wine glass	verre *m* à vin	vär ä veN
knife	couteau *m*	kōōtō
mustard jar	moutardier *m*	mōōtärdyā
napkin	serviette *f*	servyet
pepper mill	moulin *m* à poivre	mōōleN ä pô·äv(ər)
pepper shaker	poivrier *m*	pô·ävrēyā
pitcher	pichet *m*	pēshā
– cream pitcher	pot *m* à lait	pōtä lā
plate	assiette *f*	äsyet
– bread plate	petite assiette *f*	pətēt äsyet
– soup plate	assiette *f* à soupe	äsyet ä sōōp
pot	pot *m*	pô
– coffee pot	cafetière *f*	käfetyär
– tea pot	théière *f*	tā·ēyär
salt shaker	salière *f*	sälēyär
serving dish	plat *m*	plä
silverware	argenterie *f*	ärzhäNtərē
spoon	cuiller *f*	kē·ēyär
– soup spoon	cuiller *f* à soupe	kē·ēyär ä sōōp
– teaspoon	petite cuiller *f*	pətēt kē·ēyär
sugar bowl	sucrier *m*	sēkrēyä
tablecloth	nappe *f*	näp
toothpick	cure-dent *m*	kēr-däN
tray	plateau *m*	plätō

Breakfast

bread	pain *m*	peN
– dark bread	pain *m* bis	peN bē(s)
– rye bread	pain *m* de seigle	peN də säg′əl
– white bread	pain *m* blanc	peN bläN
– whole wheat bread	pain *m* complet	peN kôNplä
breakfast	petit déjeuner *m*	pətē dāzhānā
butter	beurre *m*	bār
cereal	céréales *f/pl.*	sārā·äl
coffee	café *m*	käfā
– black	– noir	nô·är
– decaffeinated	– décaféiné	dākäfā·ēnā
– with cream	– au lait	ō lä
– with sugar	avec du sucre	ävek dē sēk(ər)
cold cuts	tranches *f/pl.* de charcuterie	träNsh də shärkētərē
egg	œuf *m*	āf
– hard-boiled	– dur	– dēr
– soft-boiled	– à la coque	– älä kôk
– ham & eggs	œufs *m/pl.* au jambon	ā ō zhäNbôN
– fried eggs	œufs *m/pl.* sur le plat	ā sēr lə plä
– poached eggs	œufs *m/pl.* pochés	ā pôshā
– scrambled eggs	œufs *m/pl.* brouillés	ā brōōyā
fruit juice	jus *m* de fruits	zhē də frē·ē
– orange juice	jus *m* d'orange	zhē dôräNzh
– tomato juice	jus *m* de tomate	zhē də tômät
honey	miel *m*	myel
hot chocolate	chocolat *m*	shôkōlä
jam	confiture *f*	kôNfētēr
milk	lait *m*	lä
oatmeal	bouillie *f* d'avoine	bōōyē dävô·än
roll	petit pain *m*	pətē peN
sausage	saucisse *f*	sôsēs
slice	tranche *f*	träNsh
tea	thé *m*	tā
– with lemon	– au citron	ō sētróN
– with milk	– au lait	ō lä
toast	toast *m*	tōst
zwieback	biscotte *f*	bēskôt

On the European continent, breakfast is generally a simple affair, consisting of coffee or tea, rolls, butter, jam, and occasional cold cuts.

Lunch and Dinner

I'd (We'd) like to have ...
Je voudrais (On voudrait) ...
zhə vōōdrā (ôN vōōdrā) ...

Please pass ...
Voudriez-vous me passer ...
vōōdrē-ā-vōō mə päsä ...

Would you bring us ...
Pouvez-vous nous apporter...?
pōōvā-vōō nōōzäpôrtā

What's the name of this dish?
Comment s'appelle ce plat?
kômäN säpel sə plä

*Would you like seconds on anything?
Désirez-vous encore quelque chose?
dāzērā-vōō äNkôr kelke shōz

Yes, please.
Oui, s'il vous plaît.
ōō-ē, sēl vōō plä

Yes, indeed!
Volontiers.
vôlôNtyā

Just a little.
Un tout petit peu.
eN tōō pətē pä

Thanks, that's enough.
Merci, c'est assez.
mersē, setäsä

No, thanks.
Non, merci.
nôN, mersē

I've had enough.
Je n'ai plus faim.
zhə nā plē feN

Nothing more, thanks.
Plus rien, merci!
plē rē-eN, mersē

*Did you like it?
C'était bon?
sätä bôN

Delicious!
Délicieux!
dālēsyä

This dish (The wine) is delicious!
Ce plat (Le vin) est excellent!
sə plä (lə veN) ätekseläN

*Empty your glass!
Videz votre verre!
vēdā vôt(ər) vär

Cheers!
À votre santé!
ä vôt(ər) säNtä

I'am not allowed to have any alcohol (I don't care for alcohol).
L'alcool m'est défendu (Je ne prends pas d'alcool).
lälkôl mä dāfäNdē (zhə nə präN pä dälkôl)

To wish the others at the table an enjoyable meal, say Bon appétit! Before taking the first drink, you can propose a drink to the health of the company by saying À votre santé! or simply Santé!

Cooking

baked	cuit au four	kē·ē ō foor
boiled	cuit; bouilli	kē·ē; booyē
cold	froid	frô·ä
deep fried	frit	frē
fat	gras	grä
fresh	frais	frā
fried	sauté	sôtā
grilled	grillé	grēyā
hard	dur	dēr
hot	chaud	shō
hot *(spicy)*	épicé; piquant	āpēsā; pēkäN
juicy	juteux	zhētā
lean	maigre	māg(ər)
medium (done)	à point	ä pô·eN
pickled	salé	sälā
rare	saignant	senyäN
raw	cru	krē
roasted	rôti	rôtē
salted	salé	sälā
seasoned	assaisonné	äsāzônā
smoked	fumé	fēmā
soft	tendre	täNd(ər)
steamed	étuvé; cuit à la vapeur	ātēvā; kē·ē älä väpär
stewed	braisé	brāzā
stuffed	farci	färsē
stuffing	farce *f*	färs
tender	tendre	täNd(ər)
tough	coriace	kôryäs
well done	bien cuit	byeN kē·ē

Ingredients

bacon	lard *m*	lär
bay leaves	feuilles *f/pl.* de laurier	fā'ē də lôryā
butter	beurre *m*	bēr
capers	câpres *f/pl.*	käp(ər)

caraway	cumin *m*	kēmeN
chives	civette *f*	sēvet
cinnamon	cannelle *f*	känel
cloves	clous *m/pl.* de girofle	klōō də zhērôf'əl
currants	raisins *m/pl.*	räzeN
	de corinthe	də kôreNt
fat	graisse *f*	gräs
garlic	ail *m*	ā'ē
ginger	gingembre *m*	zheNzhäNb(ər)
herbs	fines herbes *f/pl.*	fēnzärb
horseradish	raifort *m*	räfôr
jelly *(aspic)*	gélatine *f*, aspic *m*	zhälätēn, äspēk
jelly *(fruit)*	gelée *f*	zhelā
ketchup	ketchup *m*	ketshäp
lard	saindoux *m*	seNdōō
lemon	citron *m*	sētrôN
margarine	margarine *f*	märgärēn
mayonnaise	mayonnaise *f*	mäyônāz
mayonnaise sauce	sauce *f* mayonnaise	sôs mäyônāz
mushrooms	champignons *m/pl.*	shäNpēnyôN
mustard	moutarde *f*	mōōtärd
nutmeg *(powder)*	muscade *f*	mēskäd
oil	huile *f*	ē·ēl
olives	olives *f/pl.*	ôlēv
onion	oignon *m*	ônyôN
paprika	paprika *m*	päprēkä
parsley	persil *m*	persē
pepper	poivre *m*	pô·äv(ər)
pickles	cornichons *m/pl.*	kôrnēshôN
raisins	raisins *m/pl.* secs	räzeN sek
rosemary	romarin *m*	rômäreN
sage	sauge *f*	sôzh
salt	sel *m*	sel
sauce	sauce *f*; jus *m*	sôs, zhē
– cream sauce	sauce *f* à la crème	sôs älä kräm
– gravy	jus *m* de rôti	zhē də rôtē
seasoning (spice)	épice *f*	āpēs
thyme	thym *m*	teN
vanilla	vanille *f*	vänē'ē
vinegar	vinaigre *m*	vēnāg(ər)
wine	vin *m*	veN

THE MENU

Appetizers

ailloli *m*	ä-ēyôlē	garlic mayonnaise
anchois *m/pl.*	äNshô·ä	anchovies
anguille *f* fumée	äNgē'ē fēmä	smoked eel
artichaut *m*	ärtēshō	artichoke
– cœur d'artichaut	kār därtēshō	heart of artichoke
– lyonnais	lē·ônä	boiled artichoke
assiette *f* anglaise	äsyet äNglāz	cold cuts
beurre *f* d'anchois	bār däNshô·ä	anchovy butter
canapé *m*	känäpā	appetizer
crabes *m/pl.*	kräb	crab
crevettes *f/pl.*	krevet	shrimp
croque-monsieur *m*	krôk-məsyā	grilled ham and cheese sandwich
croûte *f* au fromage	krōot ō frômäzh	cheese pastry
écrevisses *f/pl.*	äkrevēs	crayfish
escargots *m/pl.*	eskärgō	snails
homard *m*	ômär	lobster
huîtres *f/pl.*	ē·ēt(ər)	oysters

A simple way of selecting your meal in a French restaurant is to choose from the menu. *This full course meal is generally very good and cheaper than if you order* à la carte. *Don't get confused: the word for menu in French is* la carte.

---

jambon *m*	zhäNbôN	ham
– blanc	– bläN	– boiled
– fumé	– fēmä	– smoked
– cru	– krē	– raw
pâté *m* de foie gras	pätā də fô·ä grä	goose liver pâté
pâté *m* en croute	pätā eN krōot	paté in crust
salade *f* niçoise	säläd nēsô·äz	vegetable salad
salade *f* de tomates	säläd də tômät	tomato salad
saucisson *m*	sôsēsôN	French salami
viande *f* froide	vyäNd frô·äd	cold meat
vol-au-vent *m*	vôl-ô-väN	puff pastry pie

Soups

bisque *f*	bēsk	shellfish soup
bouillabaisse *f*	bōōyäbās	bouillabaisse
consommé *m*	kôNsômā	bouillon, broth
crème *f* d'asperges	krām däspärzh	cream of asparagus soup
garbure *f*	gärbēr	vegetable soup with goose meat
potage *m*	pôtäzh	soup
– à la printanière	– älä preNtänyär	vegetable soup
– de gibier	– də zhēbyä	game soup
– de volaille	– də vôlä′ē	chicken broth
– julienne	– zhēlyen	julienne
– Saint-Germain	– seN zhermeN	pea soup
potée *f*	pôtā	hot pot
soupe *f*	sōōp	soup
– à l'ail	– ä lä′ē	garlic soup
– à l'oignon	– ä lônyôN	onion soup
– aux choux	ō shōō	cabbage soup
– aux lentilles	ō läNtē′ē	lentil soup
– de poissons	– də pô·äsôN	fish soup
vichyssoise *f*	vēshēsô·äz	vichyssoise

Noodles

plat *m* de macaronis *or* de nouilles	plä də mäkärōnē, də nōō′ē	dish with macaroni *or* noodles
– à la crème fraîche	– älä krām frāsh	with cream
– à la sauce tomate	– älä sôs tômät	with tomato sauce
– au gratin	– ō gräteN	au gratin *(baked cheese)*
– au parmesan	– ō pärmezäN	with permesan cheese

Fish

aiglefin *m*	āgləfeN	haddock
anguille *f*	äNgē'ē	eel
barbeau *m*	bärbō	mullet
brochet *m*	brôshā	pike
cabillaud *m*	käbēyō	cod(fish)
carpe *f*	kärp	carp
colin *m*	kôleN	hake
dorade *f*	dôräd	gilthead
esturgeon *m*	estĕrzhôN	sturgeon
hareng *m*	äräN	herring
maquereau *m*	mäkərō	mackerel
morue *f*	môrē	cod(fish)
perche *f*	pärsh	perch
plie *f*	plē	plaice
poisson *m*	pô·äsôN	fish
– d'eau douce	– dō dōos	freshwater fish
– de mer	– də mär	saltwater fish
sandre *f*	säNd(ər)	pike, perch
saumon *m*	sômôN	salmon
sole *f*	sôl	sole
tanche *f*	täNsh	tench
thon *m*	tôN	tuna
truite *f*	trē̄·ēt	trout
turbot *m*	tĕrbō	turbot
– à la meunière	– älä *m*ānyär	– fried
– au bleu	– ō bl*a*	– steamed

Sea Food

coquillages *m/pl.*	kôkēyäzh	shellfish
coquilles *f/pl.* Saint-Jacques	kôkē'ē seN zhäk	scallops
crabes *f/pl.*	kräb	hard-shell crabs
crevettes *f/pl.*	krevet	shrimps
écrevisse *f*	ākrevēs	crayfish
homard *m*	ômär	lobster
huître *f*	ē̄·ēt(ər)	oyster
langouste *f*	läNgōōst	spiny lobster
moules *f/pl.*	mōōl	mussels

Poultry

abattis *m* d'oie	äbätē dô·ä	goose giblets
bécasse *f*	bākäs	woodcock
blanc *m* de poulet	bläN də poolä	chicken breast
caille *f*	kä'ē	quail
canard *m*	känär	duck
– sauvage	– sôväzh	wild duck
coq *m* au vin	kôk ō veN	stewed chicken in red wine
dinde *f*	deNd	turkey
– aux marrons	– ō märôN	– with sweet roasted chestnuts
faisan *m*	fāzäN	pheasant
oie *f*	ô·ä	goose
perdrix *f*	perdrē	partridge
pigeon *m*	pēzhôN	pigeon
poule *f*	pool	chicken
poulet *m* de grain	poolä də greN	broiler
poulet *m* rôti	poolä rôtē	roast chicken

Meat

agneau *m*	änyō	lamb
bœuf *m*	bāf	beef
cerf *m*	sār	stag
chevreau *m*	shevrō	goat kid
chevreuil *m*	shevrä'ē	venison
gibier *m*	zhēbyā	game
lapin *m*	läpeN	rabbit
lièvre *m*	lē·äv(ər)	wild rabbit
mouton *m*	mootôN	lamb
porc *m*	pôr	pork
sanglier *m*	säNglēyä	wild boar
veau *m*	vō	veal

aloyau *m* · · · · · · · · · · · ·	älô·äyō · · · · · · · · · · · · ·	sirloin
bifteck *m* · · · · · · · · · · ·	bēftek · · · · · · · · · · · · · ·	steak
– à cheval · · · · · · · · · ·	– ä sheväl · · · · · · · · · · ·	– with egg
blanquette *f* · · · · · · · · ·	bläNket · · · · · · · · · · · · ·	
de veau · · · · · · · · · ·	də vō · · · · · · · · · · · · · ·	veal stew
bœuf *m* à la mode · · ·	bûf älä môd · · · · · · · ·	braised beef with carrots
– bourguignon · · · · · ·	– bōōrgēnyôN · · · · · ·	beef stew with mushrooms and red wine
cervelle *f* · · · · · · · · · · ·	servel · · · · · · · · · · · · · ·	brains
– en beignet · · · · · · · ·	– servel äN benyä · · ·	baked brains
châteaubriand *m* · · · ·	shätôbrē·äN · · · · · · · ·	châteaubriand steak
civet *m* · · · · · · · · · · · · ·	sēvā · · · · · · · · · · · · · · ·	ragout
– de lièvre · · · · · · · · · ·	– sēvā də lē·äv(ər) · · ·	jugged hare
côtelette *f* · · · · · · · · · ·	kôtlet · · · · · · · · · · · · · ·	chop
cochon *m* de lait à la broche · · · · · ·	kôshôN də lā älä brôsh · · · · · · · · · ·	suckling pig on a spit
cuisse *f* · · · · · · · · · · · ·	kē·ēs · · · · · · · · · · · · · ·	leg
cuisses *f/pl.* de grenouilles · · · · · · · ·	kē·ēs də grenōō'ē · · · · · · · · · · ·	grenouilles legs
couscous · · · · · · · · · · ·	kōōskōōs · · · · · · · · · ·	couscous *(vegetables and semolina with meat or chicken)*
daube *f* de mouton · ·	dôb də mōōtóN · · · · ·	stewed lamb
entrecôte *f* · · · · · · · · ·	äNtr(ə)kôt · · · · · · · · ·	steak
épaule *f* · · · · · · · · · · ·	āpôl · · · · · · · · · · · · · ·	shoulder
escalope *f* · · · · · · · · ·	eskälôp · · · · · · · · · · ·	schnitzel
– à la viennoise · · · · ·	– älä vē·enô·äz · · · · · ·	Wiener schnitzel
estouffade de bœuf · ·	estōōfäd də bûf · · · · ·	stewed beef (ragout)
étuvée *f* de veau · · · ·	ātēvā də vō · · · · · · · ·	leg of veal, stewed
faux-filet *m* · · · · · · · · ·	fô-fēlā · · · · · · · · · · · · ·	rump steak
filet *m* · · · · · · · · · · · · ·	fēlā · · · · · · · · · · · · · · ·	tenderloin, fillet
foie *f* · · · · · · · · · · · · · ·	fô·ä · · · · · · · · · · · · · · ·	liver
fricandeau *m* · · · · · · ·	frēkäNdō · · · · · · · · · ·	larded roast veal
fricassé *m* · · · · · · · · · ·	frēkäsā · · · · · · · · · · ·	fricassee
gigot *m* · · · · · · · · · · · ·	zhēgō · · · · · · · · · · · · ·	leg
– d'agneau · · · · · · · · ·	– zhēgō dänyō · · · · · ·	leg of lamb, roast
grillade *f* · · · · · · · · · · ·	grēyäd · · · · · · · · · · · ·	grilled meat
– de porc · · · · · · · · · · ·	– də pôr · · · · · · · · · · ·	grilled pork

hachis *m*	äshē	roast forcemeat
haricot *m* de mouton	ärēkō də mōōtôN	lamb stew with white beans
jambonneau *m*	zhäNbônō	trotters, pickled pork
langue *f*	läNg	tongue
– de bœuf Valenciennes	– də bäf väläNsyen	smoked tongue of beef
miroton *m*	mērōtôN	stewed beef with sauce of onions
oiseaux *m/pl.* sans tête	ô·äzō säN tät	collared veal *(filled)*
pâté *m*	pätā	paté
petit salé *m*	pətē sälā	salted meat
poitrine *f*	pô·ätrēn	brisket
pot-au-feu *m*	pôtôfä	stew *(vegetables and meat)*
quenelles *f/pl.*	kenel	fish or chickenballs
ragoût *m*	rägōō	ragout, hash
ris *m* de veau	rē də vō	veal and rice
rognonnade *f* de veau	rônyônäd də vō	roast veal loin
rognons *m/pl.*	rônyôN	kidneys
rôti *m*	rôtē	joint
saucisses *f/pl.*	sôsēs	sausages
selle *f*	sel	saddle
– de chevreuil	– də shevrā′ē	saddle of venison
sauté *m* de lapin au vin blanc	sôtā də läpeN ō veN bläN	ragout of rabbit, stewed in white wine
tripes *f/pl.*	trēp	tripe

Vegetables

artichauts *m/pl.*	ärtēshō	artichokes
asperge *f*	äspärzh	asparagus
aubergine *f*	ōberzhēn	eggplant
betteraves *f/pl.*	betəräv	turnips
– rouges	– rōōzh	beets
carottes *f/pl.*	kärôt	carrots
céleri *m*	sälerē	celery

céleri-rave	sālerē-räv	**celery root**
champignons *m/pl.* ..	shäNpēnyôN	**mushrooms**
chicorée *f*	shēkôrä	**curly endive, chicory**
chou *m*	shoo	**cabbage**
– blanc	– bläN	**white cabbage**
– de Bruxelles	– də brēsel	**Brussels sprouts**
– frisé	– frēzā	**savoy cabbage**
– rouge	– roozh	**red cabbage**
choucroute *f*	shookroot	**sauerkraut**
chou-fleur *m*	shoo-flär	**cauliflower**
chou-rave *m*	shoo-räv	**kohlrabi**
concombre *m*	kôNkôNb(ər)	**cucumber**
courge *f*	koorzh	**pumpkin, squash**
endives *f/pl.*	äNdēv	**Belgian endive**
épinards *m/pl.*	āpēnär	**spinach**
haricots *m/pl.*	ärēkō	**beans**
– verts	– vār	*French (string)* **beans**
– beurre	– bār	**butter beans**
laitue *f*	lātē	**lettuce**
oignons *m/pl.*	ônyôN	**onions**
petits pois *m/pl.*	pətē pô·ä	**peas**
poivrons *m/pl.*	pô·ävrôN	**peppers**
scarole *f*	skärôl	**escarole**
pommes *f/pl.* de terre	pôm də tär	**potatoes**
– dauphine	dôfēn	**– croquettes**
– en robe des champs	äN rôb dā shäN	**– in their jackets**
– mousseline	mooslēn	**mashed potatoes**
– rôties au four	rôtē ō foor	**baked potatoes**
– sautées	sôtā	**fried potatoes**
pommes *f/pl.*nature..	pom nätēr	**boiled potatoes**
– frites	frēt	**French fries**
salade *f*	säläd	**salad**
tomates *f/pl.*	tômät	**tomatoes**

Cheese

bleu d'Auvergne	blœ̄ dōvärn(yə)	blue cheese
fromage *m*	frômäzh	cheese
– blanc	– bläN	cottage cheese
– aux fines herbes ...	– ō fēnzärb	cheese with herbs
– à pâte molle	– ä pät môl	cream cheese
– à tartiner	– ä tärtēnā	cheese spread
– de chèvre	– də shäv(ər)	goat cheese
– gruyère	– grēyär	Swiss cheese, Gruyère (cheese)

Desserts

clafoutis *m*	kläfo͞otē	pudding with cherries
crème *f*	krām	mousse, pudding, custard
– à la vanille	– älä vänē′ē	vanilla custard
– caramel	– kärämel	caramel custard
crêpe *f*	kräp	crêpe *(thin pancake)*
– suzette	– sēzet	crêpe suzette
– fourrée	– fo͞orā	– with filling
glace *f*	gläs	ice cream
meringue *f*	mereNg	meringue
mousse *f* au chocolat	mo͞os ō shôkōlä	chocolate mousse
parfait *m*	pärfā	frozen dessert
pommes *f/pl.*		
meringuées	pôm mereNgā	apple fritter
riz *m* au lait	rē·ōlā	rice pudding
sabayon *m*	säbäyôN	zabaglione *(wine mousse)*
soufflé *m* au chocolat	so͞oflā ō shôkōlä	chocolate soufflé

Fruit

ananas *m*	änänä	**pineapple**
abricot *m*	äbrēkō	**apricot**
airelles *f/pl.*	ärel	**blueberries**
– rouges	– rōozh	**cranberries**
amandes *f/pl.*	ämäNd	**almonds**
banane *f*	bänän	**banana**
cacah(o)uètes *f/pl.*	käkä·ōo·et	**peanuts**
cassis *m/pl.*	käsēs	**black currants**
cerises *f/pl.*	serēz	**cherries**
citron *m*	sētrôN	**lemon**
coco *m*	kôkō	**coconut**
coing *m*	kô·eN	**quince**
dattes *f/pl.*	dät	**dates**
figues *f/pl.*	fēg	**figs**
fraises *f/pl.*	fräz	**strawberries**
framboises *f/pl.*	fräNbô·äz	**raspberries**
fruits *m/pl.*	frĕ·ē	**fruit**
groseilles *f/pl.*	grōzā'ē	**red currants**
– à maquereau	– ä mäkərō	**gooseberries**
mandarine *f*	mäNdärēn	**tangerine**
marrons *m/pl.*	märôN	**chestnuts**
melon *m*	melôN	**(honeydew) melon**
mûres *f/pl.*	mēr	**blackberries**
noisettes *f/pl.*	nô·äzet	**hazelnuts**
noix *f/pl.*	nô·ä	**nuts**
orange *f*	ōräNzh	**orange**
pamplemousse *f*	päNpləmōos	**grapefruit**
pêche *f*	pāsh	**peach**
poire *f*	pô·är	**pear**
pomme *f*	pôm	**apple**
prune *f*	prĕn	**plum**
raisins *m/pl.*	räzeN	**grapes**
rhubarbe *f*	rĕbärb	**rhubarb**

BEVERAGES

Wine

Bordeaux	Bordeaux	bôrdō
Burgundy	(vin de) Bourgogne	(veN də) boorgôn(yə)
cider	cidre *m*	sēd(ər)
dessert wine	vin *m* de dessert	veN də desär
mulled wine	vin *m* chaud	veN shō
Muscatel	muscat *m*	mēskä
red wine	vin *m* rouge	veN roozh
rosé wine	rosé *m*	rōzā
white wine	vin *m* blanc	veN bläN

Famous French wine	
Beaujolais	bōzhôlā
Chablis	shäblē
Chateauneuf-du-Pape	shätōnâf-dē-päp
Corbières	kôrbyär
Côtes de Provence	kōtdə prôväNs
Côtes du Rhône	kōtdē rōn
Entre-deux-Mers	äNt(ər)-dā-mär
Médoc	mādôk
Muscadet	mēskädā
Saint-Emilion	seNtämēlyôN
Sauternes	sôtärn

Beer

beer	bière *f*	byär
beer mug	chope *f* bière	shôp byär
dark beer	bière *f* brune	byär brēn
a glass of beer	un verre de bière	eN vär də byär
light beer	bière *f* blonde	byär blôNd
malt liquor	bière *f* de malt	byär də mält

Other Alcoholic Beverages

alcoholic beverage ...	boisson f alcoolique ...	bô·äsôN älkôlēk
bitters	bitter m	bētär
brandy	eau-de-vie f	ōdvē
cognac	cognac m	kônyäk
gin	gin m	dzhēn
liqueur	liqueur f	lēkär
– apricot brandy	liqueur f d'abricot	lēkär däbrēkō
– cherry brandy	liqueur f de cerises	lēkär də serēz
punch	punch m	pôNtsh
rum	rhum m	rôm
vodka	vodka m	vôdkä
whiskey	whisky m	oo·ēskē

*In virtually all European countries, when you order a whiskey, you
are ordering Scotch whisky. If you would prefer rye, bourbon, or
some other beverage, you should say this when making your order.*

Non-Alcoholic Beverages

For coffee, tea, chocolate and milk, please see pp. 113–114.

fruit juice	jus m de fruits	zhē də frē·ē
– apple juice	jus m de pommes	zhē də pôm
– black currant juice	jus m de cassis	zhē də käsē
– grapefruit juice	jus m de pamplemousse	zhē də päNpləmoos
– orange juice	jus m d'orange	zhē dôräNzh
lemonade	limonade f	lēmônäd
milk shake	milk-shake m	mēlk-shäk
orangeade	orangeade f	ôräNzhäd
soda water	soda m; eau f de Seltz .	sōdä; ō də sels
soft drink	boisson f non-alcoolisée	bô·äsôN nônälkôlēzä
tonic water	eau f tonique	ō tônēk
water	eau f	ō
– mineral water	– eau f minérale	ō mēnäräl
– carbonated	– gazeuse	– gäzāz
– non-carbonated	– non-gazeuse	– nôN-gäzāz

In the Café

In France, as in most of Europe, a café is a great place to relax with a
cup of coffee, meet friends, read the paper, or most popular of all,
people-watch. If it`s pastries and cakes you`re interested in, you`ll
find the largest selection in a pâtisserie (bakery).

I'd like ...
Je voudrais ...
zhə vo͞odrā

a piece of cake	un morceau de gâteau .	eN môrsō də gätō
– of tart	– une tarte(lette)	ēn tärt(əlet)
a cup of coffee	un café	eN käfā
a cup of tea	un thé	eN tā
a dish of ice cream ..	une glace	ēn gläs
– with (without)	– avec (sans)	– ävek (säN)
whipped cream	Chantilly	shäNtēyē
a glass of orange	un verre de jus	eN vär də zhē
juice	d'orange	dôräNzh
cake	gâteau m	gätō
candy	chocolat m, bonbon m .	shôkōlä, bôNbôN
chocolate	chocolat m	shôkōlä
chocolate with ice		
cream	chocolat m glacé	shôkōlä gläsā
confectionery	pâtisserie f (fine)	pätēsərē (fēn)
cookies	petit gâteau m sec	pətē gätō säk
– almond cookies	– aux amandes	– ōzämäNd
cream..............	crème f	kräm
ice cream	glace f	gläs
– chocolate ice		
cream	glace f au chocolat	gläs ō shôkōlä
– strawberry ice		
cream	glace f à la fraise	gläs älä fräz
– vanilla ice cream ..	glace f à la vanille	gläs älä vänē'ē
– assorted ice cream .	glace f panachée	gläs pänäshä
ice cream parlor	pâtissier glacier m	pätēsyā gläsyā
meringue	meringue f	märeNg

milk	lait *m*	lā
– *cold (warm)* milk	lait *m* froid *(chaud)*	lā frô·ä (shō)
– *evaporated* milk	lait *m* condensé	lā kôNdäNsā
sherbet	sorbet *m*	sôrbā
sugar	sucre *m*	sēk(ər)
– *cube* sugar	sucre *m* en morceaux	sēkräN môrsō
sundae	coupe *f* glacée	ko͞op gläsā
sweets	bonbons *m/pl.*	bôNbôN
tart	tarte *f*, gâteau *m*	tärt, gätō
– *fruit* tart	tarte *f* aux fruits	tärt ō frē·ē
tea *(see p. 98)*	thé *m*	tā
wafers	gaufrettes *f/pl.*;	gôfret;
	cornet *m* de glace	kôrnä də gläs
whipped cream	Chantilly *f*	shäNtēyē

Incidentally, nobody will expect you to know all the names of the different cakes, pies, pastries, tarts, cookies, candies and other tempting sweets available in this part of the world. Things are always on display in any café or bakery, which means all you have to do is walk up to the counter and use the universal language, in other words, point! Your cake or pastry will be delivered to your table.

Complaints, Paying the Check

We need another *portion (set of silverware, glass).*
Ici il manque encore *un plat (un couvert, un verre).*
ēsē ēl mäNk äNkôr eN plä (eN kōōvär, eN vär)

This isn't what I ordered.	**I wanted ...**
Je n'ai pas commandé cela.	J'ai commandé ...
zhǝ nā pä kômäNdä sǝlä	zhä kômäNdä
This is not fresh any more.	**This is ...**
Ce n'est plus frais.	C'est ...
sǝ nā plē frä	sä ...

too fatty	trop gras	trō grä
too hard	trop dur	trō dēr
too hot *(temperature)*	trop chaud	trō shō
too hot *(spicy)*	trop épicé	trōäpēsä
too cold	trop froid	trō frô·ä
too salty	trop salé	trō sälä
too sour	trop aigre	trō āg(ǝr)
too tough	trop coriace	trō kôryäs

I'd like to pay. (The check, please!)
Garçon, l'addition s'il vous plaît.
gärsôN, lädēsyôN, sēl vōō plä

All together, please.	**Separate checks, please.**
Je paie tout. (C'est moi qui règle.)	Nous payons séparément.
zhǝ pā tōō (sä mó·ä kē rāg(ǝl)	nōō pāyôN säpärämäN
I don't think this is correct.	**We didn't have that.**
Cela ne me paraît pas exact.	Nous n'avons pas eu ça.
sǝlä nǝ mǝ pärä päzegsäkt	nōō nävôN päzā sä
Thanks very much.	**Keep the change.**
Merci beaucoup!	C'est pour vous.
mersē bōkōō	sä pōōr vōō

If you are pleased with the waiter's service, you can leave a small tip. Otherwise, the check includes the tip. The term taxe et service compris *on the menu means that tax and service charge are included in the price.*

DOWNTOWN

On the Street

Where is . . .?
Où est . . .?
ōō ä . . .

the bus stop	l'arrêt d'autobus	lärä dôtōb*ē*s
the Catholic Church .	l'église catholique	läglēz kätōlēk
the city hall	l'hôtel de ville	lôtel də vēl
the harbor	le port	lə pôr
the . . . Hotel	l'hôtel	lôtel
the museum	le musée	lə m*ē*zä
the police station	le commissariat de	lə kômēsärē·ä də
	police	pôlēs
the post office	le bureau de poste	lə b*ē*rō də pôst
the Protestant		
Church	le temple	lə täNp'əl
. . . Square	la place	lä pläs . . .
. . . Street	la rue	lä r*ē* . . .
the station	la gare	lä gär
the synagogue	la synagogue	lä sēnägôg
a taxi stand	une station de	*ē*n stäsyôN də
	taxis	täksē

Is it far from here?
Est-ce loin d'ici?
es lô·eN dēsē

How far is it to the . . .?
Quelle est la distance d'ici *au (à la)* . . .?
kel ä lä dēstäNs dēsē ō (älä) . . .

How many minutes by foot?
Combien de minutes à pied?
kôNbyeN də mēn*e*t ä pyä

A good distance (Not far).
Assez (Pas) loin.
äsä (pä) lô·eN

Which direction is . . .?
Dans quelle direction se trouve. . .?
däN kel dēreksyôN sə trōōv . . .

What street is . . . on?
Dans quelle rue se trouve . . .?
däN kel r*ē* sə trōōv . . .

There.	**Straight ahead.**	**To the right.**	**To the left.**
Là.	Tout droit.	À droite.	À gauche.
lä	tōō drô·ä	ä drô·ät	ä gôsh

Bus, Taxi

Can I get there by bus?
Je peux y aller en autobus?
zhə pā ē·älä änôtōbēs

Which bus goes to (the) ...?
Quel autobus va *à (au, à la)* ...?
kel ôtōbēs vä ä (ō, älä) ...

How many stops is it from here?
Combien d'arrêts y a-t-il?
kôNbyeN därä yätēl

Do I have to change?
Faut-il changer (d'autobus)?
fôtēl shäNzhā (dôtōbēs)

Where do I have to *get out (change)*?
Où faut-il *descendre (changer d'autobus)*?
ōō fôtēl desäNd(ər) (shäNzhä dôtōbēs)

Would you please tell me when we get there?
Dites-moi quand nous serons à ..., s'il vous plaît.
dēt-mō·ä käN nōō serôN ä ..., sēl vōō plä

A *one-way (transfer)* ticket to ...
Un billet *simple (de correspondance)* pour ...
eN bēyä seNp′əl (də kôrespôNdäNs) pōōr ...

Where can I get a taxi?
Je peux prendre un taxi où?
zhə pā präNdreN täksē ōō

Take me to ...
Conduisez-moi *au (à la)* ...
kôNdē·ēzä-mô·ä ō (älä) ...

To the station, please.
À la gare, s'il vous plaît!
älä gär, sēl vōō plä

How much is the fare to ...?
Ça fait combien *jusqu'à (jusqu'au,*
jusqu'à la) ...
sä fä kôNbyeN zhēskä (zhēskō, zhēskä
lä) ...

Could you show us some of the sights?
Pourriez-vous nous montrer quelques curiosités?
pōōrē·ā-vōō nōō môNträ kelke kērē·ōsētā

Please *wait (stop)* here a minute.
Attendez (Arrêtez-vous) ici un moment, s'il vous plaît.
ätäNdā (ärātā-vōō) ēsē eN mômäN, sēl vōō plä

Sightseeing and Excursions

> *Many museums and historic monuments as well as shops close for a few hours during lunchtime, so it's a good idea to take this into consideration when planning your day. Museums and other public monuments are usually closed on Tuesdays in France as well as on the public holidays.*

Two tickets for the ... tomorrow, please.
Pour demain deux places pour ..., s'il vous plaît.
pōōr demeN dä pläs pōōr ..., sēl vōō plä

Is lunch included?
Est-ce que le déjeuner est compris?
eske lə dāzhānā ā kôNprē

When do we get going?
Quelle est l'heure du départ?
kel ā lär dē dāpär

When (Where) do we meet?
Quand (Où) nous retrouvons-nous?
käN (ōō) nōō retrōōvôN-nōō

Will we be seeing the ... too?
Visitons-nous aussi ...?
vēzētôN-nōō ôsē ...

Will we have some free time?
Avons-nous du temps à notre disposition?
ävôN-nōō dē täN ä nôt(ər) dēspôzēsyôN

How much?
Combien?
kôNbyeN

Will we be able to do some shopping?
On peut faire du shopping?
ôN pə fär dē shôpēng

Will we be going to ... too?
Est-ce qu'on va aussi à ...?
eskôN vä osē ä ...

How long will we stay in ...?
Combien de temps resterons-nous à ...?
kôNbyeN də täN restərôN-nōōzä ...

When do we get back?
Quand rentrerons-nous?
käN räNtrerôN-nōō

What's worth seeing in ...?
Quelles curiosités y a-t-il à ...?
kel kērē·ōzētā yätēl ä ...

When does ... open (close)?
À quelle heure ouvre (ferme) ...?
äkelär ōōv(ər) (färm) ...

How much does the admission (guided tour) cost?
Combien coûte *l'entrée (la visite guidée)?*
kôNbyeN kōōt läNtrā (lä vēzēt gēdā)

Is there an English-speaking guide?
Y a-t-il un guide qui parle anglais?
ēyätēl eN gēd kē pärl äNglä

I'd like to see the ...
J'aimerais voir ...
zhämerä vô·är ...

Can we take a look at ... today?
Peut-on visiter aujourd'hui ...
p*ä*tôN vēzētä ōzhōōrd*ē*·ē ...

the castle	le château	lə shätō
the cathedral	la cathédrale	lä kätädräl
the church	l'église	läglēz
the fortress	la forteresse	lä fôrtəres
the exhibition	l'exposition	lekspōzēsyōN
the gallery	la galerie	lä gälerē
the memorial	le monument commémoratif	lə mônēmäN kômemôrätēf
the museum	le musée	lə mēzä
the palace	le palais	lə pälä
the zoo	le zoo	lə zô(ō)

When does the tour start?
À quelle heure commence la visite guidée?
äkel*ä*r kômäNs lä vēzēt gēdä

Can we take pictures?
On peut faire des photos?
ôN p*ä* fär dā fōtō

What is that *building (monument)?*
Quel *édifice (monument)* est-ce?
kel ādēfēs (mônēmäN) es

Who *painted this picture (sculpted this statue)?*
De qui est *ce tableau (cette statue)?*
də kē·ä sə täblō (set stät*ē*)

What period does this ... date from?
De quel siècle est ...?
dəkel sēyäk'əl ä ...

When was ... built?
Quand a été bâti ...?
käNdä ätä bätē ...

Who built ...?
Qui a bâti ...?
kē ä bätē ...

Where can I find ...?
Où se trouve ...?
ōō sə trōōv ...

Is this ...?
Est-ce que c'est ...?
eske sä ...

*****This is where ... lived (was born, died).**
Ici *vécut (naquit, mourut)* ...
ēsē väk*ē* (näkē, mōōr*ē*) ...

Vocabulary

airport	aéroport *m*	ä·ārōpôr
alley	ruelle *f*, allée *f*	rē·el, älä
amusement park	parc *m* d'attractions	pärk däträksyôN
area	région *f*	räzhē·ôN
avenue	avenue *f*	ävənē
boat trip	promenade *f* en bateau	prômenäd äN bätō
botanical gardens	jardin *m* botanique	zhärdeN bôtänēk
bridge	pont *m*	pôN
building	édifice *m*,	ādēfēs,
	immeuble *m*	ēm*a*b'əl
bus	autobus *m*	ôtōbēs
capital	capitale *f*	käpētäl
– national capital	capitale *f* nationale	käpētäl näsyônäl
castle	château *m*,	shätō
	château *m* fort	shätō fôr
cathedral	cathédrale *f*	kätādräl
cave	caverne *f*	kävärn
cemetery	cimetière *m*	sēmetyär
church	église *f*	āglēz
churchyard	cimetière *m*	sēmetyär
city	ville *f*	vēl
city hall	hôtel *m* de ville	ôtel də vēl
consulate	consulat *m*	kôNsēlä
corner	coin *m*	kô·eN
countryside	paysage *m*	pā·ēzäzh
courthouse	palais *m* de Justice	pälä də zhēstēs
covered market	marché *m* couvert	märshā kōōvär
dead-end street	voie *f* sans issue	vô·ä säNzēsē
district	région *f*	räzhē·ôN
ditch	fossé *m*	fôsā
downtown area	centre *m* (de la) ville	säNt(ər) (dəlä) vēl
embassy	ambassade *f*	äNbäsäd
environs	environs *m/pl.*	äNvērôN
excavations	fouilles *f/pl.*	fōō'ē
excursion	excursion *f*	ekskērsyôN
exhibition	exposition *f*	ekspōzēsyôN
factory	usine *f*	ēzēn
farmhouse	ferme *f*	färm
fire department	pompiers *m/pl.*	pôNpyā

first-aid station	poste *m* de secours	pôst də səkōōr
fountain	fontaine *f*, jet *m*	fôNten, zhā
	d'eau	dō
gallery	galerie *f*	gälerē
garden	jardin *m*	zhärdeN
gate	portail *m*	pôrtä'ē
government office	administration *f*	ädmēnēsträsyóN
grave	tombe *f*	tôNb
guide	guide *m*	gēd
harbor	port *m*	pôr
high-rise building	building *m*, tour *f*	bēldēng, tōōr
hiking path	sentier *m* de	säNtyā də
	randonnée	räNdônā
hill	colline *f*	kôlēn
hospital	hôpital *m*	ôpētäl
house	maison *f*	mäzôN
house number	numéro *m* de la maison	nēmārō dəlä mä-zôN
landscape	paysage *m*	pā·ēzázh
lane	ruelle *f*	rē·el
last stop	terminus *m*	termēn*e*s
library	bibliothèque *f*	bēblē·ôtāk
lost and found	bureau *m* des objets	bērō dāzôbzhā
office	trouvés	trōōvä
main street	rue *f* principale	rē preNsēpäl
memorial	monument *m*	mónēmäN
	commémoratif	kômämôrätēf
military base	base *f* militaire	bäz mēlētär
ministry	ministère *m*	mēnēstär
moat	fossé *m*	fôsā
monument	monument *m*	mónēmäN
mountain	montagne *f*	môNtän(yə)
mountain range	chaîne *f* de montagnes	shen də môNtän(yə)
motion picture theatre	cinéma *m*	sēnämä
museum	musée *m*	m*e*zā
national park	parc *m* national	pärk näsyōnäl
observatory	observatoire *m*	ôbservätô·är
old town	vieille ville *f*	vyä'ē vēl
open market	marché *m*	märshā

palace	palais *m*	pälä
park	parc *m*	pärk
part of town	quartier *m*	kärtyä
path	chemin *m*	shəmeN
pavillion	pavillon *m*	pävēyôN
pedestrian	piéton *m*	pyätôN
– pedestrian		
crossing	passage *m* clouté	päsäzh klo͞otä
police	police *f*	pôlēs
police station	commissariat *m* de	kômēsärē·ä də
	police	pôlēs
policeman	agent *m* de police	äzhäN də pôlēs
port	port *m*	pôr
post office	bureau *m* de poste	bērō də pôst
power station	centrale *f* électrique	säNträl älektrēk
public garden	parc *m*	pärk
public rest room	toilettes *f/pl.*	tô·älet
	publiques	pēblēk
river	fleuve *m*	flæv
road	rue *f*	rē
road sign	panneau *m* de	pänō də
	signalisation routière	sēnyälēzäsyôN
		ro͞otyär
ruin	ruine *f*	rē·ēn
school	école *f*	äkôl
sidewalk	trottoir *m*	trôtô·är
shop	magasin *m*	mägäzeN
shopping mall	centre *m* commercial	säNt(ər) kômersyäl
side road	rue *f* secondaire	rē sekôNdär
sightseeing	visite *f*	vēzēt
square	place *f*	pläs
stadium	stade *m*	städ
station	gare *f*	gär
stop	arrêt *m*	ärä
store	magasin *m*	mägäzeN
street	rue *f*	rē
suburb	faubourg *m*, banlieue *f*	fōbo͞or, bäNlēyä
suburban express		
train	train *m* de banlieue	treN də bäNlēyä
subway	métro *m*	mātrō
surroundings	environs *m/pl.*	äNvērôN

swimming area	piscine *f*	pēsēn
synagogue	synagogue *f*	sēnägôg
taxi	taxi *m*	täksē
taxi stand	station *f* de taxis	stäsyôN də täksē
temple	temple *m*	täNp'əl
throughway	passage *m*	päsäzh
tomb	tombe *f*	tôNb
tower	tour *f*	tōor
town	ville *f*	vēl
traffic	circulation *f*	sērkēläsyôN
traffic light	feux *m/pl.*	fā
travel agency	agence *f* de voyage	äzhäNs də vô·äyäzh
university	université *f*	ēnēversētā
valley	vallée *f*	välā
village	village *m*	vēläzh
wall	mur *m*	mēr
waterfall	cascade *f*	käskäd
zebra crossing	passage *m* clouté	päsäzh klōotā
zoo	zoo *m*	zô(ō)

Religious Services

Where is the Catholic church?
Où est l'église catholique?
ōo ā lāglēz kätōlēk

Who's preaching the sermon?
Qui fait le sermon?
kē fā lə sermóN

What time *are services (is high mass)*?
Quand a lieu *le service religieux (la grand-messe)*?
käNdä lēy*a* lə servēs relēzhē·*ä* (lä gräNmes)

Is there a *wedding (christening)* today?
Y a-t-il aujourd'hui *un mariage (un baptème)*?
ēyätēl ōzhōōrd*ē*·ē eN märē·äzh (eN bätäm)

Do they have church concerts?
Il y a des concerts de musique religieuse?
ēlyä dā kôNsär də m*ē*zēk relēzhē·*ä*z

Please call a *clergyman (priest)*!
Faites venir un *curé (prêtre)*, s'il vous plaît.
fāt venēr eN k*ē*rā (prät[ər]), sēl vōo plā

I am a	Je suis	zhə sē·ē
Christian	chrétien	krātyeN
Jew	juif	zhē·ēf
Catholic	catholique	kätōlēk
Methodist	méthodiste	mātōdēst
Moslem	musulman	mēzēlmäN
Protestant	protestant	prôtestäN

I don't belong to any religious denomination.
Je suis sans confession.
zhə sē·ē säN kôNfesyôN

abbey	abbaye *f*	äbā·ē
altar	autel *m*	ôtel
arch	arc *m*	ärk
baptism	baptême *m*	bätām
Baroque	baroque	bärôk
bell	cloche *f*	klôsh
candlestick	chandelier *m*	shäNdelēyā
cathedral	cathédrale *f*	kätädräl
(Roman) Catholic	catholique (romain)	kätōlēk (rômeN)
cemetery	cimetière *m*	sēmetyär
chapel	chapelle *f*	shäpel
choir	chœur *m*	kār
Christ	le Christ	lə krēst
christening	baptême *m*	bätām
Christian	chrétien	krātyeN
Christianity	christianisme *m*	krēstyänēsm
church	église *f*	āglēz
churchyard	cimetière *m*	sēmetyär
circumcision	circoncision *f*	sērkôNsēzyôN
clergyman	*cath.* curé *m*;	kērā;
	protest. pasteur *m*	pästār
communion	communion *f*	kômēnyôN
confess	se confesser	sə kôNfesā
confession	confession *f*	kôNfesyôN
convent	couvent *m*	kōōväN
creed	profession *f* de foi	prôfesyôN də fô·ä
cross	croix *f*	krô·ä
crucifix	crucifix *m*	krēsēfēks

cupola	coupole *f*	kōōpôl
denomination	confession *f*	kôNfesyôN
dome	coupole *f*	kōōpôl
font	fonts *m/pl.*	fôN
	baptismaux	bätēsmō
fresco	fresque *f*	fresk
God	Dieu *m*	dyä
Gospel	Evangile *m*	äväNzhēl
Gothic	gothique	gōtēk
grave	tombeau *m*	tôNbō
High Mass	grand-messe *f*	gräNmes
Islam	islamisme *m*	ēslämēsm
Jew	juif *m*	zhē̄-ēf
Jewish	juif	zhē̄-ēf
Judaism	judaïsme *m*	zhēdä·ēsm
mass	messe *f*	mes
monastery	couvent *m*	kōōväN
mosaic	mosaïque *f*	mōzä·ēk
Moslem	musulman *m*	mēzēlmäN
mosque	mosquée *f*	môskä
nave	nef *f*	nef
organ	orgue *m*	ôrg
pastor	*cath.* curé *m*;	kerā;
	protest. pasteur *m*	pästär
pillar	pilier *m*	pēlēyā
portal	portail *m*	pôrtä´ē
priest	prêtre *m*	prät(ər)
procession	procession *f*	prôsesyôN
Protestant	protestant *m*	prôtestäN
pulpit	chaire *f*	shär
rabbi	rabbin *m*	räbeN
religion	religion *f*	relēzhē·ôN
religious	religieux	relēzhē·ä
Romanesque	roman *m*	rômäN
rosary	rosaire *m*	rōzär
sacristan, sexton	sacristain *m*	säkrēsteN
sacristy	sacristie *f*	säkrēstē
sermon	sermon *m*	särmôN
service	office *m* religieux	ôfēs relēzhē·ä
Stations of the Cross	stations *f/pl.* du chemin de croix	stäsyôN dē shəmeN də krô·ä

Star of David	étoile *f* de David	ātô·äl də dävēd
statue	statue *f*	stät*ē*
synagogue	synagogue *f*	sēnägôg
tomb	tombeau *m*	tôNbō
tower	tour *f*	tōōr
vestibule	porche *m*	pôrsh

GOING SHOPPING

General Words and Phrases

Where can I *get (buy)* ...?
Où est-ce que je peux *trouver (acheter)* ...?
ōō eske zhə p*ā* trōōvā (äshtā) ...

I need ...
J'ai besoin de ...
zhā bezô·eN də

Is there a *leather (china)* shop here?
Y a-t-il un magasin *de cuir (de porcelaine)*?
ēyätēl eN mägäzeN də k*ē*·ēr (də pôrsələn)

Have you got ...?
Avez-vous ...?
ävä-vōō

I'd (We'd) like ...
Je voudrais *(Nous voudrions)* ...
zhə vōōdrā (nōō vōōdrē·ôN) ...

Please show me ...
Montrez-moi ..., s'il vous plaît.
môNtrā-mô·ä ... sēl vōō plā

Please give me ...
Donnez-moi ..., s'il vous plaît.
dônā-mô·ä ..., sēl vōō plā

a bag	un sac	eN säk
a bottle	une bouteille	*ē*n bōōtä'*ē*
a box	une boîte	*ē*n bô·ät
a few	quelques	kelke
a jar	un verre	eN vär
a pound	une livre	*ē*n lēv(ər)
a *pack (packet)*	un paquet	eN päkä
a pair	une paire	*e*n pār
a piece	un morceau	eN môrsō
a quart	un litre	eN lēt(ər)
a quarter pound	un quart	eN kär
a roll	un rouleau	eN rōōlō
a tube	un tube	eN t*ē*b
two pounds	un kilo	eN kēlō
a yard	un mètre *(approx.)*	
	(=0,914 m)	eN māt(ər)

That's plenty.	A little more.	Even more.
C'est assez.	Encore un peu.	Davantage.
set äsä	äNkôr eN pä	däväNtäzh

Can you order it for me?
Pouvez-vous le commander?
pōōvä-vōō lə kômäNdä

When will you get it in?
Quand est-ce que vous l'aurez?
käNdeske vōō lôrā

Can I exchange it?
Je peux l'échanger?
zhə pä läshäNzhä

I don't like the *shape (color)*.
La *forme (couleur)* ne me plaît pas.
lä fôrm (kōōlär) nə mə plä pä

This is ...   C'est ...   sä ...

too big	trop grand	trō gräN
too dark	trop foncé	trō fôNsä
too expensive	trop cher	trō shär
too *light (pale)*	trop clair	trō klär
too narrow	trop étroit	trōpātrô·ä
too small	trop petit	trō pətē
too wide	trop large	trō lärzh
too much	trop	trō

This is not enough.
Ce n'est pas assez.
sə nä päzäsä

Have you got something a little *nicer (less expensive)*?
Vous avez quelque chose *de mieux (de moins cher)*?
vōōzävä kelke shōz də myä (də mô·eN shär)

I like that.	I'll take it.
Cela me plaît.	Je *le (la, les)* prends.
səlä mə plä	zhə lə (lä, lā) präN

How much is that?	Thanks, that'll be all.
Ça coûte combien?	Merci, c'est tout.
sä kōōt kôNbyeN	mersē, sä tōō

Can you send my stuff to the ... Hotel please?
Pouvez-vous m'envoyer la marchandise à l'hôtel ..., s'il vous plaît?
pōōvä-vōō mäNvô·äyä lä märshäNdēz ä lôtel ..., sēl vōō plä

Do you take *credit cards (traveller's cheques)*?
Vous acceptez *des cartes de crédit (des chèques de voyage)*?
vōōzäkseptä dä kärt də krädē (dä shek də vô·äyäzh)

Stores

antique shop	magasin *m*	mägäzeN
	d'antiquités	däNtēkētä
art gallery	galerie *f*	gälerē
bakery	boulangerie *f*	bo͞oläNzhərē
barber shop	coiffeur *m*	kô·äfär
beauty parlor	institut *m* de beauté	eNstēt*ē* də bōtä
bookshop	librairie *f*	lēbrārē
butcher shop	boucherie *f*	bo͞osherē
candy store	confiserie *f*	kôNfēzerē
china shop	magasin *m* de	mägäzeN də
	porcelaine	pôrsəlen
cigar store	bureau *m* de tabac	bĕrō də täbä
clothes dyer	teinturerie *f*	teNt*ē*rerē
cobbler shop	cordonnerie *f*	kôrdónərē
cosmetic salon	institut *m* de beauté	eNstēt*ē* də bōtä
dairy	crèmerie *f*	krämerē
department store	grand magasin *m*	gräN mägäzeN
dressmaker's shop	tailleur *m* pour dames	täyär po͞or däm
drug store *(cosmetics & sundries)*	droguerie *f*	drôgerē
drug store *(prescription pharmacy)*	pharmacie *f*	färmäsē
dry cleaner's	nettoyage *m* à sec	netó·äyäzh ä sek
electrical shop	magasin *m*	mägäzeN
	d'électroménager	dälektrōmänäzhä
fashion boutique	magasin *m*	mägäzeN
	de haute couture	də ōt ko͞otēr
fish market	poissonnerie *f*	pô·äsônrē
flower shop	magasin *m* de fleurs	mägäzeN də flär
fruit market	épicerie *f*, marché *m*	āpēsərē, märshä
furrier	pelleterie *f*	peletərē
furniture store	magasin *m* de meubles	mägäzeN də m*ä*b'əl
grocery store	épicerie *f*	āpēsərē
haberdashery	mercerie *f*	märserē
hardware store	quincaillerie *f*	keNkäyerē
hat shop	chapellerie *f*	shäpelerē
jewelry store	bijouterie *f*	bēzho͞otərē

laundromat	laverie *f* automatique . .	läverē ôtōmätēk
laundry	blanchisserie *f*	bläNshēsərē
leather goods store . .	maroquinerie *f*	märōkēnərē
lingerie shop	magasin *m* de lingerie .	mägäzeN də leN-zhərē
liquor store	vins et spiritueux	veN ä spērēt*ē·ā*
music store	magasin *m* de musique .	mägäzeN də m*ē*zēk
newsdealer	marchand *m* de journaux	märshäN də zhōōrnō
optician	opticien *m*	ôptēsyeN
perfume shop	parfumerie *f*	pärfēmərē
pet shop	magasin *m* d'animaux .	mägäzeN dänēmō
photo shop	photographe *m*	fōtōgräf
photographer's studio	photographe *m*	fōtōgräf
poultry shop	commerce *m* de volaille(s)	kômers də vôlä'ē
real estate agency . . .	agence *f* immobilière . .	äzhäNs ēmôbēlēyär
record store	magasin *m* de disques .	mägäzeN də dēsk
second-hand book-shop	librairie *f* d'occasion . . .	lēbrärē dôkäzyôN
self-service	libre-service *m*	lēb(ər)-servēs
shoemaker's shop . . .	cordonnerie *f*	kôrdônərē
shoe store	magasin *m* de chaussures	mägäzeN də shōsēr
souvenir shop	magasin *m* de souvenirs *m/pl.*	mägäzeN də sōōvənēr
sporting goods store .	magasin *m* de sport . . .	mägäzeN də spór
stationery store	papeterie *f*	päpätərē
super market	supermarché *m*	sēpermärshā
tailor shop	tailleur *m*	täyär
textile store	magasin *m* de tissu . . .	mägäzeN də tēs*ē*
toy store	magasin *m* de jouets . . .	mägäzeN də zhōō·ā
travel agency	agence *f* de voyage	äzhäNs də vô·äyäzh
vegetable market	marchand *m* de légumes	märshäN də läg*ē*m
watchmaker's shop . .	horlogerie *f*	ôrlôzhərē
wine shop	marchand *m* de vin . . .	märshäN də veN

Flowers

bouquet	bouquet *m* de fleurs ...	bōokā də flār
chrysanthemums	chrysanthèmes *m/pl.* ...	krēsäNtäm
flower pot	pot *m* de fleurs	pô də flār
flowers	fleurs *f/pl.*	flār
gladioli	glaïeuls *m/pl.*	gläyál
lilacs	lilas *m*	lēlä
orchids	orchidées *f/pl.*	ôrkēdä
roses	roses *f/pl.*	rōz
tulips	tulipes *f/pl.*	tēlēp
vase	vase *m*	väz
violets	violettes *f/pl.*	vē·ôlet

Bookshop

autobiography	autobiographie *f*	ôtōbē·ōgräfē
biography	biographie *f*	bē·ōgräfē
book	livre *m*	lēv(ər)
catalogue	catalogue *m*	kätälóg
children's book	livre *m* pour enfants ...	lēv(ər) pōōr äNfäN
city map	plan *m* de la ville	pläN dəlä vēl
detective novel	roman *m* policier	rômäN pôlēsyä
dictionary	dictionnaire *m*	dēksyônär
guide book	guide *m* touristique	gēd tōōrēstēk
map	carte *f* géographique	kärt zhē·ōgräfēk
novel	roman *m*	rômäN
paperback	livre *m* de poche	lēv(ər) də pôsh
phrase book	guide *m* de conversation	gēd də kôNverzäsyôN
poetry book	recueil *m* de poésie	reka'ē də pō·äzē
record	disque *m*	dēsk
reference book	ouvrage *m* de référence	ōōvräzh də räfäräNs
road map	carte *f* routière	kärt rōōtyär
story book	livre *m* de contes	lēv(ər) də kôNt
text book	manuel *m*	mänē·el
thriller	roman *m* policier	rômäN pôlēsyä
translation	traduction *f*	trädēksyôN
travel reading	lecture *f* de voyage	lektēr də vô·äyäzh
volume	volume *m*	vôlēm

Photo Shop

Would you please develop this film?
Développez-moi ce rouleau, s'il vous plaît.
dāvālôpā-mó·ä sə ro͞olō, sēl vo͞o plä

One *print (enlargement)* of each negative, please.
Une épreuve (Un agrandissement) de chaque négatif, s'il vous plaît.
ēn äprāv (eNägräNdēs·mäN) də shäk nägätēf, sēl vo͞o plä

– three by four (inches).	**– three and a half by three and a half.**
– sept (sur) dix.	– neuf (sur) neuf.
– set (sēr) dēs	– nāf (sēr) nāf

– three and a half by five and a half (inches).
– neuf (sur) treize.
– nāf (sēr) trāz

Could you retouch this for me?
Est-ce que vous pouvez retoucher un peu?
eske vo͞o po͞ovā reto͞oshā eN pā

I'd like ...	**– a cartridge film.**
Je voudrais ...	– un film à châssis.
zhə vo͞odrā ...	– eN fēlm ä shäsē

– a super eight color film.	**– a sixteen millimeter color film.**
– un film en couleurs super huit.	– un film en couleurs seize mm.
– eN fēlm äN ko͞olár sēpär ē·ēt	– eN fēlm äN ko͞olár säz mēlēmät(ər)

– a black and white eight millimeter film.
– un film noir et blanc huit millimètres.
– eN fēlm nó·är ā bläN ē·ē mēlēmät(ər)

– a thirty-five millimeter film.	**– a film for color slides.**
– un film trente cinq millimètres.	– une pellicule de diapositives.
– eN fēlm träNt seNk mēlēmät(ər)	– ēn pelēkēl də dē·äpôzētēv

– a *twenty (thirty-six)* exposure film.
– une pellicule de *vingt (trente-six)* poses.
– ēn pelēkēl də veN (träNt-sēs) pōz

Would you please put the film in the camera for me?
Vous pourriez me mettre la pellicule dans l'appareil, s'il vous plaît?
vo͞o po͞orē·ā mə met(ər) lä pelēkēl däN läpärä′ē, sēl vo͞o plä

camera	appareil *m*	äpärä′ē
	photographique	fōtōgräfēk
color film	pellicule *f* en couleurs	pelēkĕl äN kooˉlär
color negative film	pellicule *f* négative	pelēkĕl nägätēv
	en couleurs	äN kooˉlär
develop	développer	dävelôpā
development	développement *m*	dävelôpmäN
diaphragm	diaphragme *m*	dē·äfrägm
8-mm film	film *m* de huit	fēlm də ēˉ·ē
	millimètres	mēlēmāt(ər)
enlargement	agrandissement *m*	ägräNdēsmäN
exposure	exposition *f*	ekspōzēsyóN
exposure meter	posemètre *m*	pōzmāt(ər)
film	film *m*, pellicule *f*	fēlm, pelēkĕl
film *(take moving*		
pictures)	filmer	fēlmā
flash bulb	ampoule *f* flash	äNpooˉl fläsh
flash cube	cube *m* flash	kĕb fläsh
lens	objectif *m*	ôbzhektēf
movie camera	caméra *f*	kämärä
negative	négatif *m*	nägätēf
paper	papier *m*	päpyā
– glossy *(matte)*	– brillant *(mat)*	– brēyäN (mä)
photo, picture	photo(graphie) *f*	fōtō(gräfē)
photograph *(verb)*	prendre des photos	präNd(ər) dā fōtō
print	épreuve *f*	āprāv
– color print	épreuve *f* en couleurs	āprāv äN kooˉlär
reversal film	film *m* inversible	fēlm eNversēb′əl
roll film	pellicule *f*, rouleau *m*	pelēkĕl, rooˉlō
shutter	obturateur *m*	obtērätär
shutter (release)	déclencheur *m*	däkläNshär
– automatic shutter	déclencheur *m*	däkläNshär
	automatique	ôtōmätēk
slide	diapositive *f*	dē·äpōzētēv
slide frame	petit cadre *m* pour	pətē käd(ər) poor
	diapositives	dē·äpōzētēv
snapshot	instantané *m*	eNstäNtänä
take a picture	prendre une photo	präNdrĕn fōtō
tripod	pied *m*	pyä
view finder	viseur *m*	vēzär
yellow filter	filtre *m* jaune	fēlt(ər) zhōn

Jeweler

amber	ambre *m* jaune	äNb(ər) zhōn
bracelet	bracelet *m*	bräslā
brooch	broche *f*	brôsh
costume jewelry	bijoux *m/pl.* fantaisie	bēzhoo fäNtäzē
cufflinks	boutons *m/pl.*	bootôN
	de manchette	də mäNshet
diamond	brillant *m*	brēyäN
ear clips	clips *m/pl.*	klēp
earrings	boucles *f/pl.*	book'əl
	d'oreille	dôrä'ē
emerald	émeraude *f*	ämerōd
gold	or *m*	ôr
gold plated	doré	dôrā
jewelry	parure *f*	pärēr
necklace	chaîne *f*	shen
pearls	perles *f/pl.*	pärl
pendant	pendant *m*	päNdäN
ring	bague *f*	bäg
ruby	rubis *m*	rēbē
sapphire	saphir *m*	säfēr
silver	argent *m*	ärzhäN
silver plated	argenté	ärzhäNtā
wedding ring	alliance *f*	älyäNs

Clothing

May I try it on?	**I take a size ...**	**This is ...**
Je peux l'essayer?	Je fais du ...	C'est ...
zhə *pā* lesāyā	zhə fā dē ...	sā ...

too long	trop long	trō lôN
too short	trop court	trō koor
too tight	trop étroit	trōpātrô·ä
too wide	trop large	trō lärzh

Can it be altered? ....*fits just fine (doesn't fit).*
On peut faire des retouches? ... me va bien (ne me va pas).
ôN *pā* fār dā retoosh ... mə vä byeN (nə mə vä pä)

apron	tablier *m*	täblēyā
bathing cap	bonnet *m* de bain	bônā də beN
bathing trunks/suit	maillot *m* de bain	mäyô də beN
bathrobe	peignoir *m*	penyô·är
belt	ceinture *f*	seNtēr
bikini	bikini *m*	bēkēnē
blouse	chemisier *m*	shemēzyā
blue jeans	blue-jeans *m/pl.*	blōōdzēn
bra, brassière	soutien-gorge *m*	sōōtyeN-gôrzh
cap	casquette *f*	käsket
cardigan	veste *f* de tricot	vest də trēkō
coat	manteau *m*	mäNtō
corset	corselet *m*; corset *m*	kôrsəlā, kôrsā
dress	robe *f*	rôb
dressing gown	robe *f* de chambre	rôb də shäNb(ər)
fur coat	(manteau *m* de)	(mäNtō də)
	fourrure *f*	fōōrēr
fur jacket	veste *f* de fourrure	vest də fōōrēr
garter belt	porte-jarretelles *f*	pôrt-zhärtel
girdle	ceinture *f*	seNtēr
gloves	gants *m/pl.*	gäN
handkerchief	mouchoir *m*	mōōshô·är
hat	chapeau *m*	shäpō
– straw hat	chapeau *m* de paille	shäpō də pä'ē
jacket *(lady's)*	veste *f*	vest
jacket *(man's)*	veston *m*	vestôN
knee socks	mi-bas *m/pl.*	mē-bä
leather coat	manteau *m* de cuir	mäNtō də kē·ēr
leather jacket	blouson *m* en cuir	blōōzôN äN kē·ēr
lingerie	lingerie *f*	leNzherē
night shirt	chemise *f* de nuit	shemēz də nē·ē
nightie	chemise *f* de nuit	shemēz də nē·ē
pajamas	pyjama *m*	pēzhämä
panties	slip *m*	slēp
pants, trousers	pantalon *m*	päNtälôN
pants suit	costume *m*	kôstēm
parka	anorak *m*	änôräk
petticoat	jupon *m*	zhēpôN
raincoat	imperméable *m*	eNpermä·äb'əl
scarf	écharpe *f*	äshärp
shirt	chemise *f*	shemēz

– **drip-dry**	– sans repassage	– säN repäsäzh
– **short-sleeved**	– à manches courtes	– ä mäNsh kōōrt
shorts	short *m*	shôrt
ski pants	pantalon *m* de ski	päNtälôN də skē
skirt	jupe *f*	zhēp
slacks	pantalon *m*	päNtälôN
slip	jupon *m*	zhēpôN
socks	chaussettes *f/pl.*	shôset
sport shirt	chemise *f* de sport	shemēz də spôr
sportswear	vêtements *m/pl.*	vätmäN
	de sport	də spôr
stockings	bas *m/pl.*	bä
stole	étole *f*	ātôl
suède coat	manteau *m* de chamois	mäNtō də shämô·ä
suède jacket	blouson *m* de chamois	blōōzôN də shä-mô·ä
suit *(lady's)*	tailleur *m*	täyär
suit *(man's)*	costume *m*	kôstēm
summer dress	robe *f* d'été	rôb dātā
suspenders	jarretelles *f/pl.*	zhärtel
sweatshirt	sweatshirt *m*	sōō·etshärt
sweater	pullover *m*	pēlōvär
swimsuit	maillot *m* de bain	mäyō də beN
tie	cravate *f*	krävat
tights	collants *m/pl.*	kôläN
track suit	survêtement *m*	sērvätmäN
trousers	pantalon *m*	päNtälôN
two-piece	tailleur *m*,	täyär,
	deux-pièces	dā-pyās
underpants	caleçon *m*	kälsôN
undershirt *(men's)*	gilet *m* du corps	zhēlä dē kôr
– **women's**	chemise *f*	shəmēz
underwear	sous-vêtements *m/pl.*	sōō-vätmäN
vest	gilet *m*	zhēlä
windbreaker	anorak *m*	änôräk

Dry Goods

accessories	accessoires m/pl.	äksesó·är
belt	ceinture f	seNtẽr
braces	bretelles f/pl.	bretel
buckle	boucle f	bo͞ok'əl
button	bouton m	bo͞otôN
buttonhole thread	fil m pour boutonnières	fẽl po͞or bo͞otônyär
darning cotton	coton m à repriser	kôtôN ä reprēzä
darning wool	laine f à repriser	len ä reprēzä
dress-shield	dessous m de bras	dəso͞o də brä
dry goods	mercerie f	märserē
elastic	élastique m	ālästēk
garters	jarretelles f/pl.	zhärtel
hooks and eyes	crochets m/pl.	krôshā
lining	doublure f	do͞oblẽr
needle	aiguille f	āgē'ē
– sewing needle	aiguille f à coudre	āgē'ē ä ko͞od(ər)
panty hose	collant m	kôläN
pin	épingle f	āpeNg'əl
ribbon	ruban m	rēbäN
safety pin	épingle f de sûreté	āpeNg'əl də sẽrtā
scissors	ciseaux m/pl.	sēzō
silk thread	soie f à coudre	sô·ä ä ko͞od(ər)
snap	bouton-pression m	bo͞otôN-presyóN
suspenders	bretelles f/pl.	brətel
synthetic thread	fil m polyester	fẽl pôlyestär
tape	ruban m	rēbäN
tape measure	centimètre m	säNtẽmät(ər)
thimble	dé m	dā
thread	fil m (à coudre)	fẽl ä ko͞od(ər)
wool	laine f	len
zipper	fermeture f éclair	färmetẽr äklär

Fabrics

cloth	drap m	drä
corduroy	velours m côtelé	velo͞or kōtlä
cotton	coton m	kôtôN
fabric	tissu m; étoffe f	tēsē, ätôf

– checked	– quadrillé	– kädrēyä
– patterned, printed	– imprimé	– eNprēmā
– solid color	– uni	– enē
– striped	– rayé	– rāyā
flannel	flanelle *f*	flänel
jersey	jersey *m*	zhersē
linen	toile *f*	tô·äl
material	tissu *m*; matière *f*	tēsē; mätyär
nylon	nylon *m*	nēlôN
silk	soie *f* naturelle	sô·ä nät*e*rel
– artificial silk	soie *f* artificielle	sô·ä ärtēfēsyel
synthetic fibre	fibre *f* synthétique	fēb(ər) seNtātēk
velvet	velours *m*	velōor
wool	laine *f*	len
– pure wool	– pure laine	– p*e*r len
– pure virgin wool	– pure laine vierge	– p*e*r len vyärzh
worsted	laine *f* peignée	len penyā

Cleaning, Alterations, Repairs

I'd like to have this *dress (suit)* cleaned.
Je voudrais faire nettoyer *cette robe (ce costume)*.
zhə vōodrā fār netô·äyā set rôb (sə kôstēm)

I'd like to have these things laundered.
Je voudrais faire laver ce linge.
zhə vōodrā fār lävä sə leNzh

Would you please *press this (take out this stain)*?
Pouvez-vous *me repasser ceci (enlever cette tache)*?
pōovä-vōo mə repäsä səsē (äNlevä set täsh)

Could you *darn this (sew on this button)*?
Pouvez-vous *repriser ceci (recoudre ce bouton)*?
pōovä-vōo reprēzä səsē (rekōod(ər) sə bōotôN)

Would you mend this run for me?
Vous pourriez me faire un remaillage?
vōo pōorē·ā mə fār eN remäyäzh

Could you *lengthen (shorten)* this?
Pouvez-vous *le (la) rallonger (raccourcir)* un peu?
pōovä-vōo lə (lä) rälôNzhä (räkōorsēr) eN p*a*

Optician

Can you fix these glasses?
Pouvez-vous réparer ces lunettes?
pōōvā-vōō rāpärā sā lĕnet

Can you replace these lenses?
Pouvez-vous remplacer ces verres?
pōōvā-vōō räNpläsā sā vär

I'm *near-sighted (far-sighted)*.
Je suis *myope (presbyte)*.
zhə sē·ē mē·ôp (presbēt)

binoculars	jumelles *f/pl.*	zhĕmel
compass	boussole *f*	bōōsôl
contact lenses	verres *m/pl.* de contact	vär də kôNtäkt
eyeglass case	étui *m* à lunettes	ātē·ē ä lĕnet
frame	monture *f*	môNtēr
glasses	lunettes *f/pl.*	lĕnet
magnifying glass	loupe *f*	lōōp
spectacles	lunettes *f/pl.*	lĕnet
sunglasses	lunettes *f/pl.* de soleil	lĕnet də sôlä′ē

Stationery

ball point pen	stylo *m* à bille	stēlō ä bē′ē
– cartridge	mine *f*; cartouche *f*	mēn; kärtōōsh
carbon paper	papier *m* carbone	päpyā kärbôn
crayons	crayons *m/pl.* de couleur	krāyôN də kōōlär
envelope	enveloppe *f*	äNvelôp
eraser	gomme *f*	gôm
fountain pen	stylo *m*	stēlō
glue	colle *f*	kôl
ink	encre *f*	äNk(ər)
pad	bloc *m*	blôk
– scratch pad	bloc-notes *m*	blôk nôt
– sketch pad	bloc *m* à dessin	blôk ä deseN
paper	papier *m*	päpyā
– typewriter paper	papier *m* machine (à écrire)	– päpyā mäshēn (ä äkrēr)
– wrapping paper	papier *m* d'emballage	päpyā däNbäläzh
– writing paper	papier *m* à lettre	päpyā ä let(ər)
pencil	crayon *m*	krāyôN

Shoes

I take a size ... J'ai la pointure ... zhā lä pô·eNt*ē*r ...	I'd like a pair of ... Je désire une paire de ... zhə dāz*ē*r ēn pär də ...

beach sandals	sandales *f/pl.*	säNdäl
bedroom slippers	pantoufles *f/pl.*	päNtoof'əl
boots	bottes *f/pl.*	bôt
ladies' shoes	chaussures *f/pl.* pour dames	shôs*ē*r poor däm
loafers	mocassins *m/pl.*	mókäseN
rubber boots	bottes *f/pl.* de caoutchouc	bôt də kä·ôtshoo
sandals	sandales *f/pl.*	säNdäl
sneakers, gym shoes .	chaussures *f/pl.* de gymnastique	shôs*ē*r də zhēmnästēk
walking shoes	souliers *m/pl.* de marche	soolyä də märsh

They're too *tight (wide)*. Ils sont trop *étroits (trop larges)*. ēl sôN trōpātrô·ä (trō lärzh)	They pinch here. Ils serrent ici. ēl sär ēsē

Could you fix these shoes for me?
Voudriez-vous me réparer ces souliers?
voodrē·ävoo mə rāpärā sā soolyä

crêpe sole	semelle *f* de crêpe	semel də krāp
heel	talon *m*	tälôN
– flat	– plat	– plä
– high	– haut	– ō
in-sole	semelle *f* intérieure	semel eNtārē·*ā*r
leather	cuir *m*	k*ē*·ēr
leather sole	semelle *f* de cuir	semel də k*ē*·ēr
rubber sole	semelle *f* de caoutchouc	semel də kä·ôtshoo
shoe horn	chausse-pied *m*	shôs-pyä
shoe laces	lacets *m/pl.*	läsä
shoe polish	cirage *m*	sēräzh
sole *(noun)*	semelle *f*	semel
sole *(verb)*	ressemeler	reseməlā
suede	daim *m*	deN

Cigar Store

A pack of ... *cigarettes (tobacco)*, please.
Un paquet de *cigarettes (tabac)*, s'il vous plaît.
eN päkä də sēgäret (täbä), sēl voo plā

Do you have American cigarettes?
Avez-vous des cigarettes américaines?
ävä-voo dā sēgäret ämārēken

A dozen cigars, please.
Douze cigares, s'il vous plaît.
dooz sēgär, sēl voo plā

Would you please refill my lighter?
Voudriez-vous me remplir le briquet, s'il vous plaît.
voodrē·ā-voo mə räNplēr lə brēkā, sēl voo plā

A box of matches, please.
Une boîte d'allumettes, s. v. p.
ēn bó·ät dälemet, sēl voo plā

Could I please have a light?
Avez-vous du feu, s'il vous plaît?
ävä-voo dē fā, sēl voo plā

cigar	cigare m	sēgär
cigarette	cigarette f	sēgäret
– filtered	– à bout filtre	– ä boo fēlt(ər)
– unfiltered	– sans filtre	– säN fēlt(ər)
flint	pierre f à briquet	pyär ä brēkā
lighter	briquet m	brēkā
– gas lighter	briquet m à gaz	brēkā ä gäz
lighter fluid	essence f à briquet	esäNs ä brēkā
matches	allumettes f/pl.	älemet
pipe	pipe f	pēp
pipe cleaner	cure-pipe f	kēr-pēp
tobacco	tabac m	täbä

Toiletries

after shave	lotion f après rasage	lôsyôN äprä räzazh
barette	barrette f	bäret
bath salts	sels m/pl. pour le bain	sel poor lə beN
bobby pins	pinces f/pl. à cheveux	peNs ä shevā
brush	brosse f	brôs
clothes brush	brosse f à habits	brôs ä äbē
comb	peigne m	pen(yə)
compact	poudrier m	poodrēyä

cream	crème *f* (de beauté)	krām (də bōtä)
curler	bigoudi *m*, rouleau *m*	bēgoodē, roolō
deodorant	déodorant *m*	dā-ōdôräN
dye	teinture *f*	teNtēr
emery board	lime *f* à ongles en carton	lēm ä oNg'əl äN kärtôN
eye liner	crayon *m* (à paupières)	krāyôN (ä pôpyär)
eye shadow	ombre *f* à paupières	ôNbrä pôpyär
eyebrow pencil	crayon *m* à sourcils	krāyôN ä soorsē
face cream	crème *f* (pour le visage)	krām (poor lə vēzäzh)
hair conditioner	sèche-cheveux *m*	sāsh-shevā
hair net	filet *m*	fēlā
hair spray	vaporisateur *m*	väpôrēzätār
hair tonic	lotion *f* capillaire	lôsyôN käpēlär
hairbrush	brosse *f* à cheveux	brôs ä shevā
hairpin	épingle *f* à cheveux	āpeNg'əl ä shevā
lipstick	rouge *m* à lèvres	roozh ä läv(ər)
mascara	rimmel *m*	rēmel
mirror	miroir *m*, glace *f*	mērô·är, gläs
mouthwash	eau *f* dentifrice	ō däNtēfrēs
nail file	lime *f* à ongles	lēm ä ôNg'əl
nail polish	vernis *m* à ongles	värnē ä ôNg'əl
nail polish remover	dissolvant *m*	dēsôlväN
nail scissors	ciseaux *m/pl.* à ongles	sēzō ä ôNg'əl
orange stick	cure-ongles *m*	kēr-ôNg'əl
perfume	parfum *m*	pärfeN
powder	poudre *f*	pood(ər)
powder puff	houppette *f*	oopet
prophylactic	préservatif *m*	präzervätēf
razor	rasoir *m* (mécanique)	räzô·är (mākänēk)
– electric shaver	rasoir *m* électrique	räzô·är ālektrēk
– safety razor	rasoir *m* de sûreté	räzô·är də sērtā
– straight razor	rasoir *m*	räzô·är
razor blades	lames *f/pl.* de rasoir	läm də räzô·är
rouge	rouge *m*	roozh
sanitary napkins	serviettes *f/pl.* hygiéniques	servyet ēzhē·änēk
scissors	ciseaux *m/pl.*	sēzō
shampoo	shampooing *m*	shäNpô·eN
shaving brush	blaireau *m*	blārō

shaving cream	crème *f* à raser	kräm ä räzä
shaving foam	mousse *f* à raser	moos ä räzä
shaving soap	savon *m* à barbe	sävôN ä bärb
soap	savon *m*	sävôN
sponge	éponge *f*	äpôNzh
sun tan cream	crème *f* solaire	kräm sôlär
– sun tan lotion	lotion *f* solaire	lôsyôN sôlär
– sun tan oil	huile *f* solaire	ē·ēl sôlär
tampons	tampons *m/pl.*	täNpôN
tissues	mouchoirs *m/pl.* en pa- pier	mooshô·är äN päpyä
toilet articles, toiletries	articles *m/pl.* de toilette	ärtēk′əl də tô·älet
toilet kit	nécessaire *m* de toilette	nāsesär də tô·älet
toilet paper	papier *m* hygiénique	päpyä ēzhē·änēk
wash cloth	gant *m* de toilette	gäN də tô·älet
tooth brush	brosse *f* à dents	brôs ä däN
tooth paste	dentifrice *m*	däNtēfrēs
tooth powder	poudre *f* dentifrice	pood(ər) däNtēfrēs
towel	serviette *f*	servyet
– bath towel	serviette *f* de bain	servyet də beN
tweezers	pincettes *f/pl.*	peNset

Watchmaker

Can you fix this *watch (clock)*?	**It's running *fast (slow)*.**
Pouvez-vous réparer cette montre?	Elle *avance (retarde)*.
poovä-voo rāpärā set môNt(ər)	el äväNs (retärd)

How much will the repair cost?
Combien va coûter la réparation?
kôNbyeN vä kootä lä rāpäräsyôN

alarm clock	réveil *m*	rāvā′ē
crystal	verre *m*	vār
clock	montre *f*	môNt(ər)
face	cadran *m*	kädräN
hand	aiguille *f*	āgē′ē
pocket watch	montre *f* de poche	môNt(ər) də pôsh

spring	ressort *m*	resôr
stop watch	chronomètre *m*	krônômāt(ər)
watch	montre *f*	môNt(ər)
watch band	bracelet *m* (pour montre)	bräslā (pŏŏr môNt(ər)
wrist watch	montre-bracelet *f*	môNt(ər)-bräslā

Sundries

ash tray	cendrier *m*	säNdrēyā
bag	sac *m*	säk
ball	balle *f*	bäl
basket	corbeille *f*, panier *m*	kôrbā'ē, pänyā
battery	batterie *f*	bätərē
beach bag	sac *m* de camping	säk də käNpēng
bottle opener	décapsuleur *m*	dākäpsēlär
briefcase	portefeuille *m*; serviette *f*	pôrtfä'ē; servyet
camp stove	réchaud *m* à alcool	rāshō ä älkôl
can opener	ouvre-boîte *m*	ōov(ər)-bô·ät
candle	bougie *f*	bōozhē
– beeswax	cire *f* d'abeille	sēr däbä'ē
candlestick	bougeoir *m*	bōozhô·är
candy	bonbons *m/pl.*	bôNbôN
canned goods	conserves *f/pl.*	kôNsärv
cassette	cassette *f*	käset
ceramics	céramique *f*	särämēk
china	porcelaine *f*	pôrsəlen
corkscrew	tire-bouchon *m*	tēr-bōoshôN
detergent	détergent *m*	dāterzhäN
– dishwashing detergent	détergent *m* à vaisselle	dāterzhäN ä väsel
doll	poupée *f*	pōopā
figurine	figure *f*	fēgēr
flashlight	flash *m*	fläsh
hammock	hamac *m*	ämäk
handbag	sac *m* à main	säk ä meN
handicrafts	objets *m/pl.* artisanaux	ôbzhā ärtēzänō
handkerchief	mouchoir *m*	mōoshô·är
jackknife	couteau *m* de poche	kōotō də pôsh

leash	laisse *f*	lās
mat	soucoupe *f*	sōōkōōp
paper napkins	serviettes *f/pl.* en papier	servyet äN päpyā
phonograph record	disque *m*	dēsk
picture	image *f*	ēmäzh
plastic bag	sac *m* en plastique	säk äN plästēk
playing cards	cartes *f/pl.* à jouer	kärt ä zhōō·ā
pocket knife	couteau *m* de poche	kōōtō də pôsh
purse	porte-monnaie *m*	pôrt-mônā
recording tape	bande *f* magnétique	bäNd mänyātēk
rope	corde *f*	kôrd
rucksack	sac *m* à dos	säk ä dō
Scotch tape	ruban *m* adhésif, scotch	rēbäN ädāzēf, skôtsh
sled	luge *f*	lēzh
spot remover	détachant *m*	dātäshäN
string	ficelle *f*	fēsel
stuffed animal	animal *m* en peluche	änēmäl äN pelēsh
suitcase	valise *f*	välēz
tape recorder	magnétophone *m*	mänyātōfôn
thermometer	thermomètre *m*	termōmāt(ər)
thermos bottle	thermos *f*	termôs
toy	jouets *m/pl.*	zhōō·ā
umbrella	parapluie *m*	päräplē'ē
vase	vase *m*	väz
video cassette	cassette-vidéo *f*	käset vēdä·ō
wallet	portefeuille *m*	pôrtfä'ē
washing line	corde *f* à linge	kôrd ä leNzh
wood carving	sculpture *f* sur bois	skēlptēr sēr bô·ä

AT THE POST OFFICE

The activities of European post offices are far broader in scope than they are in the United States. In addition to all the usual mail services, the post office is also the telegraph and telephone company, and provides full banking services, including checking and savings accounts. They will also hold mail for travelers. Simply tell your correspondents to write you "poste restante" (póst restäNt) in the city of your destination.

Post Office

Where is the post office?
Où est le bureau de poste?
ōōä lə bĕrō də pôst

Where is there a mail box?
Où y a-t-il une boîte aux lettres?
ōōyätēl ēn bô·ät ō let(ər)

How much does this *letter (card)* cost?
C'est combien pour cette *lettre (carte)?*
sā kôNbyeN pōōr set let(ər) (kärt)

– to the United States.
– pour les États-Unis.
– pōōr lāzātäzēnē

– to Canada.
– pour le Canada.
– pōōr lə känädä

What's the postage on ...
Le port, c'est combien pour ...
lə pôr, sā kôNbyeN pōōr

Five ... stamps please.
Cinq timbres à ..., s'il vous plaît.
seNk teNb(ər)-pôst ä ..., sēl vōō plā

this air mail letter ...	cette lettre par avion	set let(ər) pär ävyôN
this letter abroad	cette lettre pour l'étranger	set let(ər) pōōr läträNzhä
this local letter	cette lettre locale	set let(ər) lôkäl
this parcel	ce colis	sə kôlē
this picture post card	cette carte postale illustrée	set kärt pôstäl ēlēsträ
this post card	cette carte postale	set kärt pôstäl
this printed matter ..	cet imprimé	set eNprēmä
this registered letter	cette lettre recommandée	set let(ər) rekômäNdä
this small parcel	ce petit colis	sə pətē kôlē
this special delivery letter	cette lettre exprès	set let(ər) eksprä

Do you have any special issues?

Vous avez aussi des timbres de collection?

voozävä ôsē dā teNb(ər) də kôleksyôN

Two of each, please.

Deux de chaque, s'il vous plaît.

dā də shäk, sēl voo plä

This set of stamps, please.

Cette série de timbres-poste, s'il vous plaît.

set sārē də teNb(ər)-pôst, sēl voo plä

I'd like to send this letter *by registered mail (special delivery).*

Cette lettre *recommandée (par exprès)*, s'il vous plaît.

set let(ər) rekômäNdä (pär eksprä), sēl voo plä

A *postal transfer (money order),* **please.**

Un *mandat-poste (mandat-carte)*, s'il vous plaît.

eN mäNdä-pôst (mäNdä-kärt), sēl voo plä

How long does it take for a *letter (package)* **to get to ...?**

Combien de temps met *une lettre (un colis)* pour ...?

kôNbyen də täN metēn let(ər) (eN kôlē) poor

Is there any mail here for me?

Y a-t-il du courrier pour moi?

ēyätēl dē kooryä poor mô·ä

My name ist ...

Je m'appelle ...

zhə mäpel ...

Where can I *mail (pick up)* **a package?**

Où est le guichet *d'enregistrement (de remise)* des colis postaux?

oo ā lə gēshā däNrezhēstrəmäN (də remēz) dā kôlē pôstō

Do I need a customs declaration?

Je dois faire une déclaration de douane?

zhə dô·ä fär ēn däkläräsyôN də doo·än

***Sign here, please.**

Signez ici, s'il vous plaît.

sēnyā ēsē, sēl voo plä

I'd like to have my mail forwarded.

J'aimerais faire suivre mon courrier.

zhāmerä fär sē·ēv(ər) môN kooryä

This is my new address.

Voici ma nouvelle adresse.

vô·äsē mä noovel ädres

You can pay bills at the post office simply by transferring the money to your creditor's postal account or having a money order delivered to him by mail. Of course, the French Post Offices can help jou send money to the United States, or almost any other country in the world. Inquire at the "mandats" window.

Telegrams · Telephone

A telegram form, please.
Une formule de télégramme, s. v. p.
ēn fôrmēl də tālägräm, sēl voo plä

I'd like to send . . .
Je voudrais envoyer . . .
zhə voodrā äNvô·äyā

a telegram. . . . . un télégramme . . . . eN tālägräm
a night letter . . . . un télégramme-lettre . . eN tālägräm-let(ər)

How much do ten words to . . . cost?
Combien coûtent dix mots pour . . .?
kôNbyeN koot dē mō poor . . .

When will it arrive at . . .?
Quand sera-t-il à (en) . . .?
käN sərätēl ä (äN) . . .

Will the wire get to . . . today?
Le télégramme arrivera encore aujourd'hui à (en) . . .?
lə tālägräm ärēvərä äNkôr ōzhoordē·ē ä (äN) . . .

> *In most European countries it is wise to place long distance calls at the post office, as many hotels make sizable surcharges for use of the phone.*

Where is the nearest phone booth?
Où est la cabine téléphonique la plus proche?
oo ā lä käbēn tālāfōnēk lä plē prôsh

Where can I make a phone call?
Où est-ce que je peux téléphoner?
oo eske zhə pā tālāfōnā

Can I direct dial to . . .?
Je peux faire un numéro interurbain automatique?
zhə pā fär eN nēmārō eNterērbeN ôtōmätēk

The phone book, please.
L'annuaire (du téléphone), s. v. p.
länē·är dē tālāfôn, sēl voo plä

What's the area code for . . .?
Quel est l'indicatif pour. . .?
kel ā leNdēkätēf poor . . .

> *You can direct dial the United States from almost any telephone in Europe. The country code for the U.S. and Canada is 001, followed, of course by the area code and the subscriber's number. You will need operator assistance for person-to-person or collect calls.*

A long distance call to ... please.
Une communication *interurbaine* (*or:*
internationale) pour ... s'il vous plaît.
ēn kômēnēkäsôN eNterērben (eNternä-
syônàl) po͞or ..., sēl vo͞o plä

How long will that take?
Quelle sera la durée
d'attente?
kel serä lä dērä dätäNt

Can I have some coins for the pay phone?
Avez-vous des jetons pour le taxiphone?
ävä-vo͞o dā zhetôN po͞or lə täksēfôn

How much does a *local call* (*call to ...*) cost?
Combien coûte une *communication urbaine* (*communication pour ...*)?
kôNbyeN ko͞ot ēn kômēnēkäsyôN ērben (kômēnēkäsyôN po͞or)

What time does the night rate begin?
Le tarif de nuit, c'est à partir de quelle heure?
lə tärēf də nē·ē, sätä pärtēr də kelār

*Your call is ready in booth four.
Votre communication: cabine quatre.
vôt(ər) kômēnēkäsyôN käbēn kät(ər)

*What's your number?
Quel est votre numéro?
kel ä vôt(ər) nēmärō

Please connect me with ...
Passez-moi ..., s'il vous plaît.
päsä-mô·ä ..., sēl vo͞o plä

There's no answer at that number.
Le correspondant ne répond pas.
lə kôrespôNdäN nə räpôN pä

The line is *busy* (*out of order*).
La ligne est *occupée* (*en dérangement*).
lä lēn(yə) ätôkēpä (äN däräNzhmäN)

Wrong number!
C'est un faux numéro.
säteN fô nēmärō

May I speak to *Mr.* (*Mrs., Miss*) ...?
Je voudrais parler à *Monsieur* (*Madame, Mademoiselle*) ...?
zhə vo͞odrä pärlä ä məsyä (mädäm, mädəmô·äzel) ...

Speaking!
Allô (oui)?
älō (o͞o·ē)

This is ... speaking.
C'est ...
sä ...

Who is this?
Qui est à l'appareil?
kē ätäläpärä′ē

Please hold the line.
Ne quittez pas!
nə kētä pä

Would you please cancel that call.
Veuillez annuler la communication.
vāyä änēlä lä kômēnēkäsyôN

Code Alphabet

A	=Anatole	änätôl	**N**	=Nicolas	nēkôlä
B	=Berthe	bärt	**O**	=Oscar	ôskär
C	=César	säzär	**P**	=Paul	pôl
D	=Désiré	dāzērä	**Q**	=Québec	kābek
E	=Emile	ämēl	**R**	=Robert	rôbär
F	=François	fräNsô·ä	**S**	=Suzanne	sēzän
G	=Gaston	gästôN	**T**	=Théodore	tā·ôdôr
H	=Henri	äNrē	**U**	=Ursule	ērsēl
I	=Isidore	ēsēdôr	**V**	=Victor	vēktôr
J	=Jean	zhäN	**W**	=Wagon	ōō·ägóN
K	=Kléber	klābär	**X**	=Xavier	gzävyä
L	=Louis	lōō·ē	**Y**	=Yvonne	ēvôn
M	=Marie	märē	**Z**	=Zoé	zō·ā

address	adresse *f*	ädres
addressee	destinataire *m*	destēnätär
air mail	poste *f* aérienne	pôst ä·ārē·en
area code	indicatif *m*	eNdēkätēf
c.o.d.	remboursement *m*	räNbōōrsmäN
coin changer	changeur *m* de monnaie automatique	shäNzhär də mônä ôtōmätēk
collect call	communication *f* payable à l'arrivée	kômēnēkäsyôN päyäb'əl älärēvä
counter	guichet *m*	gēshä
customs declaration	déclaration *f* de douane	dākläräsyôN də dōō·än
destination	lieu *m* de destination	lēyä də destēnäsyôN
dial *(noun)*	cadran *m*	kädräN
dial *(verb)*	composer le numéro	kôNpōzä lə nēmärō
direct dialing	automatique *m*	ôtōmätēk
general delivery	poste *f* restante	pôst restäNt
information	renseignement *m*	räNsen(yə)mäN
insured mail	courrier *m* avec valeur déclarée	kōōryä ävek välär dāklärä
letter	lettre *f*	let(ər)
local call	communication *f* urbaine	kômēnēkäsyôN ērben

long distance call	communication *f*	kômēnēkäsyôN
	interurbaine	eNterērben
mail box	boîte *f* aux lettres	bô·ät ō let(ər)
mail man	facteur *m*	fäktār
operator	téléphoniste *m/f*	tālāfōnēst
package, parcel	colis *m*	kôlē
package card	bulletin *m*	bēlteN dekspädē-
	d'expédition	syôN
person to person	communication *f*	kômēnēkäsyôN
call	avec avis d'appel	ävek ävē däpel
picture postcard	carte *f* postale	kärt pôstäl
	illustrée	ēlēsträ
post card	carte *f* postale	kärt pôstäl
post office box	boîte *f* postale	bô·ät pôstäl
postage	port *m*	pôr
postal clerk	employé *m* des postes .	äNplô·äyā dā pôst
postal savings book ..	livret *m* de caisse	lēvrā də kes
	d'épargne postale	dāpärn(ye) pôstäl
postman	facteur *m*	fäktār
printed matter	imprimé *m*	eNprēmā
pushbutton telephone	téléphone *m* à touches	tālāfôn ä tōosh
receipt	quittance *f*	kētäNs
register	recommajder	rekômäNdā
registered letter	lettre *f* recommandée ..	let(ər) rekômäNdā
registered parcel with	colis *m* avec valeur	kôlē ävek välār
declared value	déclarée	dāklärā
return postage	port *m* de retour	pôr də retōor
sender	expéditeur *m*	ekspädētār
small parcel	petit colis *m*	pətē kôlē
special delivery	exprès *m*	eksprā
special issue stamp ..	timbre *m* d'émission	teNb(ər) dāmēsyôN
	spéciale	spāsyäl
stamp *(noun)*	timbre-poste *m*	teNb(ər)-pôst
stamp *(verb)*	affranchir	äfräNshēr
stamp machine	machine *f* à	mäshēn ä
	affranchir	äfräNshēr
telegram	télégramme *m*	tālāgräm
telephone	téléphone *m*	tālāfôn
unstamped	non affranchi	nôN äfräNshē
value declaration	valeur *f* déclarée	välār dāklärā

BANK, CURRENCY EXCHANGE

French Franc (FF) – FF 1 = 100 c *(centimes)*

Where can I change some money?
Où est-ce que je peux changer de l'argent?
ōō eske zhə pā shäNzhā də lärzhäN

Where ist the bank?
Où est la banque?
ōō ā lä bäNk

I need a hundred dollars in ...
Je voudrais changer cents dollars en ...
zhə vōōdrā shäNzhā säN dôlär äN ...

How much will I get for...?
Je touche combien pour ...?
zhə tōōsh kóNbyeN pōōr ...

What's the rate of exchange?
Quel est le cours?
kel ā lə kōōr

Can you change ... into ... for me?
Pouvez-vous me changer ... en ...?
pōōvā-vōō mə shäNzhā ... äN ...

Could I have some change please?
Donnez-moi aussi de la monnaie, s'il vous plaît.
dônā-mô·ä ôsē də lä mônā, sēl vōō plā

Can you change this?
Pouvez-vous changer?
pōōvā-vōō shäNzhā

I'd like to cash this *check (traveller's cheque).*
Je voudrais encaisser ce *chèque (chèque de voyage).*
zhə vōōdrā äNkesā sə shek (shek də vô·äyäzh)

Has some money arrived for me?
Y a-t-il eu un versement à mon compte?
ēyätēl ē eN versmäN ä môN kôNt

amount	montant *m*	môNtäN
bank	banque *f*	bäNk
bank account	compte *m* bancaire	kôNt bäNkär
bank charges	frais *m/pl.* bancaires	frā bäNkär
bank note	billet *m* de banque	bēyā də bäNk
bank transfer	virement *m* bancaire	vērmäN bäNkär
bill	billet *m* de banque	bēyā də bäNk
bond	obligation *f*	ôblēgäsyôN
branch manager	directeur *m* de banque	dērektär də bäNk

cash *(adj.)*	comptant	kôNtâN
cash *(noun)*	espèces *f/pl.*	espâs
check	chèque *m*	shek
coin	pièce *f* de monnaie	pyäs də mónā
credit	crédit *m*	krādē
– take out a loan	prendre un crédit	präNdreN krādē
credit card	carte *f* de crédit	kärt də krādē
currency	monnaie *f*	mónā
daily rate	cours *m* du jour	kōor dē zhōor
deposit	versement *m*	versmäN
foreign currency	devises *f/pl.*	dəvēz
form	formulaire *m*	fôrmēlär
letter of credit	lettre *f* de crédit	let(ər) də krādē
money	argent *m*	ärzhäN
Canadian dollars	dollars *m/pl.* canadiens	dólär känädyeN
French francs	francs français *m/pl.*	fräN fräNsā
Swiss Francs	francs *m/pl.* suisses	fräN sē·ēs
American dollars	dollars *m/pl.* américains	dólär ämārēkeN
money exchange	change *m*	shäNzh
mortgage	hypothèque *f*	ēpōtāk
pay out	payer; verser	pâyä; versä
payment	paiement *m*	pāmäN
rate of exchange	cours *m* du change	kōor dē shäNzh
receipt	quittance *f*	kētäNs
savings bank	caisse *f* d'épargne	kes dāpärn(yə)
savings book	livret *m* d'épargne	lēvrā dāpärn(yə)
security	valeur *f*	välär
share of stock	coupon *m* d'action	kōopóN däksyóN
signature	signature *f*	sēnyätēr
stock	action *f*	äksyóN
telegraphic	télégraphique	tālāgräfēk
teller	caissier *m*	kesyā
transfer	virement *m*	vērmäN
traveller's cheque	chèque *m* de voyage	shek də vó·äyäzh
withdraw	résilier	räzēlyä

AT THE POLICE STATION

Reporting

STOP

POLICE

I'd like to report ...
Je voudrais déposer une plainte au sujet ...
zhə voodrä däpōzā ĕn pleNt ō sĕzhĕ ...

an accident	d'un accident	denäksēdäN
a blackmail attempt	d'un chantage	deN shäNtäzh
a hold up	d'une agression	dĕn ägresyóN
a kidnapping	d'un enlèvement	denäNlĕävmäN
a loss	d'une perte	dĕn pärt
a murder	d'un meurtre	deN märt(ər)
a theft	d'un vol	deN vól

My ... has been stolen.
On m'a volé ...
ôN mä völä ...

I lost my ...
J'ai perdu ...
zhā perdĕ ...

bag	le sac	lə säk
billfold	le portefeuille	lə pôrtfä′ē
bracelet	le bracelet	lə bräslä
briefcase	le portefeuille, la serviette	lə pôrtfä′ē, la servyät
camera	l'appareil photographique	läpärä′ē fōtōgräfēk·
car key	les clés de voiture	lä klā də vó·ätēr
handbag	le sac à main	lə säk ä meN
jewelry	les bijoux	lä bēzhoo
key	la clé	lä klā
money	l'argent	lärzhäN
necklace	la chaîne	lä shen
purse	le porte-monnaie	lə pórt-mónä
ring	la bague	lä bäg
suitcase	la valise	lä välēz
umbrella	le parapluie	lə päräplē′ē
wallet	le portefeuille	lə pôrtfä′ē
watch	la montre	lä môNt(ər)
– wrist watch	la montre-bracelet	lä môNt(ər)-bräslä

I have nothing to do with *it (this business).*
Je n'ai rien à voir *là-dedans (dans cette affaire).*
zhə närē·eN ä vô·är lä-dədäN (däN set äfär)

I'm innocent.	**I didn't do it.**
Je suis innocent.	Je n'ai pas fait cela.
zhə sē·ē ēnôsäN	zhə nä pä fä səlä

How long do I have to stay here?
Combien de temps dois-je rester ici?
kôNbyeN də täN dô·äzh restä ēsē

This man is *bothering (following)* **me.**
Cet homme *m'importune (me poursuit).*
setôm meNpôrtēn (mə po͞orsē·ē)

arrest	arrêter	ärätā
attorney	avocat *m*	ävōkä
confiscate	confisquer	kôNfēskä
court	tribunal *m*	trēbēnäl
crime	crime *m*	krēm
criminal	criminel *m*	krēmēnel
criminal investigation		
division	police *f* judiciaire	pôlēs zhēdēsyär
custody	détention *f*	dätäNsyóN
– **pre-trial**	détention *f*	dätäNsyóN
custody	préventive	präväNtēv
drugs	drogues *f/pl.*	drōg
guilt	culpabilité *f*	kēlpäbēlētā
hold-up	agression *f*	ägresyóN
judge	juge *m*	zhēzh
lawyer	avocat *m*	ävōkä
narcotics	stupéfiants *m/pl.*	stēpäfē·äN
police	police *f*	pôlēs
police car	voiture *f* de police	vô·ätēr də pôlēs
police station	commissariat *m*	kômēsärē·ä
	de police	də pôlēs
prison	prison *f*	prēzóN
smuggling	contrebande *f*	kôNtrəbäNd
thief	voleur *m*	vôlēr
verdict	jugement *m*	zhēzhmäN

BEAUTY SHOP / BARBER SHOP

At the Beauty Shop

May I make an appointment for Saturday?
Je voudrais un rendez-vous pour samedi.
zhə vōōdrā eN räNdä-vōō pōōr sämdē

Would you put me down for a permanent wave?   **For tomorrow?**
Vous pouvez me prendre pour une permanente?   Pour demain?
vōō pōōvā mə präNd(ər) pōōr ēn pärmänäNt   pōōr dəmeN

Will I have to wait?   **Will it take long?**
Faut-il attendre?   Cela mettra combien de temps?
fôtēl ätäNd(ər)   səlä meträ kôNbyeN də täN

Wash and set, please.
Faites-moi un shampoing et une mise en plis.
fāt-mó·ä eN shäNpô·eN ā ēn mēz äN plē

I'd like a *permanent (set)*, please.
Je voudrais *une permanente (une mise en plis)*.
zhə vōōdrā ēn pärmänäNt (ēn mēz eN plē)

Please set my hair for the evening.
Faites-moi une coiffure du soir, s'il vous plaît.
fāt-mó·ä ēn kô·äfēr dē sô·är, sēl vōō plä

Please *dye (rinse)* my hair ...
Une teinture (Un rinçage), s'il vous plaît.
ēn teNtēr (eN reNsäzh), sēl vōō plä

Please cut my hair a little shorter.
Coupez-moi les cheveux un peu plus court, s'il vous plaît.
kōōpā-mó·ä lä shevē eN pä plē kōōr, sēl vōō plä

Just trim it, please.
Coupez-moi juste les pointes, s'il vous plaît.
kōōpā-mó·ä zhēst lä pô·eNt, sēl vōō plä

Please cut it wet.   **Please pin it up.**
Coupez-moi les cheveux   Relevez-moi les cheveux,
mouillés.   s'il vous plaît.
kōōpā-mó·ä lä shevā mōōyä   rəlevā-mó·ä lä shevä,
                             sēl vōō plä

Please tease it a little on the *top (sides).*
Crêpez-moi un peu les cheveux *en haut (sur les côtés).*
krāpā-mô·ä eN pä lä shevä äN ō (sēr lä kôtā)

It's a little too hot under the drier.
Le séchoir est trop chaud.
lə sāshó·är ā trö shō

No *setting lotion (hair spray),* **please.**
Pas de *fixateur (laque),* s'il vous plaît.
päd fēksätär (läk), sēl vōō plä

Could you give me a *manicure (pedicure)?*
Pourriez-vous me faire la *manucure (pédicure)?*
pōōrē·ä-vōō mə fär lä mänēkēr (pādēkēr)

Please file my nails *round (to a point).*
Limez les ongles *ronds (pointus),* s'il vous plaît.
lēmā lāzóNg'əl rôN (pô·eNtē), sēl vōō plä

Just polish them, please.
Faites-les seulement briller,
s'il vous plaît.
fāt-lā sälmäN brēyä,
sēl vōō plä

With (Without) **nail polish.**
Avec (Sans) vernis.
ävek (säN) värnē

Please *tweeze (shave)* **my eyebrows.**
Épilez (Rasez-moi) les sourcils, s'il vous plaît.
āpēlā (räzä-mô·ä) lā sōōrsē, sēl vōō plä

A *facial mask (face massage),* **please.**
Un masque facial (Un massage facial), s'il vous plaît.
eN mäsk fäsyäl (eN mäsäzh fäsyäl), sēl vōō plä

Would you please put this *hairpiece (wig)* **on for me?**
Mettez-moi *ce postiche (cette perruque),* s'il vous plaît.
metä-mô·ä sə pôstēsh (set perēk), sēl vōō plä

Yes, thank you, that's just fine.
Oui, merci, c'est bien.
ōō·ē, mersē, sā byeN

Very nice!
Très bien!
trā byeN

At the Barber Shop

(Shave and) A haircut, please.
Une coupe de cheveux (et la barbe), s'il vous plaît.
ēn kōop də shvā (ā lä bärb), sēl vōo plä

Not too short, please.
Pas trop courts, s'il vous plaît.
pä trō kōor, sēl vōo plä

(Very) Short, please.
(Très) Courts, s'il vous plaît.
(trā) kōor, sēl vōo plä

– at the back.	– on top.	– in front.	– on the sides.
– derrière.	– en haut.	– devant.	– sur les côtés.
– deryär	– äN ō	– dəväN	– sēr lä kótä

A razor cut, please.
Une coupe au rasoir, s'il vous plaît.
ēn kōop ō räzó·är, sēl vōo plä

With (Without) part, please.
Avec (Sans) raie, s'il vous plaît.
ävek (säN) rä, sēl vōo plä

Part on the *left (right)*, please.
La raie *à gauche (à droite)*, s'il vous plaît.
lä rä ä gósh (ä dró·ät), sēl vōo plä

A shampoo too, please!
Lavez-moi aussi les cheveux,
s'il vous plaît.
lävä-mô·ä ósē lā shvā,
sēl vōo plä

Scalp massage, please.
Un massage de la tête,
s'il vous plaît.
eN mäsäzh dəlä tāt,
sēl vōo plä

Would you trim my *beard (moustache)*, please?
Taillez-moi *la barbe (les moustaches)*, s'il vous plaît.
täyā-mô·ä lä bärb (lā mōostäsh), sēl vōo plä

Just a shave, please.
Rien que la barbe, s'il vous plaît.
rē·eN kə lä bärb, sēl vōo plä

Some hair tonic (A little brilliantine), please.
Avec de la lotion (Un peu de brillantine), s'il vous plaît.
ävek dəlä lôsyóN (eN pā də brēyäNtēn), sēl vōo plä

Please leave it dry.
Ne les mouillez pas, s'il vous plaît.
nə lā mōoyä pä, sēl vōo plä

Yes, thank you, that's just great.
Oui, merci, c'est parfait.
ōo·ē, mersē, sā pärfā

barber	coiffeur *m*	kô·äfär
	(pour hommes)	(pōōr ôm)
beard	barbe *f*	bärb
beauty parlor	salon *m* de beauté	sälóN də bōtä
brilliantine	brillantine *f*	brēyäNtēn
cold wave	permanente *f* à froid	pärmänäNt ä frô·ä
comb *(noun)*	peigne *m*	pen(yə)
comb *(verb)*	peigner	penyä
curls	boucles *f/pl.*	bōōk'əl
cut	couper	kōōpä
dandruff	pellicules *f/pl.*	pelēkēl
do *s.o.'s* hair	coiffer	kô·äfä
dye	teindre	teNd(ər)
hair	cheveux *m/pl.*	shvä
– dry hair	– secs	– sek
– greasy hair	– gras	– grä
haircut	coupe *f* de cheveux	kōōp də shvä
hair-do	coiffure *f*	kô·äfēr
hairdresser	coiffeur *m*	kô·äfär
hair drier	séchoir *m*	säshô·är
hair loss	chute *f* des cheveux	shet dä shvä
hair style	coiffure *f*	kô·äfēr
hairpiece	postiche *m*	póstēsh
manicure	manucure *f*	mänēkēr
moustache	moustaches *f/pl.*	mōōstäsh
part	raie *f*	rä
pedicure	pédicure *f*	pädēkēr
permanent wave	permanente *f*	pärmänäNt
scalp massage	massage *m* de la tête	mäsäzh dəlä tät
set	mettre en plis	metreN plē
shave	faire la barbe	fär lä bärb
sideburns	favoris *m/pl.*	fävôrē
strand	mèche *f*	mäsh
tease	crêper	kräpä
tint	colorer	kôlôrä
toupé	postiche *m*	póstēsh
wash	laver	lävä
wig	perruque *f*	perek
wisp	mèche *f*	mäsh

HEALTH

Pharmacy

Where is the next pharmacy?
Où est la pharmacie la plus proche?
o͞o ā lä färmäsē lä pl*ē* prôsh

Which pharmacy has night duty?
Quelle pharmacie assure le service de nuit?
kel färmäsē äs*ē*r lə servēs də n*ē*·ē

I'd like this medicine, please.
Ce médicament, s'il vous plaît.
sə mādēkämäN, sēl vo͞o plä

I'd like ...
Je voudrais ...
zhə vo͞odrä ...

Please give me something for ...
Je vous prie de me donner quelque chose contre ...
zhə vo͞o prē də mə dônā kelke shôz kôNt(ər) ...

Do I need a prescription for this medicine?
Ce remède est délivré sur ordonnance?
sə remäd ā dālēvrä s*ē*r ôrdônäNs

Can you order this medicine for me?
Pouvez-vous me procurer ce médicament?
po͞ovä-vo͞o mə prōk*ē*rā sə mādēkämäN

When can I pick it up?
Je peux l'avoir quand?
zhə p*ā* lävô·är käN

Can I wait for it?
Puis-je attendre?
p*ē*·ēzhätäNd(ər)

for external use ...	usage externe	*ē*zäzh ekstärn
for internal use	usage interne	*ē*zäzh eNtärn
before meals	avant le repas	äväN lə repä
after meals	après le repas	äprä lə repä
three times a	trois fois par	trô·ä fô·ä pär
day	jour	zho͞or
as prescribed	comme prescrit ...	kôm preskrē
on an empty		
stomach	à jeun	ä zh*ā*n

Medication and Bandages

absorbent cotton	coton *m* hydrophile	kôtôN ēdrōfēl
lace bandage	pansement *m* élastique	päNsmäN ālästēk
adhesive bandage	sparadrap *m*	spärädrä
alcohol	alcool *m*	älkôl
ampule	ampoule *f*	äNpool
antidote	contrepoison *m*	kôNtrəpô-äzôN
boric acid ointment	acide *m* borique	äsēd bôrēk
burn ointment	pommade *f* contre	pômäd kôNt(ər)
	les brûlures	lā brēlēr
camomile tea	infusion *f* camomille *f*	eNfēzyôN kämō-
		mē'ē
castor oil	huile *f* de ricin	ē·ēl də rēseN
cardiovascular drug	remède *m* pour la	remäd poor lä
	circulation	sērkēläsyôN
charcoal pills	poudre *f* de charbon	pood(ər) de shär-
		bôN
contraceptive pills	pilules *f/pl.*	pēlēl
	contraceptives	kôNträseptēv
corn plaster	pansement *m* pour les	päNsmäN poor lä
	cors	kôr
cotton swabs	cotons-tiges *m/pl.*	kôtôN-tēzh
cough medicine	remède *m* (sirop *m*)	remäd (sērō)
(-syrup)	contre la toux	kôNt(ər) lä too
dextrose	glucose *m*	glēkōz
diaphoretic	sudorifique *m*	sēdôrēfēk
digestive tablets	comprimés *m/pl.* pour	kôNprēmä poor
	la digestion	lä dēzhestyôN
digestive tonic	gouttes *f/pl.* pour	goot poor
	la digestion	lä dēzhestyôN
disinfectant	désinfectant *m*	dāzeNfektäN
diuretic	diurétique *m*	dē·ērätēk
drops	gouttes *f/pl.*	goot
ear drops	gouttes *f/pl.* pour	goot poor
	les oreilles	lāzôrā'ē
elastic bandage	bande *f* élastique	bäNd ālästēk
elastic stocking	bas *m* élastique	bä ālästēk
emetic	vomitif *m*	vômētēf
enema	lavement *m*	lävmäN

eye drops/ointment ..	gouttes f/pl./pommade f	go͞ot/pômäd po͞or
	pour les yeux	läzyä
fever cure	fébrifuge m	fābrēfēzh
first-aid kit	pansements m/pl.	päNsmäN
gargle	gargarisme m	gärgärēsm
gauze bandage	bandage m de gaze	bäNdäzh də gäz
glycerine	glycérine f	glēsärēn
hydrogen peroxide ..	eau f oxygénée	ō ôksēzhānā
injection	injection f	eNzheksyôN
insect repellent	remède m contre les	remäd kôNt(ər) lā
	piqûres d'insectes	pēkēr deNsekt
iodine	teinture f d'iode	teNtēr dyōd
laxative	purgatif m	pērgätēf
liniment	liniment m; friction f ..	lēnēmäN; frēksyôN
medicine, remedy	remède m	remäd
mouthwash	eau f dentifrice	ō däNtēfrēs
ointment	pommade f	pômäd
pain pills	comprimés m/pl.	kôNprēmä
	contre la douleur	kôNt(ər) lä do͞olär
peppermint	menthe f	mäNt
pill	pilule f; comprimé m ..	pēlēl; kôNprēmä
powder	poudre f	po͞od(ər)
prophylactics	préservatifs m/pl.	prāzervätēf
quinine	quinine f	kēnēn
salve	pommade f; onguent m	pômäd; ôNgäN
sanitary napkins	serviettes f/pl.	servyet
	hygiéniques	ēzhē·änēk
sleeping pills	somnifère m	somnēfär
styptic pencil	bâton m hémostatique .	bätôN āmôstätēk
suppository	suppositoire m	sēpôzētô·är
talcum powder	poudre f de talc	po͞od(ər) də tälk
tincture	teinture f	teNtēr
tonic	fortifiant m	fôrtēfē·äN
tranquilizer	calmant m	kälmäN
valerian drops	gouttes f/pl. de	go͞ot də
	valériennes	välärē·en
vaseline	vaseline f	väzlēn
vitamin pills	comprimés m/pl. de	kôNprēmä də
	vitamines	vētämēn
wound salve	pommade f cicatrisante	pômäd sēkätrēzäNt

The doctor is in

Quick, call a doctor!
Appelez d'urgence un médecin, s'il vous plaît.
äplä dērzhäNs eN mädəseN, sēl vōō plä

Is there a doctor in the house?
Y a-t-il un médecin dans la maison?
ēyätēl eN mädəseN däN lä mäzôN

Can he come here?
Peut-il venir?
pᾱtēl venēr

Where is there a doctor?
Où y a-t-il un médecin?
ōō yätēl eN mädəseN

Please get a doctor!
Faites venir un médecin, s'il vous plaît.
fāt venēr eN mädəseN, sēl vōō plä

Where is there a hospital?
Où se trouve l'hôpital?
ōō sə trōōv lôpētäl

When does the doctor have office hours?
Quand le médecin a-t-il ses consultations?
käN lə mädəseN ätēl sä kôNsēltäsyôN

Would you please come to the ...
Venez s'il vous plaît, *au (à la)* ...
venä sēl vōō plä, ō (älä) ...

I'm sick.
Je suis malade.
zhə sē̄-ē mäläd

My husband (My wife, Our child) is sick.
Mon mari (Ma femme, Notre enfant) est malade.
môN märē (mä fäm, nôträNfäN) ä mäläd

doctor	médecin *m*	mädəseN
dermatologist	dermatologue *m*	därmätōlôg
ear, nose and throat specialist	oto-rhino-laryngologiste *m*	ōtō-rēnō-läreNgōlōzhēst
eye doctor	oculiste *m*	ôkēlēst
general practitioner	médecin *m* de médecine générale	mädəseN də mädəsēn zhänäräl
gynecologist	gynécologue *m*	zhēnäkōlôg
neurologist	neurologue *m*	nārōlôg
ophthalmologist	oculiste *m*	ôkēlēst
orthopedist	orthopédiste *m*	ôrtōpädēst
otolaryngologist	O.R.L. *m*	ō-är-el
pediatrician	pédiatre *m*	pädē-ät(ər)
psychiatrist	psychiatre *m*	psēkyät(ər)

psychologist	psychologue *m*	psēkōlôg
specialist	spécialiste *m*	späsyälēst
surgeon	chirurgien *m*	shērĕrzhē·eN
– plastic surgery	chirurgie *f* plastique ...	shērĕrzhē plästēk
urologist	urologue *m*	ĕrōlôg
doctor's office	cabinet *m* de	käbēnä də
	consultation	kôNsĕltäsyôN
office hours	(heures *f/pl.* des)	(är dā)
	consultations *f/pl.*	kôNsĕltäsyôN
waiting room	salle *f* d'attente	säl dätäNt

I haven't felt well the last few days.
Depuis quelques jours je ne me sens pas bien.
depĕ·ē kelke zhōor zhə nə mə säN pä byeN

My *head (throat, stomach)* hurts.
J'ai mal *à la tête (au cou, au ventre)*
zhā mäl älä tāt (ō kōo, ō väNt[ər])

It hurts here.
J'ai mal ici.
zhā mäl ēsē

I've got a *severe (sharp)* pain here.
J'ai *très (horriblement)* mal ici.
zhā trā (ôrēbləmäN) mäl ēsē

I've got a *(high)* fever.
J'ai *de la (beaucoup de)* fièvre.
zhā dəlä (bōkōo də) fē·āv(ər)

I've caught a cold.
J'ai pris froid.
zhā prē frô·ä

I can't handle the *heat (food)* here.
Je ne supporte pas *la chaleur (la nourriture)*.
zhə nə sĕpôrt pä lä shälär

I must have done something to my stomach.
J'ai une indigestion, je suppose.
zhā ĕn eNdēzhestyóN, zhə sĕpōz

I ate ...
J'ai mangé ...
zhā mäNzhā ....

I threw up.
J'ai vomi.
zhä vômē

I feel sick.
J'ai mal au cœur.
zhā mäl ō kär

I have *no appetite (diarrhea)*.
Je n'ai pas d'appétit (J'ai la diarrhée.)
zhə nā pä däpätē (zhā lä dē·ärä)

I'm constipated.
Je suis constipé(e).
zhə sĕ·ē kóNstēpä

My eyes hurt.
J'ai mal aux yeux.
zhā mäl ōzy$\bar{a}$

I can't sleep.
Je ne peux pas dormir.
zhə nə p$\bar{a}$ pä dôrmēr

I've got chills.
J'ai des frissons.
zhā dā frēsôN

I'm diabetic.
Je suis diabéthique.
zhə s$\bar{e}$-ē dē-äbātēk

I fell.
J'ai fait une chute.
zhā f$\bar{a}$ $\bar{e}$n sh$\bar{e}$t

... is (are) swollen.
... est (sont) enflé(s).
... $\bar{a}$ (sôN) äNflä

I have an earache.
J'ai mal aux oreilles.
zhā mäl ōzôr$\bar{a}$'ē

I feel nauseated.
J'ai mal au cœur.
zhā mäl ō k$\bar{a}$r

I can't move ...
Je ne peux pas bouger ...
zhə nə p$\bar{a}$ pä b$\overline{oo}$zhä ...

I'm expecting a baby.
J'attends un bébé.
zhätäN eN bābā

I sprained my ankle.
Je me suis foulé la cheville.
zhə mə s$\bar{e}$•ē f$\overline{oo}$lä lä shevē'ē

Is it serious?
Est-ce grave?
es gräv

I'm feeling a little (much) better.
Je me sens un peu (beaucoup) mieux.
zhə mə säNseN p$\bar{a}$ (b$\bar{o}$k$\overline{oo}$) my$\bar{a}$

Could you give me a prescription for ...?
Pouvez-vous me prescrire ...?
p$\overline{oo}$vä-v$\overline{oo}$ mə präskrēr ...

I'd like to be vaccinated against ...
J'aimerais me faire vacciner contre le (la) ...
zhāmerā mə fär väksēnä kôNt(ər) lə (lä) ...

Suppositories are used frequently for various ailments, so don't be surprised if they are prescribed to you!

The doctor will tell you:

Take your clothes off, please.
Déshabillez-vous, s'il vous plaît.
dāzäbēyä-vōō, sēl vōō plä

Breathe deeply!
Respirez (Aspirez) profondément!
respērä (äspērä) prōfóNdämäN

Does this hurt?
Cela vous fait mal ici?
sälä vōō fä mäl ēsē

Open your mouth.
Ouvrez la bouche!
ōōvrä lä bōōsh

Let me see your tongue.
Tirez la langue!
tērä lä läNg

Cough.
Toussez!
tōōsä

What have you been eating?
Qu'avez-vous mangé?
kävä-vōō mäNzhā

How long have you been ill?
Depuis quand êtes-vous malade?
depē·ē käN ät-vōō mäläd

We'll have to do *a blood test (an urinalysis)*.
Il faut faire une analyse *de sang (d'urine)*.
ēl fō fär ēn änälēz də säN (dērēn)

You're going to need an operation.
Il faut vous faire opérer.
ēl fō vōō fär ōpārā

I'll have to refer you to . . .
Je vais vous envoyer chez . . .
zhə vä vōōzäNvó·äyä shā . . .

You must stop *drinking (smoking)*!
Il ne faut pas *boire d'alcool (fumer)*.
ēl nə fō pä bó·är dälkôl (fēmä)

Spend the next few days in bed.
Restez quelques jours au lit!
restä kelke zhōōr ō lē

You'll have to stay *in bed (on a strict diet)*.
Il faut *rester couché (observer un régime sévère)*.
ēl fō restä kōōshä (ôbservä eN räzhēm sävär)

Take *two tablets (ten drops)* three times a day.
Prenez-en *deux comprimés (dix gouttes)* trois fois par jour.
prenäzäN dä kôNprēmä (dē gōōt) trô·äfô·ä pär zhōōr

It's nothing serious.
Ce n'est rien de grave!
sə nä rē·eN də gräv

Come back and see me a week from now.
Revenez dans huit jours.
revənä däN ē·ē zhōōr

Parts of the Body and their Functions

abdomen	ventre *m*;	väNt(ər),
	bas-ventre *m*	bä-väNt(ər)
ankle	jointure *f*;	zhô-eNt*ĕ*r,
	(foot) cheville *f*	shevĕ'ē
appendix	appendice *m*	äpäNdēs
arm	bras *m*	brä
armpit	aisselle *f*	āsel
artery	artère *f*	ärtār
back	dos *m*	dō
bile	bile *f*	bēl
bladder	vessie *f*	vesē
blood	sang *m*	säN
blood pressure	tension *f* artérielle	täNsyóN ärtārē·el
body	corps *m*	kór
circulation	circulation *f*	sērk*ĕ*läsyóN
bone	os *m*	ôs (*pl.*: ō)
bowel movement	selle *f*	sel
brain	cerveau *m*	sārvō
breast	poitrine *f*	pô·ätrēn
breathing	respiration *f*	respēräsyóN
buttocks	fesses *f*/*pl.*	fes
calf	mollet *m*	môlā
cheek	joue *f*	zhōō
chest	poitrine *f*	pô·ätrēn
chin	menton *m*	mäNtóN
collarbone	clavicule *f*	klävēk*ĕ*l
digestion	digestion *f*	dēzhestyóN
disc	disque *m*	dēsk
ear	oreille *f*	ôrä'ē
eardrum	tympan *m*	teNpäN
elbow	coude *m*	kōōd
eye	œil *m* (*pl.* yeux)	ä'ē (*pl.* yä)
– **eyeball**	globe *m* oculaire	glôb ók*ĕ*lär
– **eyelid**	paupière *f*	pōpyär
face	visage *m*	vēzäzh
finger	doigt *m*	dô·ä
– **thumb**	pouce *m*	pōōs
– **index finger**	index *m*	eNdeks

– middle finger	médius *m*	mādyēs
– ring finger	annulaire *m*	änēlär
– pinkie	auriculaire *m*	órēkēlär
foot	pied *m*	pyā
forehead	front *m*	frôN
frontal sinus	sinus *m* frontal	sēnēs frôNtäl
gall bladder	vésicule *f* biliaire	vāzēkēl bēlyär
genital organs	organes *m/pl.* génitaux	órgän zhänētō
gland	glande *f*	gläNd
hair	cheveux *m/pl.*	shvā
hand	main *f*	meN
head	tête *f*	tät
heart	cœur *m*	kär
heel	talon *m*	tälôN
hip	hanche *f*	äNsh
instep	cou-de-pied *m*	kōō-də-pyā
intestine	intestin *m*	eNtesteN
– large intestine	gros intestin *m*	grō eNtesteN
– small intestine	intestin grêle *m*	eNtesteN gräl
jaw	mâchoire *f*	mäshô·är
– upper jaw	mâchoire supérieure	mäshô·är sēpärē·är
– lower jaw	mâchoire inférieure	mäshô·är eNfärē·är
joint	articulation *f*	ärtēkēläsyóN
kidney	rein *m*	reN
knee	genou *m*	zhenōō
kneecap	rotule *f*	rótēl
larynx	larynx *m*	lareNks
leg	jambe *f*	zhäNb
– thigh	cuisse *f*	kē·ēs
– lower leg	jambe *f*	zhäNb
limbs	membres *m/pl.*	mäNb(ər)
lip	lèvre *f*	läv(ər)
liver	foie *f*	fô·ä
lung	poumon *m*	pōōmóN
male organ	verge *f*	värzh
maxillary sinus	sinus *m*	sēnēs
menstruation	règles *f/pl.*	räg'əl
metabolism	métabolisme *m*	mätäbōlēsm
mouth	bouche *f*	bōōsh
mucous membrane	muqueuse *f*	mēkāz
muscle	muscle *m*	mēsk'əl

nail	ongle *m*	ôNg'əl
neck	cou *m*; nuque *f*	kōō, nĕk
– back of the neck	nuque *f*	nĕk
– nape of the neck	nuque *f*	nĕk
nerve	nerf *m*	nār
nerves	nerfs *m/pl.*	nār
nose	nez *m*	nä
palate	palais *m*	pälā
pancreas	pancréas *m*	päNkrä·äs
pelvis	bassin *m*, bas-ventre *m*	bäseN, bä-väNt(ər)
penis	pénis *m*	pānēs
pregnancy	grossesse *f*	grōses
respiration	respiration *f*	respēräsyôN
rib	côte *f*	kôt
shin	tibia *m*	tēbē·ä
shoulder	épaule *f*	āpôl
sinew	tendon *m*	täNdóN
skin	peau *f*	pō
skull	crâne *m*	krän
sole	plante *f* du pied	pläNt dē pyä
spinal cord	moelle *f* épinière	mô·äl āpēnyär
spine	épine *f* dorsale, colonne *f* vertébrale	āpēn dórsäl, kôlôn vertābräl
spleen	rate *f*	rät
stomach	estomac *m*	estōmä
temple	tempe *f*	täNp
tendon	tendon *m*	täNdóN
thorax	thorax *m*	tôräks
throat	gorge *f*	gôrzh
toe	orteil *m*	ôrtā'ē
tongue	langue *f*	läNg
tonsils	amygdales *f/pl.*	ämēgdäl
tooth	dent *f*	däN
urin	urine *f*	ērēn
uterus	utérus *m*	ētārēs
vagina	vagin *m*	väzheN
vein	veine *f*	ven
wrist	poignet *m*	pô·änyā

What's wrong?

abscess	abcès *m*	äbsä
airsickness	mal *m* de l'air	mäl də lär
allergy	allergie *f*	älerzhē
anemia	anémie *f*	änämē
appendicitis	appendicite *f*	äpäNdēsēt
arthritis	rhumatisme *m*	rēmätēsm
	articulaire	ärtēkēlär
asthma	asthme *m*	äsm
attack	attaque *f*	ätäk
backache	mal *m* au dos	mäl ō dō
bleeding	hémorragie *f*	āmôräzhē
blood poisoning	septicémie *f*	septēsāmē
blood pressure	tension *f*	täNsyóN
– high	– haute	– ōt
– low	– basse	– bäs
boil	furoncle *m*	fērôNk'əl
breathing problem	troubles *m/pl.*	trōōb'əl
	respiratoires	respērätô·är
bronchitis	bronchite *f*	brôNshēt
bruise	contusion *f*	kôNtēzyóN
burn	brûlure *f*	brēlēr
cancer	cancer *m*	käNsär
cardiac infarction	infarctus *m* du	eNfärktēs dē
	myocarde	mē·ōkärd
chicken pox	varicelle *f*	värēsel
chills	frissons *m/pl.*	frēsôN
cholera	choléra *m*	kólärä
circulatory problem	troubles *m/pl.*	trōōb'əl
	circulatoires	sērkēlätô·är
cold	rhume *m*	rēm
colic	colique *f*	kólēk
concussion	commotion *f*	kômôsyóN
	cérébrale	sārābräl
conjunctivitis	conjonctivite *f*	kôNzhóNktēvēt
constipation	constipation *f*	kôNstēpäsyóN
cough	toux *f*	tōō
cramp	crampe *f*	kräNp
cut	coupure *f*	kōōpēr
diabetes	diabète *m*	dē·äbät

diarrhea	diarrhée *f*	dē·ärä
diphtheria	diphthérie *f*	dēftärē
disease	maladie *f*	mälädē
– **contagious**	– contagieuse	– kôNtäzhē·äz
dislocation	luxation *f*	lēksäsyôN
dizziness	vertige *m*	värtēzh
dysentery	dysenterie *f*	dēzäNtərē
eye inflammation	inflammation *f* de l'œil	eNflämäsyôN də lä'ē
fever	fièvre *f*	fē·äv(ər)
fit	attaque *f*	ätäk
flatulence	ballonnements *m/pl.*	bälôn·mäN
flu	grippe *f*	grēp
food poisoning	intoxication *f* alimentaire	eNtôksēkäsyôN älēmäNtär
fracture	fracture *f*	fräktēr
frostbite	engelure *f*	äNzhelēr
gall stones	calculs *m/pl.* biliaires	kälkēl bēlyär
German measles	rubéole *f*	rēbä·ôl
hemorrhage	hémorragie *f*	ämôräzhē
hay fever	rhume *m* des foins	rēm dā fô·eN
heart attack	crise *f* cardiaque	krēz kärdē·äk
heart problems	troubles *m/pl.* cardiaques	trōōb'əl kärdē·äk
heartburn	aigreurs *f/pl.* d'estomac	ägrēr destōmä
hemorrhoids	hémorroïdes *f/pl.*	ämôrō·ēd
hoarseness	enrouement *m*	äNrōōmäN
hypertension	hypertension *f*	ēpärtäNsyôN
illness	maladie *f*	mälädē
indigestion	embarras *m* gastrique	äNbärä gästrēk
inflammation	inflammation *f*	eNflämäsyôN
influenza	grippe *f*	grēp
injury	blessure *f*	blesēr
insomnia	insomnie *f*	eNsômnē
intestinal catarrh	entérite *f*	äNtärēt
jaundice	jaunisse *f*	zhōnēs
kidney stones	calculs *m/pl.* rénaux	kälkēl rānō
leukemia	leucémie *f*	lāsämē
liver problem	maladie *f* du foie	mälädē dē fô·ä
lockjaw	constriction *f* des mâchoires	kôNstrēksyôN dā mäshô·är

lumbago	lumbago *m*	lôNbägō
measles	rougeole *f*	rōōzhôl
middle ear inflammation	otite *f*	ôtēt
mumps	oreillons *m/pl.*	ôrāyóN
nausea	nausées *f/pl.*	nōzä
nephritis	néphrite *f*	nāfrēt
neuralgia	névralgie *f*	nāvrälzhē
nosebleed	saignements *m/pl.* du nez	sän(yə)mäN dē nā
pain	douleurs *f/pl.*	dōōlär
paralysis	paralysie *f*	pärälēzē
passing out	évanouissement *m*	āvänōō-ēsmäN
peptic ulcer	ulcère *m* d'estomac	ēlsär destōmä
piles	hémorroïdes *f/pl.*	āmōrō-ēd
pleurisy	pleurésie *f*	plärāzē
pneumonia	pneumonie *f*	pnämōnē
poisoning	empoisonnement *m*	eNpô-äzônmäN
injury	blessure *f*	bläsēr
pulled tendon	déchirement *m* des tendons	däshērmäN dā täNdôN
rash	éruption *f*	ārēpsyóN
rheumatism	rhumatisme *m*	rēmätēsm
scarlet fever	scarlatine *f*	skärlätēn
sciatica	sciatique *f*	sē-ätēk
seasickness	mal *m* de mer	mäl də mär
shock	choc *m* nerveux	shôk nervā
skin disease	maladie *f* de la peau	mälädē dəlä pō
skin lesion	égratignures *f/pl.*	āgrätēnyēr
smallpox	variole *f*	värē·ôl
sore throat	mal *m* de gorge	mäl də gôrzh
sprain	foulure *f*	fōōlēr
stitch in the side	point *m* de côté	pô·eN də kôtā
stomach pains	maux *m/pl.* d'estomac	mō destōmä
stroke	apoplexie *f*	äpôpleksē
sunburn	coup *m* de soleil	kōō də sólä'ē
sunstroke	insolation *f*	eNsōläsyóN
suppuration	suppuration *f*	sēpērāsyóN
swelling	enflure *f*	äNflēr
tetanus	tétanos *m*	tātänós
tonsilitis	angine *f*	äNzhēn
tuberculosis	tuberculose *f*	tēbärkēlōz

tumor	enflure *f*; tumeur *f*	äNflĕr; tēmär
typhoid fever	typhus *m*	tēfēs
ulcer	ulcère *m*	ēlsär
venereal disease	maladie *f* vénérienne	mälädē vānārē·en
vomiting	vomissement *m*	vômēsmäN
whooping cough	coqueluche *f*	kôklēsh
wound	plaie *f*	plä

In the Hospital

anesthetic	narcose *f*	närkōz
bed pan	bassin *m*	bäseN
blood count	hémogramme *m*	āmōgräm
blood test	prise *f* de sang	prēz də säN
blood transfusion	transfusion *f*	träNsfēzyóN
diagnosis	diagnostic *m*	dē·ägnôstēk
discharge	sortie *f* de clinique	sôrtē də klēnēk
doctor	médecin *m*	mädəseN
examination	examen *m*, analyse *f*	egzämeN, änälēz
examine	examiner	egzämēnā
hospital	hôpital *m*	ôpētäl
infusion	infusion *f*	eNfēzyóN
injection	injection *f*; piqûre *f*	eNzheksyóN; pēkĕr
intensive care unit	service *m* de réanimation	servēs də rā·änēmäsyóN
medical director	médecin *m* chef	mädəseN shef
night nurse	infirmière *f* de nuit	eNfĕrmyär də nē·ē
nurse	infirmière *f*	eNfĕrmyär
operate on	opérer	ôpārā
operating room	salle *f* d'opération	säl dôpäräsyôN
operation	opération *f*	ôpāräsyôN
patient	malade *m*	mäläd
surgeon	chirurgien *m*	shērērzhē·eN
temperature	température *f*	täNpärätĕr
temperature chart	courbe *f* de température	kōōrb de täNpärätĕr
visiting hours	heures *f/pl.* de visite	ĕr də vēzēt
ward	service *m*	servēs
x-ray *(noun)*	radiographie *f*	rädē·ōgräfē
x-ray *(verb)*	radiographier	rädē·ōgräfyā

Nurse, could you give me a *pain killer (sleeping pill)*.
Mademoiselle, donnez-moi *quelque chose contre la douleur (un somnifère)*.
mädəmô·äzel, dônä-mô·ä kelke shōz kôNt(ər) lä dōōlār (eN sômnēfär)

When can I get out of bed?
Quand est-ce que je pourrai me lever?
käNdeske zhə pōōrā mə levä

What's the diagnosis?
Quel est le diagnostic?
kel ä lə dē·ägnôstēk

At the Dentist's

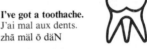

Where is there a dentist here?
Où y a-t-il un dentiste?
ōō yätēl eN däNtēst

I've got a toothache.
J'ai mal aux dents.
zhā mäl ō däN

I'd like to make an appointment.
J'aimerais prendre rendez-vous.
zhämerā präNd(ər) räNdä-vōō

This tooth hurts.
Cette dent me fait mal.
set däN mə fā mäl

– *up here (an upper tooth)*.
– *en haut (une dent du haut)*.
– äN ō (ēn däN dē ō)

– *down here (a lower tooth)*.
– *en bas (une dent du bas)*.
– äN bä (ēn däN dē bä)

I've lost a filling.
Un plombage est parti.
eN plôNbäzh ā pärtē

This tooth is loose.
La dent branle.
lä däN bräN'əl

... broke off.
... s'est cassée.
... sā käsā

Does this tooth have to be pulled?
Il faut arracher la dent?
ēl fōtäräshā lä däN

Can you do a temporary repair on this tooth?
Pouvez-vous soigner la dent provisoirement?
pōōvā-vōō sô·änyā lä däN prōvēzō·är·mäN

Can you fix these dentures?
Pouvez-vous réparer cette prothèse?
pōōvā-vōō rāpärā set prōtās

*Please don't *eat anything (smoke)* for two hours.
Ne *mangez rien (fumez pas)* pendant deux heures, s'il vous plaît.
nə mäNzhä rē·eN (fēmā pä) päNdäN dāzər, sēl vōō plā

When do you want me to come back?
Quand dois-je revenir?
käN dô·äzh rəvenēr

abscess	abcès *m*	äbsā
anesthesia	anesthésie *f*	änestäzē
– local	anesthésie *f* locale	änestäzē lôkäl
– general	anesthésie *f* générale	änestäzē zhänäräl
braces	appareil *m* (dentaire)	äpärä′ē (däNtär)
bridge	bridge *m*	brēdzh
cavities	carie *f*	kärē
crown	couronne *f*	kōōrôn
cuspid	canine *f*	känēn
dental clinic	clinique *f* dentaire	klēnēk däNtār
dentist	dentiste *m*	däNtēst
denture	dentition *f*	däNtēsyôN
extract	arracher, extraire	äräshā, ekstrār
false tooth	fausse dent *f*	fōs däN
fill	plomber	plôNbā
filling	plombage *m*	plôNbäzh
gums	gencive *f*	zhäNsēv
incisor	incisive *f*	eNsēzēv
injection	injection *f*	eNzheksyôN
jaw	mâchoire *f*	mäshô·är
molar	molaire *f*	mōlār
nerve	nerf *m*	nār
oral surgeon	chirurgien *m* dentiste	shērērzhē·eN däNtēst
orthodontist	orthodonto-stomato-logiste *m*	ôrtōdôNtō-stōmä-tōlōzhēst
plaster cast	plâtre *m*	plät(ər)
plate	plaque *f*	pläk
root	racine *f*	räsēn
root canal work	traitement *m* de la racine	trätmäN dəlä räsēn
tartar	tartre *m*	tärt(ər)
temporary filling	pansement *m*	päNsmäN
tooth	dent *f*	däN
tooth cervix	collet *m* d'une dent	kôlā dĕn däN
toothache	mal *m* aux dents	mäl ō däN
wisdom tooth	dent *f* de sagesse	däN də säzhes

Taking a Cure

bath	bain *m*	beN
bath attendant	maître *m* nageur	māt(ər) näzhár
convalescent home	maison *f* de convalescence	māzōN də kôNvälesäNs
cure	cure *f*	kēr
cure tax	taxe *f* de cure	täks də kēr
cure vacation	cure *f*	kēr
diet	régime *m*, diète *f*	räzhēm, dē·ät
gymnastics	gymnastique *f*	zhēmnästēk
health resort	station *f* climatique	stäsyōN klēmätēk
hot spring	source *f* chaude	sōors shaud
inhale	faire des inhalations	fār dāzēnäläsyóN
massage *(noun)*	massage *m*	mäsäzh
massage *(verb)*	masser	mäsā
masseur	masseur *m*	mäsᴂr
masseuse	masseuse *f*	mäsᴂz
medicinal spring	source *f* médicinale, thermes *f*/*pl*.	sōors mādēsēnäl, tärm
mineral bath	bain *m* thermal	beN tärmäl
mineral spring	source *f* thermale	sōors tärmäl
minerals	minéraux *m*/*pl*.	mēnärō
mud	boue *f* minérale	bōo mēnäräl
mud bath	bain *m* de boue	beN də bōo
mud pack	enveloppement *m* de boue	äNvelôpmäN də bōo
pump room	buvette *f*	bᴂvet
radiation therapy	traitement *m* par les rayons	trätmäN pär lā räyōN
rest cure	cure *f* de repos	kēr də rəpō
sanatorium	sanatorium *m*	sänätóryóm
sauna	sauna *m*	sōnä
sea water	eau *f* de mer	ō də mār
short wave	onde *f* courte	ôNd kōort
spa	station *f* balnéaire *(thermale)*	stäsyōN bälnā·ᾱr (tärmäl)
steam bath	bain *m* de vapeur	beN də väpᾱr
sunlamp	rayons *m*/*pl*. ultraviolets	räyōN ēlträvē·ōlā
ultrasonics	écographie *f*	äkōgräfē

CONCERT, THEATRE, MOVIES

> *Most continental European theatres are repertory theatres, featuring a permanent company performing a different play, opera or operetta each evening.*

At the Box Office

What's on tonight?
Qu'est-ce qu'on joue ce soir?
keskôN zhoo sə sô·är

When does *the performance (the concert)* start?
À quelle heure commence *la représentation (le concert)*?
äkelär kômäNs lä repräzäNtäsyôN (le kôNsär)

Where can we get tickets?
Où est-ce qu'on prend les billets?
oo eskôN präN lä bēyä

Are there any discounts for ....?
Il y a une réduction pour ...?
ēlyä ən rādēksyôN poor ...

> *Many European theatres and concert halls provide discount tickets for the disabled, for students and senior citizens.*
> *If you're a student, be sure to get an international student identity card (ISIC) before leaving home. It entitles you to many reductions.*

Are there still tickets available for *this (tomorrow)* evening?
Y a-t-il encore des billets pour *ce soir (demain soir)*?
ēyätēl äNkôr dā bēyä poor sə sô·är (demeN sô·är)

One ticket in the *third (tenth)* row, please.
Une place au *troisième (dixième)* rang, s'il vous plaît.
ēn pläs ō trô·äzyäm (dēzyäm) räN, sēl voo plä

Two seats in the third row, first balcony, please.
Deux places au premier balcon, troisième rang, s'il vous plaît.
dä pläs ō prəmyä bälkôN, trô·äzyäm räN, sēl voo plä

– in the middle.	– on the side.
– au milieu.	– sur le côté.
– ō mēlēyä	– sēr lə kôtä

accompanist	accompagnateur *m*	äkôNpänyätär
act	acte *m*	äkt
actor	acteur *m*	äktär
actress	actrice *f*	äktrēs
advance ticket sales	location *f*	lôkäsyóN
alto	alto *m*	ältō
applause	applaudissements *m/pl.*	äplôdēsmäN
aria	aria *f*	ärē·ä
ballet	ballet *m*	bälā
balcony	balcon *m*	bälkôN
band	orchestre *m*	ôrkest(ər)
baritone	baryton *m*	bärētôN
bass	basse *f*	bäs
box office	caisse *f*; vente *f* de billets	kes; väNt də bēyā
chamber music	musique *f* de chambre	mēzēk də shäNb(ər)
check room	vestiaire *m*	vestyär
chorus	chœur *m*	kär
coat check	ticket *m* de vestiaire	tēkā də vestyär
comedy	comédie *f*	kômādē
composer	compositeur *m*	kôNpōzētär
concert	concert *m*	kôNsär
concert hall	salle *f* de concert	säl də kôNsär
conductor	chef *m* d'orchestre	shef dôrkest(ər)
contralto	contralto *m*	kôNträltō
costumes	costumes *m/pl.*	kôstēm
costume designer	costumier *m*	kôstēmyä
curtain	rideau *m*	rēdō
curtain time	lever *m* de rideau	ləvā də rēdō
dancer	danseur *m*, danseuse *f*	däNsär, däNsāz
director	metteur *m* en scène	metär äN sän
drama	drame *m*	dräm
duett	duo *m*	dē·ō
final curtain	fin *f*	feN
grand piano	piano *m* à queue	pē·änō ä kā
intermission	entracte *m*	äNträkt
legitimate theatre	théâtre *m*	tā·ät(ər)
libretto	livret *m*	lēvrä
lobby	foyer *m*	fô·äyā
music	musique *f*	mēzēk

musical	musical *m*	mēzēkäl
musician	musicien *m*	mēzēsyeN
opera	opéra *m*	ōpärä
opera glasses	jumelles *f/pl.* de théâtre	zhēmel də tä·ät(ər)
operetta	opérette *f*	ōpäret
orchestra	orchestre *m*	ôrkest(ər)
orchestra seats	fauteuils *m/pl.* d'orchestre	fôtā'ē dôrkest(ər)
overture	ouverture *f*	ōōvärtēr
part/role	rôle *m*	rôl
– leading role	premier rôle *m*	prəmyā rôl
performance	représentation *f*	rəprāzäNtäsyôN
pianist	pianiste *m*	pē·änēst
piano recital	récital *m* de piano	räsētäl də pē·änō
piece of music	morceau *m* de musique	môrsō də mēzēk
play	pièce *f* (de théâtre)	pyäs (də tä·ät(ər))
producer	producteur *m*	prōdēktär
production	production *f*	prōdēksyôN
program	programme *m*	prōgräm
scenery/settings	décors *m/pl.*	dākôr
set designer	décorateur *m*	dākôrätär
singer	chanteur *m*; cantatrice *f*	shäNtär; käNtätrēs
singing	chant *m*	shäN
soloist	soliste *m*	sōlēst
song	chanson *f*	shäNsôN
– folk song	chanson *f* populaire	shäNsôN pôpēlär
song recital	récital *m* de chant	räsētäl də shäN
soprano	soprano *m*	sōpränō
stage	scène *f*	sän
stage director	metteur *m* en scène	metär äN sän
symphony concert	concert *m* symphonique	kôNsär seNfōnēk
tenor	ténor *m*	tänôr
theatre	théâtre *m*	tä·ät(ər)
theatre schedule	affiche *f* de théâtre	äfēsh də tä·ät(ər)
ticket	billet *m*	bēyā
ticket sales	vente *f* de billets	väNt də bēyā
tragedy	tragédie *f*	träzhädē
violin recital	récital *m* de violon	räsētäl də vē·ōlôN
work	œuvre *f*	āv(ər)

At the Movies

What's on tonight at the movies?
Qu'est-ce qu'on joue au cinéma ce soir?
keskôN zhōō ō sēnämä sə sô·är

What time does *the box office open (the film start)*?
A quelle heure commence *la location (le film)*?
äkelär kômäNs lä lôkäsyôN (lə fēlm)

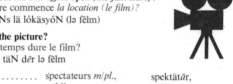

How long is the picture?
Combien de temps dure le film?
kôNbyeN də täN dēr lə fēlm

audience	spectateurs *m/pl.*, public *m*	spektätär, pēblēk
auditorium	salle *f* de spectacle	säl də spektäk'əl
cartoon	dessin *m* animé	deseN änēmä
cinema	cinéma *m*	sēnämä
color film	film *m* en couleurs	fēlm äN kōōlär
documentary	(film *m*) documentaire *m*	(fēlm) dôkēmäNtär
dubbed	synchronisé	seNkrōnēzä
dubbing	synchronisation *f*	seNkrōnēzäsyôN
educational film	(film *m*) documentaire	(fēlm) dôkēmäNtär
feature film	long métrage *m*	lôN mäträzh
film	film *m*	fēlm
film actor	acteur *m* de cinéma	äktär də sēnämä
film festival	festival *m* du film	festēväl dē fēlm
film screening	écran *m*	äkräN
motion picture theatre	cinéma *m*	sēnämä
movie	film *m*	fēlm
movie house	cinéma *m*	sēnämä
newsreel	actualités *f/pl.* de la semaine	äktē·älētä dəlä smen
preview	prochains films *m/pl.*	prôshen fēlm
screen	écran *m*	äkräN
screenplay	scénario *m*	sänärē·ō
short subject	court métrage *m*	kōōr mäträzh
subtitled	sous-titré	sōō-tēträ
thriller	film *m* policier	fēlm pólēsyä
usher	ouvreuse *f*	ōōvräz

PASTIMES

Fun and Games

Where is there ...?
Où y a-t-il ici ...?
ōō yätēl ēsē ...

a bar	un bar	eN bär
a discotheque	une discothèque	ēn dēskōtāk
an ice skating rink	une pâtinoire	ēn pätēnô·är
a miniature golf course	un minigolf	eN mēnē-gôlf
a night club	une boîte de nuit	ēn bô·ät də nē·ē
a pool hall	un billard	eN bēyär
a riding stable	une école d'équitation	ēn äkôl dākētä-syôN
a sailing school	une école de yachting	ēn äkôl də yôtēng
a tennis court	un court de tennis	eN kōōr də tenēs

I'd like to...
J'aimerais ...
zhāmerā ...

play badminton	jouer au volant	zhōō·ā ō vôläN
play miniature golf	jouer au mini-golf	zhōō·ā ō mēnē-gôlf
play ping pong	jouer au ping-pong	zhōō·ā ō pēn(yə)-pôNg
watch the fashion show	aller voir le défilé de mode	älä vô·är lə dāfēlā də môd

Do you have television?
Vous avez la télévision?
vōōzävā lä tālāvēzyôN

Can I listen to the radio here?
Je peux écouter la radio ici?
zhə pəzäkōōtā lä rädē·ō ēsē

What station is that?
Quelle station est-ce?
kel stäsyôN es

What's on today?
Quel est le programme aujourd'hui?
kel ā lə prōgräm ōzhōōrdē·ē

Do you play chess (ping pong)?
Jouez-vous aux échecs (au ping-pong)?
zhōō·ā·vōō ōzäshek (ō pēn(yə)-pôNg)

amusement	distraction *f*	dēsträksyôN
beauty contest	concours *m* de beauté	kóNko͞or də bōtä
bowling alley	piste *f* de bowling	pēst də bo͞olēng
card game	jeu *m* de cartes	zhä də kärt
– **cut**	couper	ko͞opä
– **deal**	donner	dônä
– **shuffle**	battre	bät(ər)
– **ace**	as *m*	äs
– **jack**	valet *m*	välā
– **queen**	dame *f*	däm
– **king**	roi *m*	rô·ä
– **clubs**	trèfle *m*	trāf'əl
– **diamonds**	carreau *m*	kärō
– **hearts**	cœur *m*	kȧr
– **spades**	pique *m*	pēk
– **joker**	joker *m*	zhōkär
– **trick**	levée *f*	levā
– **trump**	atout *m*	äto͞o
checkers	(jeu *m* de) dames	(zhä də) däm
chess	échecs *m/pl.*	āshek
– **board**	échiquier *m*	āshēkyā
– **chessman**	pièce *f*	pyās
– **square**	case *f*	käz
– **bishop**	fou *m*	fo͞o
– **castle**	tour *f*	to͞or
– **king**	roi *m*	rô·ä
– **knight**	cavalier *m*	kävälyā
– **pawn**	pion *m*	pyóN
– **queen**	reine *f*	ren
– **rook**	tour *f*	to͞or
chip	jeton *m*	zhetóN
circus	cirque *m*	sērk
club	club *m*	klȧb
country fair	fête *f* populaire	fāt pôpēlär
dice	dé *m*	dā
– **shoot dice**	jouer aux dés	zho͞o·ā ō dā
gambling casino	casino *m*	käzēnō
gambling game	jeu *m* de hazard	zhä də äzär
– **banker**	banquier *m*	bäNkyā
– **bet**	miser (sur)	mēzā (sēr)
– **draw**	faire un coup	fār eN ko͞o

– move	coup *m*	kōo
– piece	pion *m*	pyôN
– play	jouer	zhōo·ā
– stake	mise *f*	mēz
magazine	revue *f*, magazine *m*	revē̄, mägäzēn
– fashion magazine	journal *m* de modes	zhōornäl də mód
– glossy	illustré *m*	ēlē̄strā
newspaper	journal *m*	zhōornäl
party games	jeux *m*/*pl.* de société	zhā də sôsē·ātā
pastime	passe-temps *m*	päs-täN
ping pong	ping-pong *m*	pēn(yə)-pôNg
radio	radio *f*	rädē·ō
– FM	modulations *f*/*pl.* de fréquence	mōdē̄läsyôN də frākäNs
– long wave	grandes ondes *f*/*pl.*	gräNdzóNd
– medium wave	ondes *f*/*pl.* moyennes	ôNd mô·äyen
– short wave	ondes *f*/*pl.* courtes	ôNd kōort
– radio play	pièce *f* radiophonique	pyäs rädē·ōfōnēk
record	disque *m*	dēsk
record player	électrophone *m*	ālektrōfôn
recording tape	bande *f* magnétique	bäNd mänyätēk
table tennis	ping-pong *m*; tennis *m* de table	pēn(yə)-pôNg; tenēs də täb'əl
tape recorder	magnétophone *m*	mänyätōfôn
television	télévision *f*	tālāvēzyóN
– announcer	speaker *m*	spēkär
– breakdown	perturbation *f*	pertĕrbäsyóN
– news	informations *f*/*pl.*	eNfôrmäsyóN
– program	programme *m*	prōgräm
– program schedule	prochaines émissions	prôshen āmēsyóN
– turn off	éteindre	āteNd(ər)
– turn on	allumer	älēmā
– television play	jeu *m* télévisé	zhā tālāvēzā

Getting acquainted

Hope you don't mind if I talk to you.
Excusez-moi de vous adresser la parole.
ekskēzā-mô·ä də vōozädresā lä pärôl

Mind if I join you?
Vous permettez que je m'asseye à côté de vous?
vōo pärmetā ke zhə mäsä ä kôtā də vōo

May I treat you to a *drink (coffee, tea)*?
Vous prenez *quelque chose (un café, un thé)*?
vōo prenā kelke shōz (eN käfā, eN tā)

You got something on for this evening?
Vous êtes déjà pris(e) ce soir?
vōozät dāzhä prē(z) sə sô·är

Shall we dance?
Vous voulez danser?
vōo vōolā däNsā

Is there a *discotheque (a dance hall)* here?
Y a-t-il ici *une discothèque (un dancing)*?
ēyätēl ēsē ēn dēskōtāk (eN däNsēng)

May I have the next dance?
(Voulez-vous m'accorder cette danse) Mademoiselle?
(vōolā-vōo mäkôrdā set däNs) mädəmô·äzel

We can chat undisturbed here.
Ici, nous pouvons bavarder sans être dérangés.
ēsē, nōo pōovôN bävärdā säNzät(ər) dāräNzhā

May I invite you to a party?
Je voudrais vous inviter à une fête.
zhə vōodrā vōozeNvētā ä ēn fāt

I'll be expecting you at . . .
Je vous attends *chez (à)* . . .
zhə vōozätäN shā (ä) . . .

You look good in that dress.
Cette robe vous va très bien.
set rôb vōo vä trā byeN

When can you come visit me?
Quand est-ce que vous viendrez me voir?
käNdeske vōo vyeNdrā mə vô·är

When can we meet again?
Quand pouvons-nous nous revoir?
käN pōovôN-nōo nōo revô·är

May I give you a lift home?
Je peux vous raccompagner?
zhə pā vōo räkôNpänyā

Where do you live?
Où habitez-vous?
ōo äbētā-vōo

Won't you come in for a minute?
Vous voulez entrer un moment?
vōō vōōlā äNtrā eN mōmäN

May I walk part of the way with you?
Je peux vous accompagner un moment?
zhə pā vōōzäkôNpänyā eN mômäN

Thanks very much for a nice evening.
Merci beaucoup pour cette agréable soirée.
mersē bōkōō pōōr set ägrā·äb'əl sô·ärä

accompany	accompagner	äkôNpänyä
dance *(noun)*	danse *f*	däNs
dance *(verb)*	danser	däNsä
dance hall	dancing *m*	däNsēng
dicotheque	discothèque *f*	dēskôtäk
enjoy oneself	s'amuser	sämēzā
expect somebody	attendre qn.	ätäNd(ər) kelkeN
flirting	flirt *m*	flärt
invite	inviter	eNvētä
kiss *(noun, only!)* ...	baiser *m*	bāzä
kiss *(verb)*	embrasser	äNbräsä
live	habiter	äbētä
love *(noun)*	amour *m*	ämōōr
love *(verb)*	aimer	āmā
make love	flirter	flärtä
meet	(se) rencontrer,	(sə) räNkôNträ,
	retrouver	rətrōōvä
meet again	se revoir	sə rəvô·är
party	fête *f*	fāt
take a walk	se promener	sə prômənä
visit	visiter	vēzētä
visit *(chat)* *(verb)* ...	causer	kôzä

On the Beach

Where can we go swimming here?
Où peut-on se baigner ici?
ōō pātôN sə bānyā ēsē

Can we go swimming here?
On a le droit de se baigner ici?
ônä lə drô·ä də sə bānyā ēsē

Two tickets (with cabana), please.
Deux billets (avec cabine), s'il vous plaît.
dä bēyä (ävek käbēn), sēl vōō plä

How far out can we swim?
Jusqu'où peut-on nager?
zhēskōō pätôN näzhā

Can we swim *topless (nude)* here?
Nous pouvons-nous baigner *sans soutien-gorge (nus)?*
nōō pōōvóN-nōō bänyä säN sōōtyeN-gôrzh (nē)

How *deep (warm)* is the water?
Quelle est la *profondeur (température)* de l'eau?
kel ā lä prôfôNdār (täNpärätēr) dəlō

Is it dangerous for children?
Est-ce dangereux pour les enfants?
es däNzhārā pōōr läsäNfäN

*No swimming!
Interdiction de se baigner!
(Baignade interdite)
eNterdēksyôN də sə bänyä
(bänyäd eNterdēt)

Is there an undertow here?
Y a-t-il des courants?
ēyätēl dä kōōräN

Where is the lifeguard?
Où est le maître-nageur?
ōō ā lə māt(ər)-näzhär

A *deck chair (umbrella)*, please.
Une chaise-longue (Un parasol), s'il vous plaît.
ēn shāz-lông (eN päräsôl), sēl vōō plä

How much does . . . cost?
Combien coûte . . .?
kôNbyeN kōōt . . .

I'd like to rent a *cabana (boat)*.
Je voudrais louer *une cabine (un bateau).*
zhə vōōdrä lōō·ä ēn käbēn (eN bätō)

Where *is (are)* . . .?
Où *est (sont)* . . .?
ōō ā (sóN) . . .

I'd like to go water skiing.
Je voudrais faire du ski nautique.
zhə vōōdrä fär dē skē nôtēk

Where can I go fishing?
Où peut-on pêcher à la ligne?
ōō pätôN pāshä älä lēn(yə)

Would you be good enough to keep an eye on my gear.
Vous pourriez surveiller mes affaires, s'il vous plaît?
vōō pōōrē·ä sērvāyā mäzäfär, sēl vōō plä

air mattress	matelas *m* pneumatique	mätlä pnämätēk
air temperature	température *f* de l'air . .	täNpärätēr də lār
bathing cap	bonnet *m* de bain	bônä də beN
bathing suit	maillot *m* de bain	mäyō də beN
– trunks	slip *m* de bain	slēp də beN
bathrobe	peignoir *m*	penyô·är
bay	baie *f*	bā

boat	bateau m	bätō
– dinghy	canot m pneumatique	känō pnämätĕk
– motorboat	bateau m à moteur	bätō ä mōtär
– pedal boat	pédalo m	pädälō
– sailboat	voilier m	vô·älēyā
cabana	cabine f de bain	käbēn də beN
dive	plonger	plôNzhā
diving board	tremplin m	träNpleN
dune	dune f	dēn
jellyfish	méduse f	mādēz
locker room	vestiaire m	vestyär
non-swimmer	non-nageur m	nôN-näzhär
nude beach	plage f de nudistes	pläzh də nēdēst
	(naturistes)	(nätērēst)
saline content	teneur f en sel	tenär äN sel
sandy beach	plage f de sable	pläzh də säb'əl
scuba diving	plongée f sous-marine	plôNzhā sōō-märēn
scuba equipment	équipment m de	äkēpmäN də
	plongée sous-marine	plôNzhā sōō-märēn
shells	coquillages m/pl.	kôkēyäzh
shower	douche f	dōōsh
swim	nager	näzhā
swimmer	nageur m	näzhär
swimming pier	passerelle f	päsərel
take a sunbath	prendre un bain de soleil	präNdreN beN də sôlā'ē
water	eau f	ō
water temperature	température f de l'eau	täNpärätēr dəlō
wave	vague f	väg

Sports

What sports events do they have here?
Quelles manifestations sportives y a-t-il ici?
kel mänēfestäsyôN spôrtēv ēyätēl ēsē

Where's the *stadium (soccer field)*?
Où est *le stade (le terrain de football)*?
ōō ä lə städ (lə tereN də fōōtbôl)

*. . . is playing . . . today.

Aujourd'hui . . . joue contre . . .
ōzho͞ordē·ē . . . zho͞o kôNt(ər)

I'd love to see the *game (race, fight)*.

J'aimerais bien voir *le jeu (la course, le combat)*.
zhämrā byeN vô·är lə zh*ä* (lä ko͞ors, lə kôNbä)

When (Where) is the soccer game?

Quand (Où) le match de football a-t-il lieu?
käN (o͞o) lə mätsh də fo͞otbôl ätēl lēy*ä*

Can you get us tickets for it?	**Goal!**
Pourriez-vous nous procurer des *cartes (billets)*?	But!
po͞orē·ā-vo͞o no͞o prôkērā dā kärt (bēyā)	bē(t)

What's the score?   ***The score is three to two for . . .**

Où en est le match?   Le score est de trois à deux pour . . .
o͞o änä lə mätsh   lə skôr ā də trô·ä ä d*ä* po͞or . . .

Is there an _outdoor (indoor)_ swimming pool here?

Y a-t-il une piscine *découverte (couverte)*?
ēyätēl *ē*n pēsēn däko͞ovärt (ko͞ovärt)

What sports do you like to play?

Qu'est-ce que *vous faites (tu fais)* comme sport?
keske vo͞o fät (t*ē* fä) kôm spôr

I'm . . .	**I play . . .**	**I'm fond of . . .**
Je suis . . .	Je joue au . . .	Je me passionne pour . . .
zhə sē·ē . . .	zhə zho͞o ō . . .	zhə mə päsyôn po͞or . . .

athlete	athlète *m/f*	ätlāt
auto racing	course *f* automobile · · ·	ko͞ors ôtōmōbēl
– race	course *f* · · · · · · · · · · · · ·	ko͞ors
– race car driver	coureur *m* automobile ·	ko͞orär ôtōmōbēl
– racing car	voiture *f* de course · · · ·	vô·ätēr də ko͞ors
bicycling	cyclisme *m*	sēklēsm
– bicycle	bicyclette *f*	bēsēklet
– bicycle race	course *f* cycliste · · · · · ·	ko͞ors sēklēst
– bicycle rider	cycliste *m*	sēklēst
– ride a bike	aller à bicyclette · · · · · ·	älä ä bēsēklet
boat racing	régates *f/pl.*	rāgät
– racing boat	bateau *m* de course · · ·	bätō də ko͞ors
bowling	bowling *m*	bo͞olēng (bōlēng)

– bowling alley	piste *f* de bowling	pēst də bōolēng
boxing	(match *m* de) boxe *f*	(mätsh də) bôks
– box	boxer	bôksā
– boxer	boxeur *m*	bôks*a*r
competition	compétition *f*	kôNpātēsyôN
– championship	championnat *m*	shäNpyónä
– defeat	défaite *f*	dāfāt
– draw	match *m* nul	mätsh n*e*l
– free style	exercices *m/pl.* libres	eksersēs lēb(ər)
– game	jeu *m*	zh*a*
– goal	but *m*	b*e*(t)
– half time	mi-temps *m*	mē-täN
– match	jeu *m*	zh*a*
– play	jouer	zhōo·ā
– point	point *m*	pô·eN
– practice	entraînement *m*	äNtränmäN
– result	résultat *m*	räz*e*ltä
– start	départ *m*	dāpär
– victory	victoire *f*	vēktó·är
– win	gagner	gänyā
dog races	course *f* de lévriers	kōors də lāvrē·ā
fencing	escrime *f*	eskrēm
figure skating	patinage *m*	pätēnäzh
– skate	patiner	pätēnā
– skates	patins *m/pl.*	päteN
– skater	patineur *m*	pätēn*a*r
fishing	pêche *f* à la ligne	pāsh älä lēn(yə)
– fishing rod	canne *f* à pêche	kän ä pāsh
– go fishing	pêcher à la ligne	pāshā älä lēn(yə)
– fishing license	permis *m* de pêche	permē də pāsh
golf	golf *m*	gôlf
gymnastics	gymnastique *f*	zhēmnästēk
– gymnast	gymnaste *m*	zhēmnäst
– gymnastics with apparatus	gymnastique *f* aux agrès	zhēmnästēk ōzägrä
– balance beam	poutre *f* horizontale	pōotrôrêzôNtäl
– horizontal bar	barre *f* fixe	bär fēks
– parallel bars	barres *f/pl.* parallèles	bär päräläl
– rings	anneaux *m/pl.*	änō
handball	handball *m*	äNdbôl
hockey	hockey *m*	ókā

hunting	chasse *f*	shäs
– hunting license	permis *m* de chasse	permē də shäs
judo	judo *m*	zhēdō
marksmanship	tir *m*	tēr
– clay pigeon shooting	tir *m* au pigeon	tēr ō pēzhôN
– rifle range	(stand *m* de) tir *m*	(stäN də) tēr
– shoot	tirer	tērā
– target	cible *f*	sēb′əl
mountain climbing	alpinisme *m*	älpēnēsm
– mountain climber	alpiniste *m*	älpēnēst
ninepins	jeu *m* de quille	zhē də kē′ē
player	joueur *m*	zhoo·är
referee	arbitre *m*	ärbēt(ər)
riding	hippisme *m*; équitation *f*	ēpēsm; ākētäsyôN
– horse	cheval *m*	shəväl
– horse race	course *f* de chevaux	koors də shəvō
– jumping	saut *m*	sō
– ride	monter à cheval	môNtä ä shəväl
– rider	cavalier *m*	kävälyā
– trotting race	course *f* de trot attelé	koors də trô ätəlā
rowing	aviron *m*	ävērôN
– scull	rame *f*	räm
– oarsman	rameur *m*	rämär
– coxswain	barreur *m*	bärär
sailing	voile *f*; yachting *m*	vô·äl; yôtēng
– sail *(noun)*	voile *f*	vô·äl
– sail *(verb)*	faire de la voile	fär dəlä vô·äl
– sailboat	voilier *m*	vô·älyā
skiing	ski *m*	skē
– ski *(noun)*	ski *m*	skē
– ski *(verb)*	faire du ski	fär dē skē
– ski binding	fixation *f*	fēksäsyôN
– ski jump	tremplin *m* (de saut)	träNpleN (də sō)
– ski lift	téléski *m*	tāläskē
– ski wax	fart *m*	färt
soccer	football; "foot"	footbôl; foot
– ball	ballon *m*	bälôN
– corner	corner *m*	kôrnär
– forward	avant *m*	äväN
– free kick	coup *m* franc	koo fräN

– fullback	arrière *m*	äryär
– kick a goal	marquer un but	märkā eN bē̄(t)
– goal	but *m*	bē̄(t)
– goalie	gardien *m* de but	gärdyeN də bē̄(t)
– halfback	demi *m*, libero *m*	dəmē, lēbārō
– off-side	hors-jeu *m*	ôr-zhā
– penalty kick	penalty *m*	pānältē
– play soccer	jouer au football	zhoo͞·ā ō foo͞tbôl
– player	joueur *m*	zhoo͞·är
– throw-in	touche *f*	too͞sh
sports	sport *m*	spôr
– athletic club	association *f* sportive	äsôsyäsyóN spôrtēv
– sports fan	passionné *m* de sport	päsyônā də spôr
swimming	natation *f*	nätäsyóN
– dive	plongeon *m*	plôNzhóN
– diving board	plongeoir *m*	plôNzhô·är
– swimmer	nageur *m*	näzhär
team	équipe *f*	ākēp
tennis	tennis *m*	tenēs
– singles/doubles	simple *m*/double *m*	sēNp′əl/doo͞b′əl
– play tennis	jouer au tennis	zhoo͞·ā ō tenēs
– tennis ball	balle *f* de tennis	bäl də tenēs
– tennis court	court *m* de tennis	koo͞r də tenēs
– badminton	badminton *m*, volant *m*	bädmēntôn, vóläN
tobogganing	luge *f*	lēzh
– toboggan	luge *f*	lēzh
track and field	athlétisme *m*	ätlātēsm
umpire	arbitre *m*	ärbēt(ər)
volleyball	volley-ball *m*	vôlā-bôl
wrestling	lutte *f*	lēt
– wrestle	lutter	lētā
– wrestler	lutteur *m*	lētär

The most popular sport (especially for spectators) in France is soccer, called le football *or* le foot.
Another very popular sport is bicycle racing, le cyclisme, *which culminates in the gruelling* Tour de France *race. Sailing, tennis and skiing are also quite popular. Especially in the south of France, rugby enjoys enormous popularity.*

APPENDIX

Signs

À LOUER	ä lōō·ā	to let
À VENDRE	ä väNd(ər)	for sale
ARRÊT	ärā	stop
ARRIVÉE	ärēvā	arrival
ATTENTION	ätäNsyôN	caution
AVIS AU PUBLIC ...	ävē ō pēblēk	public notices
BUVETTE (BAR)	bĕvet (bär)	refreshments
DAMES	däm	ladies
DANGER	däNzhā	danger
DANGER DE MORT	däNzhā də môr	mortal danger
DÉFENSE D'AFFICHER	dāfäNs däfēshā	post no bills
DÉFENSE DE FUMER	dāfäNs də fēmā	no smoking
DÉFENSE DE SE BAIGNER	dāfäNs də sə bānyā .	no swimming allowed
DEUXIÈME ÉTAGE .	dāzyām ātäzh	third floor
ENTRÉE	äNtrā	entrance
ENTRÉE INTERDITE	äNtrā eNterdēt	no admittance
ENTRÉE LIBRE	äNtrā lēb(ər)	admission free
ESCALIER ROULANT	eskälyā rōōläN	escalator
EXTINCTEUR	eksteNktŭr	fire extinguisher
FERMÉ	färmā	closed
MESSIEURS	mesyŭ	gentlemen
NE PAS OUVRIR	nə päzōōvrēr	do not open
NE PAS SE PENCHER AU DEHORS	nə pä sə päNshä ō də·ôr	do not lean out the window
PEINTURE FRAÎCHE	peNtŭr fräsh	wet paint
POUSSEZ	pōōsā	push
PREMIER ETAGE ...	prəmyär ātäzh	second (!) floor
PRIÈRE DE NE PAS TOUCHER	prēyär də nə pä tōōshā	do not touch
PRIVÉ	prēvā	private (road)
SORTIE	sôrtē	exit
SORTIE DE SECOURS	sôrtē də səkōōr	emergency exit
TIREZ	tērā	pull

Abbreviations

A.C.F.	Automobile Club de France ... [ôtōmōbēl klẽb də fräNs]	**French Automobile Association**
A.J.	Auberge de Jeunesse .... [ōbärzh də zhā̃nes]	**youth hostel**
arr.	arrivée; arrondissement .... [ärēvā̃; ärôNdēsmäN]	**arrival; district**
bd.	boulevard [boōlvär]	**boulevard**
B.P.	boîte postale [bô·ät pôstäl]	**post-office box**
c.-à-d.	c'est-à-dire [setädēr]	**that is**
C.C.P.	compte de chèques postaux ... [kôNt də shek pôstō]	**postal check account**
C.J.	camp de jeunesse .... [käN də zhā̃nes]	**youth camp**
ct.	(du mois) courant .... [(dẽ mô·ä) koōräN]	... **instant**
C.U.	Cité Universitaire .... [sētā ēnēversētär]	**university camp**
dép.	départ [dāpär]	**departure**
dépt.	département [dāpärtmäN]	**department**
M.	Monsieur [məsyā̃]	**Mister**
Mlle	Mademoiselle [mädəmó·äzel] ..	**Miss**
MM	Messieurs [mesyā̃]	**Messieurs**
Mme	Madame [mädäm]	**Mistress**
O.R.T.F. ..	Office de la Radiotélévision française	**French Broadcasting Corporation**
P. et T.	Postes et Télécommunications . [pôst ã tālākômēnēkäsyôN]	**Post and Telecommunication**
pl.	place [pläs]	**square**
R.E.R.	Réseau express régional ..... [rāzō ekspres räzhē·ônäl]	**system of suburban express trains**
R.N.	route nationale .... [roōt näsyônäl]	**Federal Highway**
S.A.M.U...	service d'aide médicale d'urgence .... [servēs dād mādēkäl dẽrzhäNs]	**life-saving-service**
S.N.C.F. ..	Société Nationale des Chemins de Fer Français	**French Railroad**
S.I.	syndicat d'initiative .... [seNdēkä dēnēsyätēv]	**tourist office**

Weights and Measures

1 millimeter	un millimètre (mm)	eN mēlēmāt(ər)
1 centimeter	un centimètre (cm)	eN säNtēmāt(ər)
1 decimeter	un décimètre (dm)	eN dāsēmāt(ər)
1 meter	un mètre (m)	eN māt(ər)
	(=1.0936 yards)	
1 kilometer	un kilomètre (km)	eN kēlōmāt(ər)
	(=0.6214 miles)	
1 inch	un pouce (=2.54 cm)	eN pōos
1 foot	30.48 cm	
1 yard	0.914 m	
1 (statute) mile	une lieue (=1.609 km)	ēn lēyä
1 nautical mile	un mille marin	eN mēl märeN
	(=1.853 km)	
1 square foot	0.0929 m²	
1 square yard	0.836 m²	
1 square meter	un mètre carré (m²)	eN māt(ər) kärā
	(=1.196 square yards)	
1 square mile	2.59 kilomètres carrés (km²)	kēlōmāt(ər) kärā
1 cubic foot	0.028 mètres cube (m³)	mātrə kēb
1 liter	un litre (l)	eN lēt(ər)
	(=2.113 pints)	
1 pint	0.473 l	
1 quart	0.946 l	
1 gallon	3.785 l	
1 ounce	28.349 grammes (g)	gräm
1 pound	un demi kilo (une livre)	eN dəmē kēlō/ ēn lēv(ər)
1 hundredweight	un quintal	eN keNtäl
	(=45.359 kg)	
1 ton	une tonne	ēn tôn
a piece (of ...)	un morceau (de...)	eN môrsō (də ...)
a pair (of ...)	une paire (de ...)	ēn pär (də ...)
a dozen	une douzaine (de ...)	ēn dōozen (də ...)
a pack(et) (of ...)	un paquet (de ...)	eN päkā (də ...)

Colors

beige	beige	bāzh
black	noir	nô·är
blonde	blond	blóN
blue	bleu	blā
– light blue	bleu clair	blā klār
– navy blue	bleu foncé	blā fôNsā
brown	brun	breN
– chestnut brown	châtain	shäteN
color	couleur *f*	kōōlär
– colored	coloré	kôlôrā
– colorful	multicolore	mēltēkôlôr
– solid-colored	uni	ēnē
gold	doré	dôrā
green	vert	vār
– dark green	vert foncé	vār fôNsā
– light green	vert clair	vār klār
gray	gris	grē
– ash gray	gris cendré	grē säNdrā
– dark gray	gris foncé	grē fôNsā
– pale gray	gris clair	grē klār
lavender/mauve	lavande/mauve	läväNd, môv
orange	orange	ôräNzh
pink	rose	rōz
purple	pourpre	pōōrp(ər)
red	rouge	rōōzh
– bright red	rouge clair	rōōzh klār
– fire engine red	rouge vif	rōōzh vēf
– dark red/maroon	rouge foncé	rōōzh fôNsā
silver	argenté	ärzhäNtā
violet	violet	vē·ôlā
white	blanc (blanche)	bläN (bläNsh)
yellow	jaune	zhōn

BASIC FRENCH GRAMMAR RULES

I. The Article

1. There are two genders in French, masculine and feminine.

2. The **definite** article in the **masculine** singular is **le** [lə], e.g. *le livre* [lə lēv(ər)] the book.

3. The **definite** article in the **feminine** singular is **la** [lä], e.g. *la maison* [lä mäzôN] the house.

4. The masculine and feminine **plural** is always **les** [lā], e.g. *les livres* [lā lēv(ər)] the books, *les maisons* [lā mäzôN] the houses.

5. The **indefinite** article in the **masculine** singular is **un** [eN], e.g. *un cheval* [eN shəväl] a horse.

6. The **indefinite** article in the **feminine** singular is **une** [ēn], e.g. *une lettre* [ēn let(ər)] a letter.

7. Nouns expressing an indefinite amount or an indefinite number of items take the **partitive,** which is formed by the preposition **de** and the definite article, e.g. *du pain* [dē peN] bread, *de la viande* [də lä vē·äNd] meat, des *amis* [dāzämē] friends. There is no English equivalent for the partitive.

II. The Noun

1. As in English, the subject and object function of the noun is indicated by its place in the sentence.

2. The possessive case can be indicated by *de* [də] or *à* [ä].

3. *de* and *à* are combined with *le* and *les* in the following ways: *de le* becomes *du* [dē], *de les* becomes *des* [dā], *à le* becomes *au* [ō], *à les* becomes *aux* [ō].

III. The Adjective and Adverb

1. **Adjectives** agree in number and gender with the nouns they modify.

2. **Adverbs** are formed by adding **-ment** to the feminine form of the adjective.

3. The feminine form of the adjective is formed by adding *-e* to the masculine (*m*) form (if this does not already end in *-e*), e.g. *m grand* [gräN], *f grande* [gräNd] big; *m poli* [pôlē], *f polie* [pôlē] polite; but *m* and *f* sage [säzh] wise.

IV. Comparison

1. The **comparative** is formed by placing *plus* [plē] more, before the adjective or adverb, e.g. *beau* [bō] beautiful, *plus beau* [plē bō] more beautiful; *rapidement* [räpēd·mäN] fast, *plus rapidement* [plē räpēd·mäN] faster.

2. The following adjectives are irregular in the comparative: *bon* [bôN] good, *meilleur* [māyār] better; *mauvais* [mōvā] bad, *pire* [pēr] worse; *petit* [pətē] little, small, *moindre* [mô·eNd(ər)] less, (*plus petit* [plē pətē] smaller).

3. The following adverbs are irregular in the comparative: *bien* [byeN] well, *mieux* [myā] better; *mal* [mäl] badly, *pis* [pē] worse; *peu* [pā] little, *moins* [mô·eN] less; *beaucoup* [bōkoo] much, *plus* [plē] more.

4. "Than" after a comparative is *que*, e.g. *il est plus fort que moi* [ēlā plē fôr kə mô·ä], he is stronger than I.

5. The **superlative** of adjectives and adverbs is formed by placing the definite article before the comparative, e.g. *le plus beau voyage* [lə plē bō vô·äyäzh] the most beautiful trip; *le meilleur ami* [lə māyārämē] the best friend; *le plus rapidement* [lə plē räpēd·mäN] the fastest.

V. Formation of Plurals

1. As in English, the plural is generally formed by adding *s* to the singular noun, e.g. *le livre* [lə lēv(ər)] the book, *les livres* [lā lēv(ər)] the books.

2. Nouns ending in *s*, *x* and *z* do not change in the plural, e.g. *la souris* [lä soorē] the mouse, *les souris* [lā soorē] the mice; *la voix* [lä vô·ä] the voice, *les voix* [lā vô·ä] the voices.

3. Some nouns ending in *-ou* and all nouns ending in *au*, *eau*, *eu* and *œu* form the plural by adding *-x*, e.g. *le chou* [lə shoo] the cabbage, plural: *les choux* [lā shoo]; *le genou* [lə zhenoo] the knee, plural: *les genoux* [lā zhenoo]; *le cheveu* [lə shevā] the (strand of) hair, plural: *les cheveux* [lā shevā] hair; *le tableau* [lə täblō] the picture, plural: *les tableaux* [lā täblō].

4. Most nouns ending in *-al* and some nouns ending in *-ail* form the plural by *-aux*, e.g. *le cheval* [lə shəväl] the horse, plural: *les chevaux* [lā shəvō]; *le travail* [lə trävä·ē] work, plural: *les travaux* [lā trävō].

VI. Pronouns

Personal Pronouns

I. Subject Pronouns

je [zhə] I; *tu* [tē] you; *il* [ēl] he; *elle* [el] she; *nous* [no͞o] we; *vous* [vo͞o] you (*pl.*); *ils* [ēl] they (*m*); *elles* [el] they (*f*).

II. Direct and Indirect Object Pronouns

1. The **conjunctive** personal pronouns are:

Indirect Object			Direct Object		
me	[mə]	me	me	[mə]	me
te	[tə]	you	te	[tə]	you
lui	[lē·ē]	him, it	le	[lə]	him, it
lui	[lē·ē]	her, it	la	[lä]	her, it
se	[sə]	yourself, himself, herself, itself	se	[sə]	himself, herself, yourself, itself
nous	[no͞o]	us	nous	[no͞o]	us
vous	[vo͞o]	you [*pl.*]	vous	[vo͞o]	you [*pl.*]
leur	[lär]	them	les	[lä]	them [*m*]
			les	[lä]	them [*f*]

In general, these personal pronouns precede the verb, e.g. *il me donne* [ēl mə dôn] he gives me.

2. The **disjunctive** personal pronouns are *moi* [mô·ä] me; *toi* [tô·ä] you; *lui* [lē·ē] him; *elle* [el] her; *nous* [no͞o] us; *vous* [vo͞o] you; *eux* [ä] them (*m*); *elles* [el] them (*f*), e.g. *Qui est venu? – Moi!* [kē ā vənē? – mô·ä!] Who has come? – I!

3. The **possessive** is formed by the preposition *de* [də] preceding the disjunctive personal pronoun, e.g. *Il se souvient de moi (vous)* [ēl sə so͞ovyeN də mô·ä (vo͞o)] He remembers me (you).

4. The **indirect object** is formed by the preposition *à* preceding the disjunctive personal pronoun, e.g. *à moi* [ä mô·ä] to me, *à eux* [ä ä] to them.

Possessive Pronouns

1. **adjective function** (preceding a noun):

Singular

masculine *mon* [môN] my; *ton* [tôN] your; *son* [sôN] his, feminine *ma* [mä] my; *ta* [tä] your; *sa* [sä] her; *notre* [nôt(ər)] our; *votre* [vôt(ər)] your; *leur* [lär] their.

Plural (masc. and fem.)

mes [mā] my; *tes* [tā] your; *ses* [sā] his, her; *nos* [nō] our; *vos* [vō] your; *leurs* [lär] their.

These pronouns agree with gender and number of the thing(s) possessed.

A noun in the third person singular can take *son, sa* or *ses* depending on the number and gender of the thing(s) possessed, e.g. *La famille prend ses repas au restaurant* [lä fämē·ē präN sä repä ō restôräN] The family has its meals at a restaurant.

A noun in the third person plural takes *leur(s)*, e.g. *Ces familles ont vendu leurs meubles* [sā fämē·ē ôN väNdē lär māb'əl] These families have sold their furniture.

The possessive pronoun "your" (polite form) is always *votre*, e.g. *Où prenez-vous votre petit déjeuner?* [oo prənā voo vôt(ər) pətē dāzhānā] Where do you have breakfast?

2. **nominative function** (combined with an article):

le mien	[lə myeN],	*la mienne*	[lä myān]	mine (*m/f*)
le tien	[lə tyeN],	*la tienne*	[lä tyān]	yours (*m/f*)
le sien	[lə syeN],	*la sienne*	[lä syān]	his, hers, its
le nôtre	[lə nôt(ər)]	*la nôtre*	[lä nôt(ər)]	ours
le vôtre	[lə vôt(ər)],	*la vôtre*	[lä vôt(ər)]	yours (*pl.*)
le leur	[lə lär],	*la leur*	[lä lär]	theirs

The plural is formed by the addition of *-s*.

Demonstrative Pronouns

1. **adjective function** (preceding a noun)

ce [sə], *cet* [set], *cette* [set] this (*m/f*), *ces* [se] these (*m/f*)

Note: *cet* is the masculine singular before vowels and vowel sounds (*h*), e.g. *ce cheval* [sə shəväl] this horse, *cet homme* [setôm] this man, *cette femme* [set fäm] this woman, *ces enfants* [sezäNfäN] these children.

2. **nominative function** (standing alone)

celui-ci	[selē·ēsē],	*celle-ci*	[selsē]	this one here (*m/f*)
ceux-ci	[sāsē],	*celles-ci*	[selsē]	these here (*m/f*)
celui-là	[selē·ēlä],	*celle-là*	[sel-lä]	that one there (*m/f*)
ceux-là	[sālä],	*celles-là*	[sel-lä]	those over there (*m/f*)

celui, celle [selē·ē, sel] this, that
ceux, celles [sā, sel] these, those
ceci [sesē] this
cela [selä] that (informally: *ça*)

Relative Pronouns

qui	[kē]	who (persons), which, that (things)
dont	[dôN]	of whom, about whom (persons), of which, about which (things)
à qui	[äkē]	to whom
que	[kə]	whom (persons), which, that (things)

Interrogative Pronouns

1. **adjective function** (preceding a noun):

quel?	[kel],	*quelle?*	[kel]	what? which? (*m/f sing.*)
quels?	[kel],	*quelles?*	[kel]	what? which? (*m/f pl.*)

e.g. *quel livre?* [kelēv(ər)] which book?; *quelle fille?* [kel fē·ē] which girl?; *quels garçons?* [kel gärsôN] which boys?; *quelles villes?* [kel vēl] which cities?

2. **nominative function** (standing alone):

lequel?	[ləkel],	*laquelle?*	[läkel]	which one? (*m/f sing.*)
lesquels?	[lekel],	*lesquelles?*	[lekel]	which ones? (*m/f pl.*)

e.g. *lesquels de tes amis?* [lekel də tāzämē] which of your friends?

qui?	[kē]	who?	*de qui?*	[də kē] of whom?
à qui?	[äkē]	to whom?	*qui?*	[kē] whom? (as object)

qu'est-ce qui? [keskē] who?
qu'est-ce que? [keskə] or *que?* [kə] what?
de quoi? [də kô·ä] from what?
à quoi? [äkô·ä] what about?

VII. The Verb

A. The Auxiliary Verbs avoir and être

	Present	Imperfect	Past Definite	Future	Imperative
avoir	to have				
j'	ai	avais	eus	aurai	aie
tu	as	avais	eus	auras	ayons
il	a	avait	eut	aura	ayez
nous	avons	avions	eûmes	aurons	**Past**
vous	avez	aviez	eûtes	aurez	**Participle:**
ils	ont	avaient	eurent	auront	eu

	Present	Imperfect	Past Definite	Future	Imperative
être	to be				
je	suis	j'étais	fus	serai	sois
tu	es	étais	fus	seras	soyons
il	est	était	fut	sera	soyez
nous	sommes	étions	fûmes	serons	**Past**
vous	êtes	étiez	fûtes	serez	**Participle:**
ils	sont	étaient	furent	seront	été

B. The Regular Verbs

First Conjugation

	Present	Imperfect	Past Definite	Future	Imperative
blâmer	to blame				
je	blâme	blâmais	blâmai	blâmerai	blâme
tu	blâmes	blâmais	blâmas	blâmeras	blâmons
il	blâme	blâmait	blâma	blâmera	blâmez
nous	blâmons	blâmions	blâmâmes	blâmerons	**Past**
vous	blâmez	blâmiez	blâmâtes	blâmerez	**Participle:**
ils	blâment	blâmaient	blâmèrent	blâmeront	blâmé(e)

Second Conjugation

punir to punish

	Present	Imperfect	Past Definite	Future	Imperative
je	punis	punissais	punis	punirai	punis
tu	punis	punissais	punis	puniras	punissons
il	punit	punissait	punit	punira	punissez
nous	punissons	punissions	punîmes	punirons	**Past**
vous	punissez	punissiez	punîtes	punirez	**Participle:**
ils	punissent	punissaient	punirent	puniront	puni(e)

Third Conjugation

recevoir to receive

	Present	Imperfect	Past Definite	Future	Imperative
je	reçois	recevais	reçus	recevrai	reçois
tu	reçois	recevais	reçus	recevras	recevons
il	reçoit	recevait	reçut	recevra	recevez
nous	recevons	recevions	reçûmes	recevrons	**Past**
vous	recevez	receviez	reçûtes	recevrez	**Participle:**
ils	reçoivent	recevaient	reçurent	recevront	reçu(e)

Fourth Conjugation

	Present	Imperfect	Past Definite	Future	Imperative
vendre	to sell				
je	vends	vendais	vendis	vendrai	vends
tu	vends	vendais	vendis	vendras	vendons
il	vend	vendait	vendit	vendra	vendez
nous	vendons	vendions	vendîmes	vendrons	**Past**
vous	vendez	vendiez	vendîtes	vendrez	**Participle:**
ils	vendent	vendaient	vendirent	vendront	vendu(e)

THE FRENCH ALPHABET

A a	B b	C c	D d	E e	F f	G g
[ä]	[bā]	[sā]	dā]	[ə]	[āf]	[zhā]

H h	I i	J j	K k	L l	M m	N n
[äsh]	[ē]	[zhē]	[kä]	[el]	[ām]	[ān]

O o	P p	Q q	R r	S s	T t
[ō, ô]	[pā]	[kē̄]	[ār]	[es]	[tā]

U u	V v	W w	X x	Y y	Z z
[ē̄]	[vā]	[do͞ob'əlvā]	[ēks]	[ēgräk]	[zād]

ENGLISH – FRENCH DICTIONARY

The translations are followed by phonetic transcriptions and page references, so that this dictionary serves as an index as well.

A

abbey abbaye *f* [äbā] 124

abdomen ventre *m* [väNt(ər)] 166
bas-ventre *m* [bäväNt(ər)] 166

above au-dessus de [ōdəsē də] 25

abscess abcès *m* [äbsā] 174

absorbent cotton coton *m* hydrophile [kôtôN ēdrōfēl] 160

accelerate accélérer [äkselärā] 51

accelerator accélérateur *m* [äkselerätär] 51

access road route *f* d'accès [rōōt däksā] 42

accessories accessoires *m/pl* [äksesō·är] 136

accident accident *m* [äksēdäN] 153

accommodations logis *m* [lôzhē] 90

accompanist accompagnateur *m* [äkôNpänyätär] 177

accompany accompagner [äkôNpänyā] 184

act acte *m* [äkt] 176

actor acteur *m* [äktär] 176

actress actrice *f* [äktrēs] 176

adapter plug fiche *f* intermédiaire [fēsh eNtermādyär] 90

address adresse *f* [ädres] 149

addressee destinataire *m* [destenätär] 149

admission entrée *f* [äNtrā] 118

admission free entrée libre [äNtrā lēb(ər)] 191

advance reservation réservation *f* [räzerväsyôN] 95

advance ticket sales location *f* [lôkäsyôN] 177

after après [äprā] 159

after shave lotion *f* après rasage [lôsyôN äprä räzäzh] 140

afternoon après-midi *m* [äprämēdē] 31; **in the ~** l'après-midi [läprämēdē] 31; **this ~** cet après-midi [setäprä-mēdē] 31

against contre [kôNt(ər)] 164

age âge *m* [äzh 35]; **under ~** mineur [mēnär] 34

ago: a month ~ il y a un mois [ēlyä eN mô·ä] 32

air air *m* [är] 26; **~ conditioning** climatisation *f* [klēmätēzäsyôN] 75; **~ filter** filtre *m* d'air [fēlt(ər) där] 51; **~ jet** buse *f* d'aération [bēz dä·äräsyôN] 70; **~ mail** par avion [pär ävyôN] 145; **~ mattress** matelas *m* pneumatique [mätlä pnämätēk] 185; **~ pump** pompe *f* à air [pôNpä är] 57; **~ sickness** mal *m* de l'air [mäl də lär] 169; **~ temperature** température *f* de l'air [täNpärätēr də lär] 185

aircraft avion *m* [ävyôN] 70

airline compagnie *f* aérienne [kôNpänyē ä·ärē·en] 70

airport aéroport *m* [ä·ārōpôr] 68; **~ service charge** taxe *f* d'aéroport [täks dä·ārōpôr] 68

alcohol alcool *m* [älkôl] 99

all tout [tōō] 80

allergy allergie *f* [älerzhē] 169

alley ruelle *f* [rē·el]; allée *f* [älā] 120

allow-me? vous permettez? [vōō permetā] 20

almonds amandes *f/pl* [ämäNd] 110

alone seul, -e [säl] 14

already déjà [dezhä] 84

altar autel m [ôtel] 124

alter faire des retouches [fär dä retōōsh] 133

alto alto m [àltō] 177

amber ambre m jaune [äNb(ər) zhōn] 133

ambulance ambulance f [äNbēläNs] 48

American américain [ämärēkeN] 152; **~ dollars** dollars américains [dòlär ämärēkeN] 152; **~ plan** pension f complète [päNsyòN kòNplet] 83; **~ studies** langue et littérature américaines [läNgä lētärätēr ämäräken] 39

amount montant m [mòNtäN] 151

ampule ampoule f [äNpōōl] 160

amusement distraction f [dēsträksyòN] 181; **~ park** parc m d'attractions [pärk däträksyòN] 120

anchor ancre f [äNk(ər)] 75

anchovies anchois m/pl [äNshô·ä] 102

anemia anémie f [änämē] 169

anesthesia anesthésie f [änestäzē] 174; **general ~** anesthésie f générale [änestäzē zhänäräl] 174; **local ~** anesthésie f locale [änestäzē lōkäl] 174

anesthetic narcose f [närkōz] 172

ankle jointure f [zhô·eNtēr]; (foot) cheville f [shevē'ē] 166

announcer speaker m [spēkär] 182

annually tous les ans [tōō läzäN] 32

antidote contrepoison m [kòNt(rə)pô·äzòN] 160

anti-freeze antigel m [äNtēzhel] 45

anyone quelqu'un [kelkeN] 85

anything quelque chose [kelke shōz] 80

apartment appartement m [äpärtəmäN] 81; **efficiency ~** location f

[lôkäsyòN] 82; **~ building** immeuble m de studios [ēmäb'əl də stēdē·ō] 90

appendicitis appendicite f [äpäNdēsēt] 169

appendix appendice m [äpäNdēs] 166

appetite appétit m [äpätē] 163

applause applaudissements m/pl [äplôdēsmäN] 177

apple pomme f [pòm] 110

appointment rendez-vous m [räNdävōō] 155

apprentice apprenti m [äpräNtē] 36

approach (plane) approche f [äprôsh] 70

apricot abricot m [äbrēkō] 110

April avril m [ävrēl] 33

apron tablier m [täblēyä] 134

arch arc m [ärk] 124

archaeology archéologie f [ärkä·ōlōzhē] 39

architecture architecture f [ärshētektēr] 39

area région f [räzhē·òN] 120; **~ code** indicatif m [eNdēkätēf] 149

aria aria f [ärē·ä] 177

arm bras m [brä] 166

armchair fauteuil m [fōtä'ē] 90

armpit aisselle f [äsel] 166

around (time) vers [vär] 31

arrest arrêter [ärätä] 154

arrival arrivée f [ärēvä] 60

arrive arriver [ärēvä] 34

art gallery galerie f [gälerē] 128

art history histoire f de l'art [ēstô·är də lär] 39

artery artère f [ärtär] 166

arthritis rhumatisme m articulaire [rēmätēsm ärtēkēlär] 169

artichokes artichauts m/pl [ärtēshō] 107

articles objets m/pl [òbzhä] 80

artist artiste m [ärtēst] 36

ash tray cendrier *m* [säNdrë·ä] 87
ashore: to go ~ descendre à terre [desäNdrä'tär] 72
asparagus asperge *f* [äspärzh] 107
asthma asthme *m* [äsme] 169
at *(time)* à [ä] 30; **~ night** la nuit [lä në·ē] 94
athlete athlète *m/f* [ätlät] 187
athletic club association *f* sportive [äsôsyäsyôN spôrtēv] 190
atmospheric pressure pression *f* atmosphérique [presyôN ätmôsfärēk] 26
attack attaque *f* [ätäk] 169
attend *(university)* étudier [ätēdyā] 38; *(school)* aller à [älä ä] 38
attendant pompiste *m* [pôNpēst] 45
attorney avocat *m* [ävôkä] 154
audience spectateurs *m/pl* [spektä·tär]; public *m* [pēblēk] 179
auditorium salle *f* de spectacle [säl de spektäk'el] 179
August août *m* [ōō(t)] 33
aunt tante *f* [täNt] 35
auto racing course *f* automobile [kōōrs ôtômôbēl] 187
autobiography autobiographie *f* [ôtōbē·ōgräfē] 130
automatic transmission changement *m* de vitesse automatique [shäNzh·mäN de vētes ôtômätēk] 51
automobile club club *m* automobile [klēb ôtômôbēl] 42
available *(seat)* libre [lēb(er)] 68
avenue avenue *f* [ävenē] 120
axle essieu *m* [esyē] 51

B

baby bébé *m* [bābā] 164
back en arrière [äNäryär] 40; **from … to … and ~** de … à … et retour [de … ä … ä retōōr] 73

back *(noun)* dos *m* [dō] 166; **~ seat** siège *m* arrière [syäzh äryär] 55; **~ wheel** roue *f* arrière [rōō äryär] 47
backache mal *m* au dos [mäl ō dō] 169
backfire raté *m* [rätä] 51
backwards dans le sens contraire de la marche [däN le säNs kôNträr delä märsh] 66
bacon lard *m* [lär] 100
bad: too ~! (quel) dommage! [(kel) dômäzh] 22
badminton badminton *m* [bädmēntôn]; volant *m* [vôläN] 190
bag sac *m* [säk] 126; **beach ~** sac *m* de camping [säk de käNpēng] 143; **plastic ~** sac *m* en plastique [säk äN plästēk] 144; **traveling ~** sac *m* de voyage [säk de vô·äyäzh] 64
baggage bagages *m/pl* [bägäzh] 63; **~ car** fourgon *m* [fōōrgôN] 67; **~ check** bulletin *m* d'enregistrement [bēlteN däNrezhēstremäN] 84; **~ check area** enregistrement *m* des bagages [äNrezhēstremäN dä bägäzh] 63; **~ claim area** consigne *f* [kôNsēn(ye)] 63
baked cuit au four [kē·ē ō fōōr] 100
baker boulanger *m* [bōōläNzhā] 36
bakery boulangerie *f* [bōōläNzherē] 128
balance beam poutre *f* horizontale [pōōtrôrēzôNtäl] 188
balcony balcon *m* [bälkôN] 82; *(theatre)* rang *m* [räN] 176
ball balle *f* [bäl] 143; *(soccer)* ballon *m* [bälôN] 189; **~ bearings** roulement *m* à billes [rōōlmäN ä bē'ē] 51; **~ point cartridge** mine *f* [mēn]; cartouche *f* [kärtōōsh] 138
ballet ballet *m* [bälä] 177
banana banane *f* [bänän] 110

band orchestre *m* [ôrkest(ər)] 177

bandage: adhesive ~ sparadrap *m* [spärädrä] 160; **lace ~** pansement *m* élastique [päNs·mäN älästēk] 161

bandages pansement *m* [päNs·mäN] 48

bank banque *f* [bäNk] 151; **savings ~** caisse *f* d'épargne [kes dāpärn·(yə)] 152; **~ account** compte *m* bancaire [kôNt bäNkār] 151; **~ charges** frais *m/pl* bancaires [frā bäNkär] 151; **~ note** billet *m* de banque [bēyā də bäNk] 151; **~ teller** employé *m* de banque [äN-plô·äyā də bäNk] 36; **~ transfer** virement *m* bancaire [vērmäN bäNkär] 151

bank rivage *m* [rēväzh] 75

banker banquier *m* [bäNkyä] 181

baptism baptême *m* [bätām] 124

bar bar *m* [bär] 74

barber shop salon *m* de coiffure [sälôN də kô·äfēr] 74

barette barrette *f* [bäret] 140

barge chaland *m* [shäläN] 75

baritone baryton *m* [bärētôN] 177

barometer baromètre *m* [bärō-mät(ər)] 25

Baroque baroque [bärôk] 124

barrier barrière *f* [bäryär] 67

basement sous-sol *m* [sōō-sôl] 90

bass basse *f* [bäs] 177

bath bain *m* [beN] 82; **~ attendant** maître *m* nageur [mät(ər) näzhär] 175; **~ salts** sels *m/pl* pour le bain [sel pōōr lə beN] 140; **mineral ~** bain *m* thermal [beN tärmäl] 175; **steam ~** bain *m* de vapeur [beN də väpär] 175; **take a ~** prendre un bain [präNdreN beN] 95

bathing cap bonnet *m* de bain [bô-nā də beN] 134

bathing suit maillot *m* de bain [mäyō də beN] 185

bathing trunks slip *m* de bain [slēp də beN] 185

bathrobe peignoir *m* [penyô·är] 185

bathroom salle *f* de bain [säl də beN] 90

battery batterie *f* [bätərē] 51

bay baie *f* [bā] 75

beach plage *f* [pläzh] 81; **private ~** plage *f* privée [pläzh prēvā] 92; **sandy ~** plage *f* de sable [pläzh də säb'əl] 186

beans haricots *m/pl* [ärēkō] 108; **butter ~** haricots *m/pl* beurre [ärēkō bär] 108; **French (string) ~** haricots *m/pl* verts [ärēkō vär] 108

beard barbe *f* [bärb] 157

bearing coussinet *m* [kōōsēnā] 51

beauty contest concours *m* de beauté [kôNkōōr də bōtā] 181

beauty parlor salon *m* de beauté [sälôN de bōtā] 158; institut *m* de beauté [eNstētē də bōtā] 128

bed lit *m* [lē] 90; **~ and two meals** demi-pension *f* [dəmē-päNsyôN] 90; **~ linen** draps *m/pl* de lit [drä də lē] 90; **~ rug** descente *f* de lit [desäNt də lē] 90; **day ~** canapé-lit *m* [känäpā-lē] 91

bedroom chambre *f* à coucher [shäNbrä kōōshā] 93

bedside table table *f* de nuit [täbʼəl də nē·ē] 90

beef bœuf *m* [bäf] 105

beer bière *f* [byär] 111; **~ mug** chope *f* bière [shôp byär] 111; **dark ~** bière *f* brune [byär brēn] 111; **light ~** bière *f* blonde [byär blôNd] 111

beets betteraves *f/pl* rouges [be-təräv rōōzh] 107

before *(time)* avant [äväN] 31

beige beige [bäzh] 194

bell cloche *f* [klôsh] 124; sonnette *f* [sônet] 88

below au-dessous de [ōdəsōō də] 25

belt ceinture *f* [seNter] 134

bet parier [pärē·ā]; miser (sur) [mēzä (sēr)] 181

beverage boisson *f* [bô·äsôN] 112; **alcoholic** ~ boisson *f* alcoolique [bô·äsôN älkôlēk] 112; **non-alcoholic** ~ boisson *f* non-alcoolique [bô·äsôN nôN-älkôlēk] 112

bicycle bicyclette *f* [bēsēklet] 41; **to go by** ~ aller à bicyclette [älä ä bēsēklet] 42; ~ **race** course *f* cycliste [kōōrs sēklēst] 187; ~ **rider** cycliste *m* [sēklēst] 187

bicycling cyclisme *m* [sēklēsm] 187

big grand [gräN]

bike bicyclette *f* [bēsēklet] 187; **ride a** ~ aller à bicyclette [älä ä bēsēklet] 187; ~ **lane** piste *f* cyclable [pēst sēkläb'əl] 42

bikini bikini *m* [bēkēnē] 134

bile bile *f* [bēl] 166

bill billet *m* de banque [bēyā də bäNk] 151; note *f* [nôt] 90

billfold portefeuille *m* [pôrtfä'e] 153

binoculars jumelles *f/pl* [zhēmel] 138

biography biographie *f* [bē·ōgräfē] 130

biology biologie *f* [bē·ōlōzhē] 39

birthday anniversaire *m* [änēversär] 22; **happy** ~! bon anniversaire! [bônänēversär] 23

bishop fou *m* [fōō] 181

bitters bitter *m* [bētär] 112

black noir [nô·är] 194

black currants cassis *m/pl* [käsēs] 110

blackberries mûres *f/pl* [mēr] 110

blackmail attempt chantage *m* [shäNtäzh] 153

bladder vessie *f* [vesē] 166

blanket couverture *f* [kōōverter] 75

bleeding hémorragie *f* [āmôräzhē] 169

blinker clignotant *m* [klēnyôtäN] 51

blonde blond [blôN] 194

blood sang *m* [säN] 165; ~ **count** hémogramme *m* [āmōgräm] 172; ~ **poisoning** septicémie *f* [septēsämē] 169; ~ **pressure** tension *f* artérielle [täNsyôN ärtārē·el] 166; ~ **test** analyse *f* de sang [änälēz də säN] 165; prise *f* de sang [prēz də säN] 172; ~ **transfusion** transfusion *f* [träNsfēzyôN] 172

blouse chemisier *m* [shemēzyā] 134

blown *(fuse)* fondu [fôNdē] 55; sauté [sôtā] 88

blow-out crevaison *f* [kreväzôN] 47

blue bleu [blā] 194; **light** ~ bleu clair [blā klār] 194; **navy** ~ bleu foncé [blā fôNsä] 194; ~ **jeans** blue-jeans *m/pl* [blōōdzēn] 134

blueberries airelles *f/pl* [ārel] 110

boar sanglier *m* [säNglēyā] 105

board bord *m* [bôr] 72; échiquier *m* [āshēkyā] 181

boarding house pension *f* [päNsyôN] 81

boarding school internat *m* [eNternä] 38

boat bateau *m* [bätō] 75; **pedal** ~ pédalo *m* [pādälō] 186; ~ **racing** régates *f/pl* [rägät] 187; ~ **trip** promenade *f* en bateau [prômenäd äN bätō] 120

body corps *m* [kôr] 166; *(car)* carrosserie *f* [kärôsrē] 51; ~ **and fender damage** dégâts *m/pl* matériels [dägä mätārē·el] 49

boiled cuit [kē·ē]; bouilli [bōōyē] 100

bolt vis *f* [vēs] 57; ~ **nut** écrou *m* [ākrōō] 57

bone os m [ôs] (pl: [ō]) 166

book livre m [lēv(ər)] 130; **children's ~** livre m pour enfants [lēv(ər) pōōr äNfäN] 130; **guide ~** guide m touristique [gēd tōōrēstēk] 130; **phrase ~** guide m de conversation [gēd də kôNverzäsyôN] 130; **poetry ~** recueil m de poésie [rekä'ē də pō·āzē] 130; **reference ~** ouvrage m de référence [ōōvräzh də räfäräNs] 130; **story ~** livre m de contes [lēv(ər) də kôNt] 130; **text ~** manuel m [mänē·el] 130

bookkeeper comptable m [kôNtäb'əl] 36

bookseller libraire m [lēbrär] 36

bookshop librairie f [lēbrärē] 128; **second-hand ~** librairie f d'occasion [lēbrärē dôkäzyôN] 129

booth cabine f [käbēn] 148

boots bottes f/pl [bôt] 139

border frontière f [frôNtyär] 79; **~ crossing** passage m de la frontière [päsäzh də lä frôNtyär] 80

born né [nā] 34

botanical gardens jardin m botanique [zhärdeN bôtänēk] 120

bother déranger [däräNzhā] 16; importuner [eNpôrtēnā] 154

bottle bouteille f [bōōtä'ē]. 96; **~ opener** décapsuleur m [dākäpsēlär] 143

bouquet bouquet m de fleurs [bōōkā də flär] 130

bow proue f [prōō] 75

bowel movement selle f [sel] 166

bowl terrine f [terēn] 97

bowling bowling m [bōōlēng (bōlēng)] 187; **~ alley** piste f de bowling [pēst də bōōlēng] 181

box (verb) boxer [bôksā] 188; (noun) boîte f [bô·ät] 126; **~ lunch** panier-repas m [pänyä-repä] 86; **~ office** caisse f [kes]; vente f de billets [väNt də bēyä] 177

boxer boxeur m [bôksär] 188

boxing (match m de) boxe f [(mätsh də) bôks] 188

boy garçon m [gärsôN] 35

bra soutien-gorge m [sōōtyeNgôrzh] 134

bracelet bracelet m [bräslä] 133

braces bretelles m/pl [bretel] 136; appareil m (dentaire) [äpärä'ē (däNtär)] 174

brain cerveau m [särvō] 166

brake (verb) freiner [fränā] 43; (noun) frein m [freN] 51; **~ drum** tambour m de frein [täNbōōr də freN] 51; **~ fluid** liquide m de freinage (de freins) [lēkēd də frenäzh (də freN)] 51 (45); **~ lights** feux m/pl de stop [fä də stôp] 51; **~ lining** garniture f de frein [gärnētēr də freN] 51; **~ pedal** pédale f de frein [pādäl də freN] 51

branch manager directeur m de banque [dērektär də bäNk] 151

brandy eau-de-vie f [ōdvē] 112; **apricot ~** liqueur f d'abricot [lēkär däbrēkō] 112; **cherry ~** liqueur f de cerises [lēkär də serēz] 112

brassière soutien-gorge m [sōōtyeNgôrzh] 134

bread pain m [peN] 98; **dark ~** pain m bis [peN bē(s)] 98; **white ~** pain m blanc [peN bläN] 98; **whole wheat ~** pain m complet [peN kôNplä] 98; **~ basket** corbeille f à pain [kôrbä'ē ä peN] 97

break off se casser [se käsā] 173

breakdown panne f [pän] 48

breakfast petit déjeuner m [pətē däzhänā] 83; **eat ~** prendre son petit déjeuner [präNd(ər) sôN pətē däzhänā] 90

breast poitrine f [pô·ätrēn] 166

breathe respirer [respērā] 165

breathing respiration f [respērä-syôN] 166; ~ **problem** troubles m/pl respiratoires [trŏŏb'əl respērätô·är] 169

breeze brise f [brēz] 75

bricklayer maçon m [mäsôN] 36

bridge pont m [pôN] 42; bridge m [brēdzh] 174; passerelle f de manœuvre [päserel də mänäv(ər)] 75

briefcase portefeuille m [pôrtfä'ē], serviette f [servyet] 143

brilliantine brillantine f [brēyäNtēn] 157

bring apporter [äpôrtä] 20; ~ **back** ramener [rämənä] 41

broiler poulet m de grain [pŏŏlä də greN] 105

broken cassé [käsä] 23

bronchitis bronchite f [brôNshēt] 169

broock broche f [brôsh] 133

broth consommé m [kôNsômä] 103; **chicken** ~ potage m de volaille [pôtäzh də vôlä'ē] 103

brother frère m [frär] 35; ~**-in-law** beau-frère m [bō-frär] 35

brown brun [breN] 194; **chestnut** ~ châtain [shäteN] 194

bruise contusion f [kôNtēzyôN] 169

brush brosse f [brôs] 140; **clothes** ~ brosse f à habits [brôs ä äbē] 140

Brussels sprouts chou m de Bruxelles [shŏŏ də brēsel] 108

bucket seau m [sō] 90

buckle boucle f [bŏŏk'əl] 136

building édifice m [ädēfēs] 119

bulb ampoule f [äNpŏŏl] 51; **light** ~ ampoule f (électrique) [äNpŏŏl (älektrēk)] 92

bumper pare-chocs m [pär-shôk] 51

bungalow bungalow m [beNgälō] 81

buoy bouée f [bŏŏ-ä] 75

Burgundy (vin m de) Bourgogne [(veN də) bŏŏrgôn(y)ə] 111

burn (noun) brûlure f [brēlēr] 169

burned out grillé [grēyä] 88

bus autobus m [ôtôbēs] 59; ~ **stop** arrêt m d'autobus [äre dôtôbēs] 59; ~ **terminal** termìnus m [termēnēs] 59

business administration gestion f [zhestyôN] 39; ~ **school** école f de commerce [äkôl də kômers] 38

busy occupé [ôkēpä] 148

butcher boucher m [bŏŏshä] 36

butter beurre m [bär] 98

buttocks fesses f/pl [fes] 166

button bouton m [bŏŏtôN] 136

buttonhole thread fil m pour boutonnières [fēl pŏŏr bŏŏtônyär] 136

buy acheter [äshtä] 126

C

cabaña cabine f [käbēn] 185

cabbage chou m [shŏŏ] 108

cabin cabine f [käbēn] 73; **double** ~ cabine f de deux personnes [käbēn də dä persôn] 73; **inside** ~ cabine f intérieure [käbēn eNtärē·är] 73; **outside** ~ cabine f extérieure [käbēn ekştärē·är] 73; **single** ~ cabine f individuelle [käbēn eNdēvēdē·el] 73

cabinetmaker ébéniste m [äbänēst] 36

cable câble m [käb'əl] 51

cake gâteau m [gätō] 113

calf mollet m [môlä] 166

call (verb) faire venir [fär venēr] 123; appeler [äplä] 48; (noun) communication f [kômēnēkäsyôN] 148; **long distance** ~ communication f interurbaine (internationale) [kômēnēkäsyôN eNterērben(eNternäsyônäl)] 148; **person to person** ~ **communication** f avec avis d'appel [kômênêkäsyôN ävek ävê däpel] 150; **make a phone** ~ téléphoner [täläfônä] 147; **give (someone) a** ~ téléphoner à [täläfônä ä] 17

camera appareil m photographique [äpärä'ê fôtôgräfêk] 153

camomile tea infusion f camomille [eNfêzyôN kämômê·ê] 160

camp camper [käNpä] 94; ~ **bed** lit m pliant [lê plê·äN] 95; ~ **site** terrain m de camping [tereN də käN-pêng] 94; ~ **stove** réchaud m à alcool [räshô ä älkôl] 143

camping camping m [käNpêng] 95; ~ **ID** carte f de l'A.C.C.F. [kärt dəlä sä·sä·ef] 95; ~ **site** terrain m de camping [tereN də käNpêng] 81; ~ **trailer** caravane f [kärävän] 40

camshaft arbre m à cames [ärbrä-käm] 51

can pouvoir [pōōvô·är] 18

can opener ouvre-boîte m [ōōv(ər) bô·ät] 143

canal canal m [känäl] 75

cancel annuler [änêlä] 69

cancellation fee taxe f d'annulation [täks dänêläsyôN] 69

cancer cancer m [käNsär] 169

candle bougie f [bōōzhê] 143

candlestick bougeoir m [bōōzhô·är] 143; chandelier m [shäNdelêyä] 124

candy bonbon m [bôNbôN]; chocolat m [shôkôlä] 113

canned goods conserves f/pl [kôN-särv] 143

cap casquette f [käsket] 134

capers câpres f/pl [käp(ər)] 100

capital capitale f [käpëtäl] 120

captain capitaine m [käpëten] 75;

~**'s table** table f du commandant [täb(əl) dê kômäNdäN] 75

car voiture f [vô·ätər] 40; auto f [ôtô] 73; ~ **door** portière f [pôrtyär] 52; ~ **ferry** ferry-boat [ferê-bôt] 72; ~ **key** clé f de la voiture [klä də lä vô·ätər] 52; ~ **repair service** service-entretien m [servês-äNtrətyeN] 45; **go by** ~ aller en voiture [älä äN vô·ätër] 42

carafe carafe f [käräf] 97

caraway cumin m [kêmeN] 101

carburetor carburateur m [kärbêrä-tär] 52; ~ **jet** gicleur m [zhêklär] 52

card carte f [kärt] 145; **greeting** ~ carte f de salutations [kärt də sä-lêtäsyôN] 145; **greeting** ~ **telegram** télégramme m avec carte [tälägräm ävek kärt] 147; **post** ~ carte f postale [kärt pôstäl] 145; **picture post** ~ carte f postale illustrée [kärt pôstäl êlêsträ] 145; ~ **game** jeu m de cartes [zhä də kärt] 181

cardiac infarction infarctus m du myocarde [eNfärktês dê mê·ôkärd] 169

cardigan veste f de tricot [vest də] trêkô] 134

cardiovascular drug remède m pour la circulation [remäd pōōr lä sêrkêläsyôN] 160

careful! attention! [ätäNsyôN] 49

carp carpe f [kärp] 104

carpenter menuisier m [menê·êzyä] 36

carpet tapis m [täpê] 90

carrot carotte f [kärôt] 107

cartoon dessin m animé [deseN änêmä] 179

cash (adj.) comptant [kôNtäN] 152

cassette cassette f [käset] 143

castle château m [shätô] 119;

(chess) tour f [tōōr] 181

castor oil huile f de ricin [ē·ēl də rē·seN] 160

catalogue catalogue m [kätälôg] 130

category catégory f [kätägôrē] 90

cathedral cathédrale f [kätädräl] 124

cave caverne f [kävärn] 120

cavities cave f [käv] 174

ceiling plafond m [pläfôN] 90

celery céleri m [sälerē] 107

cellar cave f [käv] 90

cemetery cimetière m [sēmetyär] 120

center strip bande f médiane [bäNd mädē·än] 42

centimeter centimètre m [säNtē-mät(ər)] 193

ceramics céramique f [särämēk] 143

cereal céréales f/pl [särā·äl] 98

certainly certainement [sär-ten·mäN] 21; **~!** bien entendu! [byeN äNtäNdē] 20; **~ not** en aucun cas [äNôkeN kä] 21

chain chaîne f [shän] 52

chair chaise f [shäz] 90; **deck ~** chaise f longue [shäz·lôNg] 91

chamber music musique f de chambre [mēzēk də shäNb(ər)] 177

championship championnat m [shäNpyônä] 188

change *(noun)* monnaie f [mônä] 151; *(verb)* changer [shäNzhä] 46, 151; *(buses, trains)* changer de [shäNzhä də] 59; *(wind)* tourner [tōōrnä] 26

chapel chapelle f [shäpel] 124

charcoalpills poudre f de charbon [pōōd(ər) də shärbôN] 160

charge *(battery)* recharger [reshärzhä] 51

charter plane charter m [shärtär] 70

chassis chassis m de la voiture [shäsē də lä vô·ätēr] 52

chat bavarder [bävärdä] 183

chauffeur chauffeur m [shôfär] 41

check *(noun)* addition f [ädēsyôN] 115; chèque m [shek] 151; *(verb)* vérifier [värēfē·ä] 45; **~ over** contrôler [kôNtrôlä] 52; **~ room** vestiaire m [vestyär] 177; **traveller's ~** chèque m de voyage [shek də vô·äyäzh] 127

checked quadrillé [kädrēyä] 137

checkers (jeu m de) dames [(zhä də) däm] 181

check-in déclaration f de séjour [dāklärāsyôN də sāzhōōr] 90

check-out déclaration f de départ [däklärāsyôN də däpär] 95

cheek joue f [zhōō] 166

cheers! à votre santé! [ä vôt(ər) säNtä] 99

cheese fromage m [frômäzh] 109; **blue ~** bleu m d'Auvergne [blā dōvärn(yə)] 109; **cottage ~** fromage m blanc [frômäzh bläN] 109; **cream ~** fromage m à pâte molle [frômäzh ä pät môl] 109; **Swiss ~** gruyère m [grēyär] 109; **~ spread** fromage m à tartiner [frômäzh ä tärtēnä] 109

chef chef cuisinier m [shef kē·ēzēnyä] 36

chemistry chimie f [shēmē] 39

cherries cerises f/pl [serēz] 110

chess échecs m/pl [āshek] 180

chessman pièce f [pyäs] 181

chest poitrine f [pô·ätrēn] 166

chicken poule f [pōōl] 105; **~ breast** blanc m de poulet [bläN də pōōlä] 105; **~ pox** varicelle f [värēsel] 169

child enfant m [äNfäN] 34

chills frissons m/pl [frēsôN] 164

chin menton *m* [mäNtôN] 166
china porcelaine *f* [pôrsəlen] 143
chip jeton *m* [zhetôN] 181
chisel ciseau *m* [sēzō] 57
chives civette *f* [sēvet] 101
chocolate chocolat *m* [shôkôlä] 113; **~ with ice cream** chocolat *m* glacé [shôkôlä gläsā] 113
choir chœur *m* [kœr] 124
cholera choléra *m* [kôlärä] 169
chop côtelette *f* [kôtlet] 106
chorus chœur *m* [kœr] 177
christening baptême *m* [bätām] 123
church église *f* [āglēz] 124; **Catholic ~** église *f* catholique [āglēz kätôlēk] 116; **Protestant ~** temple *m* [täNpʼəl] 116
churchyard cimetière *m* [sēmetyär] 124
cider cidre *m* [sēd(ər)] 111
cigar cigare *m* [sēgär] 140
cigarette cigarette *f* [sēgäret] 140; **filtered ~** cigarette *f* à bout filtre [sēgäret ä bōō fēlt(ər)] 140; **unfiltered ~** cigarette *f* sans filtre [sēgäret säN fēltr(ər)] 140
cinema cinéma *m* [sēnämä] 179
cinnamon cannelle *f* [känel] 101
circle traffic sens *m* giratoire [säNs zhērätô·är] 43
circulatory problem troubles *m/pl* circulatoires [trōōbʼəl sērkēlätô·är] 169
circus cirque *m* [sērk] 181
city ville *f* [vēl] 120; **~ hall** hôtel *m* de ville [ōtel də vēl] 120
civil servant fonctionnaire *m* [fôNksyônär] 36
claim *(luggage)* retirer [retērā] 63; **~ check** bulletin *m* d'enregistrement [bēlteN däNrezhēstrəmäN] 63
class classe *f* [kläs] 73; **first ~** première classe *f* [prəmyär kläs] 73;

tourist ~ classe *f* touriste [kläs tōōrēst] 73
clean *(out)* nettoyer [netô·äyā] 47
clear *(sky)* dégagé [dāgäzhā] 26
clergyman prêtre *m* [prät(ər)], curé *m* [kērā] 36
climate climat *m* [klēmä] 26
climb s'élever [sāləvā] 70
clock montre *f* [môNt(ər)] 31; **alarm ~** réveil *m* [rāvā'ē] 143; **it's... o'clock** il est ... heure(s) [ēlä ... är] 30
close fermer [fermā] 18
closet placard *m* [pläkär] 91
cloth chiffon *m* [shēfôN] 57; drap *m* [drä] 136
clothes hanger cintre *m* [seNt(ər)] 87
cloud nuage *m* [nē·äzh] 26; **~ cover** nuages *m/pl* [nē·äzh] 26
cloudburst pluie *f* torrentielle [plē·ē tôräNsyel] 26
cloudy couvert [kōōvär] 26; **~ skies** nuages *m/pl.* [nē·äzh] 26
cloves clous *m/pl* de girofle [klōō də zhērôfʼəl] 101
club club *m* [klēb] 181
clubs trèfle *m* [träfʼəl] 181
clutch embrayage *m* [äNbräyäzh] 52; **~ pedal** pédale *f* d'embrayage [pädäl däNbräyäzh] 52
coast côte *f* [kôt] 75
coastal road route *f* côtière [rōōt kôtyär] 43
coat manteau *m* [mäNtō] 134; **~ check** ticket *m* de vestiaire [tēkä də vestyär] 177
cobbler cordonnier *m* [kôrdônyā] 36
coconut coco *m* [kôkō] 110
cod cabillaud *m* [käbēyō]; morue *f* [môrē] 104
c.o.d. remboursement *m* [räNbōōrsmäN] 149

coffee café *m* [käfā] 98; **black ~** café *m* noir [käfā nô·är] 98; **decaffeinated ~** café *m* décaféiné [käfā dākäfā·ēnā] 98; **~ with cream** café *m* au lait [käfā ō lā] 98; **~ with sugar** café *m* avec du sucre [käfā avek dē sēk(ər)] 98

cognac cognac *m* [kônyäk] 112

coin jeton *m* [zhetôN] 148; pièce *f* de monnaie [pyäs də mônā] 152; **~ changer** changeur *m* de monnaie automatique [shäNzhär də mônā ôtōmätēk] 149

cold *(noun)* rhume *m* [rēm] 169; *(adj.)* froid [frô·ä] 25; **I'm ~** j'ai froid [zhā frô·ä] 25; **~ cuts** tranches *f/pl* de charcuterie [träNsh də shärkētərē] 98; assiette *f* anglaise [äsyet äNglāz] 102; **~ wave** permanente *f* à froid [pärmänäNt ä frô·ä] 158

colic colique *f* [kôlēk] 169

collarbone clavicule *f* [klävēkēl] 166

collect call communication *f* payable à l'arrivée [kômēnēkäsyôN päyäb'əl älärēvā] 149

collision collision *f* [kôlēzyôN] 49

color couleur *f* [kōōlär] 127; **~ of eye** couleur *f* des yeux [kōōlär dā·zyā] 79; **~ of hair** couleur *f* des cheveux [kōōlär dā shevä] 79

colored coloré [kôlôrā] 194

colorful multicolore [mēltēkôlôr] 194

comb *(noun)* peigne *m* [pen(yə)] 140; *(verb)* peigner [penyā] 158

come venir [vənēr] 16; **~ in** *(train)* arriver [ärēvā] 61; **~ in!** entrez! [äNtrā] 16

comedy comédie *f* [kômädē] 177

communion communion *f* [kômēnyôN] 124

compact poudrier *m* [pōōdrēyā] 140

compartment compartiment *m*

[kôNpärtēmäN] 67

compass boussole *f* [bōōsôl] 138

competition compétition *f* [kôNpātēsyôN] 188

complaint réclamation *f* [rāklämäsyôN] 91; **register (make) a ~** faire une réclamation [fār ēn rāklämäsyôN] 23

composer compositeur *m* [kôNpōzētär] 177

compression compression *f* [kôNpresyôN] 52

concert concert [kôNsār] 177; **~ hall** salle *f* de concert [säl də kôNsär] 177

concierge concierge · *m* [kôNsyärzh], portier *m* [pôrtyā] 91

concussion commotion *f* cérébrale [kômôsyôN särābräl] 169

condenser condensateur *m* [kôNdāNsätär] 52

condolences condoléances *f/pl* [kôNdôlā·äNs] 23

conductor contrôleur *m* [kôNtrôlär] 67; chef *m* d'orchestre [shef dôrkest(ər)] 177

confectioner pâtissier *m* [pätēsyā] 36

confectionery pâtisserie *f* (fine) [pätēsərē (fēn)] 113

confesse se confesser [sə kôNfesā] 124

confession confession *f* [kôNfesyôN] 124

confiscate confisquer [kôNfēskā] 154

congratulations! mes félicitations! [mā felēsētäsyôN] 22

conjunctivitis conjonctivite *f* [kôNzhôNktēvēt] 169

connecting rod bielle *f* [byel] 52; **~ bearing** coussinet *m* de tête de bielle [kōōsēnā də tāt də byel] 52

connection correspondance *f* [kôrespôNdäNs] 61

constipated constipé [kôNstēpä] 163

constipation constipation f [kôNstē-päsyôN] 169

consulate consulat m [kôNsẽlä] 78

contact contact m [kôNtäkt] 52; ~ **lenses** verres m/pl de contact [vär də kôNtäkt] 138

contraceptive pills pilules f/pl contraceptives [pēlẽl kôNträseptẽv] 160

convalescent home maison f de convalescence [mäzôN də kôNvä-lesäNs] 175

convent couvent m [kōōväN] 124

cook (verb) préparer les repas [prä-pärā lā repä] 95; (noun) cuisinier m [kē-ēzēnyā] 36

cookies petits gâteaux secs m/pl [pətē gätō sāk] 113

cooking utensils ustensiles m/pl de cuisine [ēstäNsēl də kē-ēzēn] 95

coolant fluide m réfrigérant [flē-ēd räfrēzhäräN] 45

cordial cordial [kôrdyäl] 12

corduroy velours m côtelé [velōōr kōtlä] 136

corkscrew tire-bouchon m [tēr-bōōshôN] 143

corn plaster pansement m pour les cors [päNsmäN pōōr lā kôr] 160

corner coin m [kô·eN] 120; (sports) corner m [kôrnär] 189

correct exact [egsäkt] 115

corridor corridor m [kôrēdôr]; couloir m [kōōlô·är] 91

corset corselet m [kôrselä]; corset m [kôrsä] 134

cosmetic salon institut m de beauté [eNstētē də bôtā] 128

cost coûter [kōōtä] 18; **how much does it ~?** combien dois-je payer? [kôNbyeN dô·äzh päyā] 69

costume costume m [kôstēm] 177; ~ **designer** costumier m [kôstē-myä] 177

cotton coton m [kôtôN] 136; ~ **swabs** cotons-tiges m/pl [kôtôN-tēzh] 160

couchette car, couchette sleeper voiture-couchette f [vô·ätēr-kōō-shet] 64, 60

cough (verb) **tousser** [tōōsä] 165; (noun) toux f [tōō] 169; ~ **medicine** remède m (sirop m) contre la toux [remäd (sērō) kôNt(ər) lä tōō] 160

counter guichet m [gēshä] 149

country fair fête f populaire [fãt pô-pēlär] 181

country road route f de campagne [rōōt də käNpän(yə)] 43

countryside paysage m [pā-ēzäzh] 120

course route f [rōōt] 75

court tribunal m [trēbēnäl] 154

courthouse palais m de Justice [pä-lä də zhēstēs] 120

cousin (male) cousin m [kōōzeN] 35; (female) cousine f [kōōzēn] 35

cover housse f d'édredon [hōōs dä-dredôN] 90

covered market marché m couvert [märshä kōōvär] 120

coxswain barreur m [bärär] 189

cramp crampe f [kräNp] 169

cranberries airelles f/pl rouges [ärel rōōzh] 110

crankshaft vilebrequin m [vēlbre-keN] 52

crawfish écrevisse f [ākrevēs] 104

crayons crayons m/pl de couleur [kräyôN də kōōlär] 138

cream crème f [krām] 141, 113; **face ~** crème f (pour le visage) [krām (pōōr lə vēzäzh)] 141; **whipped ~** Chantilly f [shäntēyē] 113

credit crédit *m* [krādē] 152; ~ **card** carte *f* de crédit [kärt də krādē] 152; **letter of** ~ lettre *f* de crédit [let(ər) də krādē] 152

creed profession *f* de foi [prôfesyôN də fô·ä] 124

crew équipage *m* [äkēpäzh] 70

crib lit *m* d'enfant [lē däNfäN] 83

crime crime *m* [krēm] 154

criminal criminel *m* [krēmēnel] 154; ~ **investigation division** police *f* judiciaire [pôlēs zhēdēsyär] 154

cross croix *f* [krô·ä] 124; ~ **road** route *f* secondaire [rōōt səgôN-där] 43

crossing traversée *f* [träversā] 72

crown couronne *f* [kōōrôn] 174

crucifix crucifix *m* [krēsēfē] 124

cruet stand huilier *m* [ē·ēlēyā] 97

cruise croisière *f* [krô·äzyär] 75

crystal verre *m* [vär] 143

cucumber concombre *m* [kôN-kôNb(ər)] 108

cufflinks boutons *m/pl* de manchette [bōōtôN də mäNshet] 133

cup tasse *f* [täs] 96

cure cure *f* [kēr] 175; ~ **tax** taxe *f* de cure [täks də kēr] 175; ~ **vacation** cure *f* [kēr] 175; **rest** ~ cure *f* de repos [kēr də rəpô] 175

curler bigoudi *m* [bēgōōdē], rouleau *m* [rōōlō] 141

curls boucles *f/pl* [bōōk'əl] 158

currency monnaie *f* [mônā] 152; **foreign** ~ devises *f/pl.* [dəvēz] 152

curtain rideau *m* [rēdō] 91; ~ **time** lever *m* du rideau [ləvā dē rēdō] 177; **final** ~ fin *f* [feN] 177

curve virage *m* [vēräzh] 42

cuspid canine *f* [känēn] 174

custody détention *f* [dātäNsyôN] 154; **pre-trial** ~ détention *f* préventive [dätäNsyôN prāväNtēv] 154

customs douane *f* [dōō·än] 80; ~ **control** passage *m* de la douane [päsäzh də lä dōō·än] 80; ~ **declaration** déclaration *f* de douane [däklärāsyôN də dōō·än] 146; ~ **examination** contrôle *m* de douane [kôNtrôl də dōō·än] 80; ~ **office** bureau *m* de douane [bērō də dōō·än] 80; ~ **officer** douanier *m* [dōō·änyā] 80

cut *(verb)* couper [kōōpā] 155, 181; *(noun)* coupure *f* [kōōpēr] 169

cutlery couvert *m* [kōōvär] 97

cylinder cylindre *m* [sēleNd(ər)] 52; ~ **head** culasse *f* [kēläs] 52; ~ **head gasket** joint *m* de culasse [zhô·eN də kēläs] 52

Canadian dollars dollars *m/pl* canadiens [dôlär känädyeN] 152

Catholic catholique [kätôlēk] 124; **Roman** ~ catholique romain [kätôlek rômeN] 124

Christ Christ *m* [krēst] 124

Christian chrétien *m* [krātyeN] 124

Christianity christianisme *m* [krēstyänēsm] 124

Christmas Noël *m* [nô·el] 33; **merry ~!** joyeux Noël! [zhô·äyä nô·el] 23

D

daily tous les jours [tōō lā zhōōr] 31; ~ **rate** cours *m* du jour [kōōr dē zhōōr] 152

dairy crèmerie *f* [krämerē] 128

damage *(noun)* dommages *m/pl* [dômäzh] 49

dance *(verb)* danser [däNsā] 183; *(noun)* danse *f* [däNs] 183; ~ **hall** dancing *m* [däNsēng] 183

dancer danseur *m* [däNsär]; danseuse *f* [däNsäz] 177

dandruff pellicules *f/pl* [pelēkēl] 158

dangerous dangereux [däNzhərā] 185

dark *(colour)* foncé [föNsā] 127

darn repriser [reprēzā] 137

darning cotton coton *m* à repriser [kôtôN ä reprēzā] 136

darning-wool laine *f* à repriser [len ä reprēzā] 136

date of birth date *f* de naissance [dät də nesäNs] 79

daughter fille *f* [fēyē] 35

dawn aube *f* [ōb] 26

day jour *m* [zhōōr]; journée *f* [zhōōrnā] 31; **New Year's Day** jour *m* de l'an [zhōōr də läN] 33; **~ room** salle *f* commune [säl kômēn] 95

dead-end street voie *f* sans issue [vô·ä säNsēsē] 120

deal donner [dônā] 181

dealership garage garage *m* concessionnaire [gäräzh kôNsesyôNār] 49

decanter carafe *f* [käräf] 97

December décembre *m* [dāsäNb(ər)] 33

deck pont *m* [pôN] 75; **boat ~** pont *m* des embarcations [pôN dāzäNbärkäsyôN] 75; **fore ~** plage *f* avant [pläzh äväN] 75; **main ~** pont *m* principal [pôN preNsēpäl] 76; **poop ~** plage *f* arrière [pläzh äryär] 76; **promenade ~** pont-promenade *m* [pôN-prômənäd] 76; **saloon ~** pont *m* de première classe [pôN də prəmyär kläs] 76; **sun ~** sundeck *m* [sändek] 76; **upper ~** pont *m* supérieur [pôN sēpārē·ār] 76; **~ chair** transat(lantique) *m* [träNsät(läNtēk] 76

declare déclarer [dāklārā] 80

deeply profondément [prôfôNdāmäN] 165

defeat défaite *f* [dāfāt] 188

delicious délicieux [dālēsyä] 99

delivery truck camionette *f* [kämyônet] 40

dental clinic clinique *f* dentaire [klēnēk däNtār] 174

dentist dentiste *m, f* [däNtēst] 36

dentistry études *f/pl* dentaires [ātēd däNtär] 39

denture dentition *f* [däNtēsyôN] 174

deodorant déodorant *m* [dā·ōdôräN] 141

depart partir [pärtēr] 67

departure départ *m* [dāpär] 67; sortie *f* [sôrtē] 79

deposit *(noun)* accompte *m* [äkôNt] 83; arrhes *f/pl* [är] 91; versement *m* [versmäN] 152; *(verb)* verser une caution [versā ēn kôsyôN] 41

dermatologist dermatologue *m* [därmätōlôg] 162

destination lieu *m* de destination [lēyä də destēnäsyôN] 149

detergent détergent *m* [dāterzhäN] 143; **dishwashing ~** détergent *m* à vaisselle [dāterzhäN ä väsel] 143

detour déviation *f* [dāvē·äsyôN] 42

develop développer [dāvelôpā] 131

development développement *m* [dāvelôpmäN] 132

dew rosée *f* [rōzā] 26

dextrose glucose *m* [glēkôz] 160

diabetes diabète *m* [dē·äbät] 170

diabetic diabéthique [dē·äbätēk] 164

diagnosis diagnostic *m* [dē·ägnôstēk] 172

dial *(noun)* cadran *m* [kädräN] 149; *(verb)* composer le numéro [kôNpōzā lə nēmārō] 149

diamond brillant *m* [brēyäN] 133

diamonds carreau *m* [kärō] 181

diaphoretic sudorifique [sēdôrēfēk] 160

diaphragm diaphragme *m* [dē·äfrägm] 132

diarrhea diarrhée f [dē·ärā] 170

dice dē m [dā] 181; **shoot ~** jouer aux dés [zhōō·ā ō dā] 181

dictionary dictionnaire m [dĕksyô-när] 130

diesel diesel m [dyezel] 45; **~ motor** moteur m diesel [môtär dyezel] 54; **~ nozzle** gicleur m diesel [zhĕklär dyezel] 52

diet régime m [räzhēm]; diète f [dē·āt] 175

differential différentiel m [dēfäräN-syel] 52

digestion digestion f [dēzhestyôN] 166

digestive tablets comprimés m/pl pour la digestion [kôNprēmā pōōr lä dēzhestyôN] 160

digestive tonic gouttes f/pl pour la digestion [gōōt pōōr lä dēzhe-styôN] 160

dinghy canot m pneumatique [känō pnämätēk] 186

dining car wagon-restaurant m [vä-gôN restôräN] 60

dining room salle f à manger [sälä mäNzhā] 74

dinner dîner m [dēnā] 91

dip stick réglette-jauge f [räglet-zhōzh] 52

diphtheria diphthérie f [dēftärē] 170

dipped headlights feux m/pl de croisement [fä də krô·äz·mäN] 53

direct direct [dērekt] 68; **~ dial** faire un numéro interurbain automatique [fär eN nēmärō eNterĕrbeN ôtōmätēk] 147; **~ dialing** automatique m [ôtōmätēk] 149

direction direction f [dēreksyôN] 59; **~ sign** panneau m indicateur [pä-nō eNdēkätär] 42

director metteur m en scène [metär äN sän] 177

disc disque m [dēsk] 166; **~ brake**

frein m à disques [freN ä dēsk] 51

discharge sortie f de clinique [sôrtē də klēnēk] 172

discotheque discothèque f [dēskô-tāk] 180

discount réduction f [rādēksyôN] 176

disease maladie f [mälädē] 170; **contagious ~** maladie f conta-gieuse [mälädē kôNtäzhē·āz] 170

disembark débarquer [dābärkā] 76

disengage débrayer [dābräyā] 53

dish plat m [plä] 99

dishes vaisselle f [vāsel] 95

disinfectant désinfectant m [däzeN-fektäN] 160

dislocation luxation f [lēksäsyôN] 170

distilled water eau f distillée [ō dē-stēlā] 45

distributor distributeur m [dēstrē-bētär] 52

district région f [räzhē·ôN] 120

ditch fossé m [fôsā] 120

diuretic diurétique m [dē·ērätēk] 160

dive (verb) plonger [plôNzhā] 186; (noun) plongeon m [plôNzhôN] 190

diving board plongeoir m [plôN-zhô·är] 190

divorced divorcé [dēvôrsā] 79

dizziness vertige m [värtēzh] 170

dock (noun) débarcadère f [däbär-kädār] 76; (verb) aborder [äbôrdā] 76; faire escale [fär eskäl] 72

doctor médecin m [mādəseN] 36; (in names) monsieur m le Docteur [məsyē lə dôktär] 13; **doctor's offi-ce** cabinet m de consultation [kä-bēnä də kôNsēltäsyôN] 163

documentary (film m) documen-taire m [(fēlm) dôkēmäNtär] 179

doll poupée f [pōōpā] 143

dome coupole f [kōōpôl] 125

door porte f [pôrt] 91; ~ **handle** poignée f [pô·änyä] 91; ~ **lock** serrure f de la portière [serēr də lä pôrtyär] 52

dormitory dortoir m [dôrtô·är] 95

doubles double m [dōōb'əl] 189

downtown area centre m (de la) ville [säNt(ər) (dəlä) vēl] 120

dozen douzaine f [dōōzän] 193

draft courant m d'air [kōōräN där] 26

drain lavabo m [läväbō] 88

drama drame m [dräm] 177

drapery rideau m [rēdō] 91

draw (verb) faire un coup [fär eN kōō] 181; (noun) match m nul [mätsh nēl] 188

drawer tiroir m [tērô·är] 91

dress robe f [rôb] 134

dressing gown robe f de chambre [rôb də shäNb(ər)] 134

dressmaker tailleur m [täyär] 36

dress-shield dessous m de bras [dəsōō də brä] 136

drier séchoir m [sāshô·är] 156

drill foret m [fôrä] 57

drink (verb) boire [bô·är] 165; (noun) boisson f [bô·äsoN] 96

drinking water eau f potable [ō pô·täb'əl] 65

drip goutter [gōōtä] 88

drip-dry sans repassage [säN repäsäzh] 135

drive aller [älä] 42; rouler [rōōlä] 50

drive shaft arbre m moteur (de couche) [ärb(ər) môtär (də kōōsh)] 52

driver chauffeur m [shôfär] 36; conducteur m [kôNdēktär] 55

driver's licence permis m de conduire [permē də kôNdē·ēr] 42

driver's seat siège m du conducteur [syäzh dē kôNdēktär] 55

driveway entrée f [äNtrā] 42

driving instructor moniteur m d'auto-école [mônētär dôtô-äkôl] 36

drops gouttes f/pl [gōōt] 160; **ear** ~ gouttes f/pl pour les oreilles [gōōt pōōr läzôrä·ē] 160; **eye** ~ gouttes f/pl pour les yeux [gōōt pōōr lāzyā] 161

druggist (pharmacist) pharmacien m [färmäsyeN] 36; (drugstore owner) droguiste m [drôgēst] 36

drugs drogues f/pl [drôg] 154

dry sécher [sāshā] 92; ~ **cleaner's** nettoyage m à sec [netô·äyäzh ä sek] 128; ~ **goods** mercerie f [märserē] 136

dubbed synchronisé [seNkrônēzä] 179

dubbing synchronisation f [seNkrônēzäsyôN] 179

duck canard m [känär] 105; **wild** ~ canard m sauvage [känär sôväzh] 105

duet duo m [dē·ō] 177

dune dune f [dēn] 186

dusk crépuscule m [krāpēskēl] 26

duty droits m/pl de douane [drô·ä də dōō·än] 80; **pay** ~ déclarer [däklärä] 80; **in** ~ **free** en franchise [äN fräNshēz] 80; **export** ~ droits m/pl de sortie [drô·ä də sôrtē] 80; **import** ~ droits m/pl d'entrée [drô·ä däNtrā] 80

dye teinture f [teNtēr] 141

dynamo dynamo f [dēnämō] 52

dysentery dysenterie f [dēzäNtərē] 170

E

ear clips clips m/pl [klēp] 133

earache mal m aux oreilles [mäl ôzôrä·ē] 164

eardrum tympan *m* [teNpäN] 166

earlier plus tôt [plē tō] 32

early tôt [tō] 31

earrings boucles *f/pl* d'oreille [bōōk'əl dôrä·ē] 133

Easter Pâques *m* [päk] 33

economics économie *f* [ākônômē] 39

economy class classe *f* économique [kläs äkônōmēk] 69

education *(subject)* pédagogie *f* [pädägōzhē] 39

eel anguille *f* [äNgē'ē] 104; **smoked** ~ anguille *f* fumée [äNgē'ē fēmä] 102

egg œuf *m* [äf] 98; **hard-boiled** ~ œuf *m* dur [äf dēr] 98; **soft-boiled** ~ œuf *m* à la coque [äf älä kôk] 98; **ham and eggs** œufs *m/pl* au jambon [ä ō zhäNbôN] 98; **fried eggs** œufs *m/pl* sur le plat [ä sēr lə plä] 98; **scrambled eggs** œufs *m/pl* brouillés [ä brōōyä] 98; ~ **cup** coquetier *m* [kôketyä] 97

eight huit [ē·ēt] 28

eighty quatre-vingts [kätrəveN] 28

elastic élastique *m* [älästēk] 136; ~ **bandage** bande *f* élastique [bäNd älästēk] 160; ~ **stocking** bas *m* élastique [bä älästēk] 160

elbow coude *m* [kōōd] 166

electric shaver rasoir *m* électrique [räzô·är älektrēk] 141

electrician électricien *m* [älektrēsyeN] 36

elevator ascenseur *m* [äsäNsär] 91

emerald émeraude *f* [ämerōd] 133

emergency: ~ **brake** signal *m* d'alarme [sēnyäl dälärm] 66; ~ **chute** glissoire *f* de secours [glēsô·är də səkōōr] 70; ~ **exit** sortie *f* de secours [sôrtē də səkōōr] 70; ~ **landing** atterrissage *m* forcé [äterēsäzh fôrsä] 70; ~ **ward** poste *m* de secours [pôst də səkōōr] 49

emetic vomitif *m* [vômētēf] 160

enema lavement *m* [lävmäN] 160

engine réacteur *m* [rä·äktär] 71; *(railroad)* locomotive *f* [lōkōmōtēv] 67

engeneer *(scientific)* ingénieur *m* [eNzhänyär] 36; *(railroad)* mécanicien *m* [mäkänēsyeN] 36

English anglais [äNglä] 24; *(subject)* langue *f* et littérature *f* anglaises [läNgä lētärätēr äNglāz] 39

enjoy oneself s'amuser [sämēzä] 184

enlargement agrandissement *m* [ägräNdēs·mäN] 131

enough assez [äsä] 46

entrance entrée *f* [äNträ] 67

entry entrée *f* [äNträ] 79; ~ **visa** visa *m* d'entrée [vēzä däNträ] 79

envelope enveloppe *f* [äNvelôp] 138

environs environs *m/pl* [äNvērôN] 120

eraser gomme *f* [gôm] 138

Eve; New Year's ~ Saint-Sylvestre *f* [seN sēlvest(ər)] 33

evening soir *m* [sô·är] 155; soirée *f* [sô·ärä] 16; **good** ~! bonsoir! [bôNsô·är] 12; **in the** ~ le soir [lə sô·är] 31; **this** ~ ce soir [sə sô·är] 31

every day tous les jours [tōō lā zhōōr] 31

everything tout [tōō] 83

exact exact [egzä(kt)] 30

exactly exactement [egzäktəmäN] 30

examination examen *m* [egzämeN]; analyse *f* [änälēz] 172

examine examiner [egzämēnä] 172

excavations fouilles *f/pl* [fōō'ē] 120

excess baggage bagages *m/pl* en excédent [bägäzh äN eksädäN] 68

exchange *(verb)* échanger [āshäN-zhā] 127; **rate of ~** cours *m* de change [kōōr də shäNzh] 152

excursion excursion *f* [ekskẽrsyôN] 72; **~ program** programme *m* d'excursion [prôgräm dekskẽr-syôN] 76; **land excursions** excursions *f/pl* (à terre) [ekskẽrsyôN (ä tär)] 76

excuse me! excusez-moi! [ekskẽzä-mô·ä] 22

excuse me? vous permettez? [vōō permetā] 20

exhaust échappement *m* [āshäp·-mäN] 52

exhibition exposition *f* [ekspōzē-syôN] 119

exit sortie *f* [sôrtē] 42; **~ visa** visa *m* de sortie [vēzä də sôrtē] 79

expect attendre [ätäNd(ər)] 85

expensive cher [shär] 127

exposure exposition *f* [ekspōzē-syôN] 132; **~ meter** posemètre *m* [pōzmät(ər)] 132

express train train *m* direct [treN dẽrekt]; express *m* [ekspres] 60

expressway autoroute *f* [ôtōrōōt] 58

extend prolonger [prōlôNzhā] 79

extension cord rallonge *f* [rälôNzh] 91

external externe [ekstärn] 159

extra week semaine *f* supplémentaire [semen sēplāmäNtär] 91

extract arracher [äräshā]; extraire [ekstrār] 174

eye œil *m* (*pl* yeux) [ä'ē (*pl* yā)] 166; **~ doctor** oculiste *m* [ôkēlēst] 162; **~ inflammation** inflammation *f* de l'œil [eNflämäsyôN də lä'ē] 170; **~ liner** crayon *m* (à paupières) [krāyôN (ä pôpyär)] 141; **~ shadow** ombre *f* à paupières [ôNbrä pôpyär] 141

eyeball globe *m* oculaire [glôb ôkē-lär] 166

eyebrows sourcils *m/pl* [sōōrsē] 156

eyebrow pencil crayon *m* à sourcils [krāyôN ä sōōrsē] 141

eyeglass case étui *m* à lunettes [ātē·ē ä lẽnet] 138

eyelid paupière *f* [pōpyär] 166

F

fabric tissu *m* [tēsē], étoffe *f* [ätôf] 137

face visage *m* [vēzazh] 166; *(of a clock)* cadran *m* [kädräN] 143; **~ massage** massage *m* facial [mä-säzh fäsyäl] 156

facial mask masque *m* facial [mäsk fäsyäl] 156

factory usine *f* [ēzēn] 120

fall *(verb)* faire une chute [fär ēn shēt] 164; *(barometer)* descendre [desäNd(ər)] 25; *(noun: season)* automne *m* [ôtôn] 33

falling rocks chute *f* de pierres [shēt də pyär] 42

false tooth fausse dent *f* [fôs däN] 174

family famille *f* [fämē·ē] 35

fan ventilateur *m* [väNtēlätär] 53; **~ belt** courroie *f* trapézoidale [kōō-rô·ä träpäzō·ēdäl] 53

far loin [lô·eN] 40

fare prix *m* du billet [prē dē bēyā] 62; **~ discount** tarif *m* réduit [tä-rēf rädē·ē] 67

farewell dinner dîner *m* d'adieu [dēnā dädyā] 76

farmer agriculteur *m* [ägrēkēltär] 36

farmhouse ferme *f* [färm] 120

far-sighted presbyte [presbēt] 138

fashion boutique magasin *m* de haute couture [mägäzeN də ōt kōōtér] 128

fashion show défilé m de mode [dä-fēlä də môd] 180

fast vite [vēt] 42; ~ **train** rapide m [räpēd] 60

fasten seat belts attacher les ceintures [ätäshā lā seNtér] 70

fat gras [grä] 100

father père m [pär] 35

father-in-law beau-père m [bō-pär] 35

fatty gras [grä] 115

faucet robinet m [rôbēnā] 88

February février m [fävrē·ā] 33

fee: rental ~ prix m de location [prē də lôkäsyôN] 95

fencing escrime f [eskrēm] 188

fender garde-boue m [gärd-bōō] 53

ferry, car ~**, train** ~ ferry-boat m [ferē-bōt] 76

fetch aller chercher [älā shärshā] 20

fever fièvre f [fē·āv(ər)] 170; ~ **cure** fébrifuge m [fābrēfēzh] 161

fiancé fiancé m [fē·äNsā] 14

fiancée fiancée f [fē·äNsā] 14

fibre fibre f [fēb(ər)] 137; **synthetic** ~ fibre f synthétique [fēb(ər) seNtātēk] 137

fight combat m [kôNbä] 187

figs figues f/pl [fēg] 110

figure skating patinage m [pätēnäzh] 188

figurine figure f [fēgēr] 143

file (verb) limer [lēmā] 156; (noun) lime f [lēm] 57

fill plomber [plôNbā] 174; ~ **her up** faites le plein [fāt lə pleN] 45; ~ **in** remplir [räNplēr] 78

filling plombage m [plôNbäzh] 174; **temporary** ~ pansement m [päNsmäN] 174

film (noun) rouleau m [rōōlō] 131; film m [fēlm] 179; pellicule f [pelēkēl] 132; (verb) filmer [fēlmā] 132;

cartridge ~ film m à chassis [fēlm ä shäsē] 131; **color** ~ pellicule f en couleur [pelēkēl äN kōōlär] 132; **color negative** ~ pellicule f négative en couleurs [pelēkēl nāgätēv äN kōōlär] 132; **educational** ~ (film m) documentaire m [(fēlm) dôkēmäNtär] 179; **feature** ~ long métrage m [lôN māträzh] 179; **reversal** ~ film m inversible [fēlm eNversēb'əl] 132; **roll** ~ pellicule f [pelēkēl]; rouleau m [rōōlō] 132; **sixteen millimeter color** ~ film m en couleur seize millimètres [fēlm äN kōōlär säz mēlēmāt(ər)] 131; **super eight color** ~ film m en couleur super huit [fēlm äN kōōlär sēpär ē·ēt] 131; **thirty five millimeter** ~ film m trente cinq millimètres [fēlm träNt seNk mēlēmāt(ər)] 131; **thirty-six exposure** ~ pellicule f de trente-six poses [pelēkēl də träNt-sē pōz] 131; **twenty exposure** ~ pellicule f de vingt poses [pelēkēl də veN pōz] 131; ~ **actor** acteur m de cinéma [äktär də sēnämä] 179; ~ **festival** festival m du film [festēväl dē fēlm] 179; ~ **screen** écran m [äkräN] 179

fine bien [byeN] 12; (weather) beau [bō] 25

finger doigt m [dô·ä] 167; **index** ~ index m [eNdeks] 167; **middle** ~ médius m [mādyēs] 167; **ring** ~ annulaire m [änēlär] 167

fire department pompiers m/pl [pôNpyä] 49

fire extinguisher extincteur m [eksteNtär] 53

fireplace cheminée f [shemēnā] 91

first premier [prəmyā] 29; ~ **class** première classe f [prəmyär kläs] 64

first-aid kit pansements *m/pl* [päNs-mäN] 161

first-aid station poste *m* de secours [pôst də səkōōr] 121; infirmerie *f* [eNfêrmərē] 60

fish *(noun)* poisson *f* [pô·äsôN] 104; *(verb)* pêcher à la ligne [pāshā älä lēn(yə)] 185; **~ market** poissonnerie *f* [pô·äsônrē] 128

fisherman pêcheur *m* [pāshār] 36

fishing pêche *f* à la ligne [pāsh älä lēn(yə)] 188; **~ license** permis *m* de pêche [permē də päsh] 188; **~ rod** canne *f* à pêche [kän ä päsh] 188; **~ trawler** bateau *m* de pêche [bätō də päsh] 75; **go ~** pêcher à la ligne [pāshā älä lēn(yə)] 188

fit *(noun)* attaque *f* [ätäk] 170

five cinq [seNk] 28

fix faire [fār] 50; réparer [rāpärā] 138

flannel flanelle *f* [flänel] 137

flash flash *m* [fläsh] 132; **~ bulb** ampoule *f* flash [äNpōōl fläsh] 132; **~ cube** cube *m* flash [kēb fläsh] 132

flashing signal avertisseur *m* lumineux [ävertēsär lēmēnā] 54

flashlight flash *m* [fläsh] 143

flat plat [plä] 139

flatulence ballonnements *m/pl* [bälôn·mäN] 170

flight vol *m* [vôl] 68; **~ attendant** hôtesse *f* de l'air [ôtes də lār] 71

flint pierre *f* à briquet [pyär ä brēkā] 140

flirting flirt *m* [flärt] 184

float *(car)* flotteur *m* [flôtär] 53

floor étage *m* [ätäzh] 91; **first ~** premier étage *m* [prəmyer ätäzh] 82; **ground ~** rez-de-chaussée *m* [rādə-shôsā] 82; **second ~** deuxième étage *m* [dāzyāmātäzh] 82

flower fleur *f* [flār] 130; **~ pot** pot *m* de fleurs [pô də flār] 130

flu grippe *f* [grēp] 170

fly voler [vôlā] 71

flying time durée *f* de vol [dērā də vôl] 71

FM modulations *f/pl* de fréquence [môdēläsyôN də frākäNs] 182

fog brouillard *m* [brōōyär] 27

follow poursuivre [pōōrsē·ēv(ər)] 154

fond of passionné pour [päsyônā pōōr]

font fonts *m/pl* batismaux [fôN bätēzmō] 125

food nourriture *f* [nōōrētēr] 163; **diet ~** menus *m/pl* diététiques [menē dē·ātätēk] 96; **vegetarian ~** menus *m/pl* végétariens [menē vāzhätärē·eN] 96; **~ poisoning** intoxication *f* alimentaire [eNtôksēkäsyôN älēmäNtär] 170

foot pied *m* [pyä] 167; **by ~** à pied [ä pyä] 116; **~ brake** frein *m* à pied [freN ä pyä] 51

footpath trottoir *m* [trôtô·är] 42

forehead front *m* [frôN] 167

forester garde *m* forestier [gärd fôrestyā] 36

forgive pardonner [pärdônā] 22

fork fourchette *f* [fōōrshet] 97

form formulaire *f* [fôrmēlār] 78

fortress forteresse *f* [fôrtəres] 119

forward *(verb)* faire suivre [fār sē·ēv(ər)] 89; *(noun; sports)* avant *m* [äväN] 189

fountain fontaine *f* [fôNten]; jet *m* d'eau, [zhä dō] 121

four quatre [kät(ər)] 28

fracture fracture *f* [fräktēr] 170

frame monture *f* [môNtēr] 138

free libre [lēb(ər)] 44; **~ kick** coup *m* franc [kōō fräN] 189; **~ style** exercices *m/pl* libres [eksersēs lēb(ər)] 188; **~ wheel hub** moyeu *m* à roue libre [mô·äyä ä rōō lĕb(ər)] 53

freeway autoroute *f* [ōtôrōōt] 58

freighter cargo *m* [kärgō] 77

French français [fräNsä] 24

fresco fresque *f* [fresk] 125

fresh frais [frä] 100

Friday vendredi *m* [väNdrədē] 33; **Good ~** vendredi *m* saint [väNdrədē seN] 33

fried sauté [sôtā] 100; **deep ~** frit [frē] 100

friend *(male)* ami *m* [ämē] 14; *(female)* amie *f* [ämē] 14

front: on the ~ of the train à l'avant du train [ä läväN dē treN] 66; **up ~** à l'avant [ä läväN] 65; **~ desk** réception *f* [räsepsyôN] 91; **~ door** porte *f* d'entrée [pôrt däNträ] 91; **~ seat** siège *m* avant [syäzh äväN] 55; **~ passenger seat** siège *m* avant droit [syäzh äväN drō·ä] 55; **~ wheel** roue *f* avant [rōō äväN] 47

frontal sinus sinus *m* frontal [sēnēs frôNtäl] 167

frost gelée *f* [zhelä] 27

frostbite engelure *f* [äNzhelēr] 170

frozen dessert parfait *m* [pärfä] 109

fruit fruits *m/pl* [frē·ē] 110; **~ market** épicerie *f m* [āpēsərē]; marché *m* [märshä] 53

fuel: ~ injector pompe *f* à injection [pôNp ä eNzheksyôN] 53; **~ lines** conduite *f* d'essence [kôNdē·ēt desäNs] 53; **~ pump** pompe *f* d'essence [pôNp desäNs] 53

full coverage insurance assurance *f* tous risques [äsēräNs tōō rēsk] 41

fullback arrière *m* [äryär] 190

funnel entonnoir *m* [äNtónô·är] 57

fur coat (manteau *m* de) fourrure *f* [(mäNtō də) fōōrēr] 134

fur jacket veste *f* de fourrure [vest

də fōōrēr] 134

furrier pelleterie *f* [peletərē] 128

fuse fusible *m* [fēsēb'əl] 53

G

gall bladder vésicule *f* biliaire [vāzēkēl bēlyär] 167

gall stones calculs *m/pl* biliaires [kälkēl bēlyär] 170

gallery galerie *f* [gälerē] 119

gambling casino casino *f* [käzēnō] 181

gambling game jeu *m* de hazard [zhä də äzär] 181

game jeu *m* [zhä] 187; *(animals)* gibier *m* [zhēbyä] 105

gangway passerelle *f* [päserel] 76

garage garage *m* [gäräzh] 44

garden jardin *m* [zhärdeN] 121

gardener jardinier *m* [zhärdēnyä] 36

gargle gargarisme *m* [gärgärēsm] 161

garlic ail *m* [ä·ē] 101

garter belt porte-jarretelles *m* [pôrtzhärtel] 134

garters jarretelles *f/pl* [zhärtel] 136

gas accélérateur *m* [äkselärätär] 53; **~ bottle** bouteille *f* de gaz [bōōtä'ē də gäz] 94; **~ station** station *f* d'essence [stäsyôN desäNs] 45

gasket joint *m* [zhô·eN] 53

gasoline essence *f* [esäNs] 45; **~ can** jerrycan *m* [dzherēkän] 45

gate portail *m* [pôrtä'ē] 121; *(airport)* pont *m* d'embarquement [pôN däNbärkmäN] 71

gauze bandage bandage *m* de gaze [bäNdäzh də gäz] 161

gear affaires *f/pl* [äfär] 185; *(car)* vitesse *f* [vētes] 53; **put it in ~** passer en … vitesse [päsä äN vētes] 53; **~ lever** levier *m* de changement de vitesse [levyä də shäNzh-mäN də vẽtes] 53; ~ **oil** huile *f* de graissage [é-él də gresäzh] 46

gear-box boîte *f* de vitesse [bô·ät də vẽtes] 53

gearshift changement *m* de vitesse [shäNzh·mäN də vẽtes] 53

general delivery poste *f* restante [pôst restäNt] 149

general practitioner médecin *m* de médecine générale [mädəseN də mädəsēn zhänäräl] 162

genital organs organes *m/pl* génitaux [ôrgän zhänétõ] 167

gentlemen messieurs *m/pl* [mesyä] 65

geology géologie *f* [zhä·ōlōzhē] 39

german allemand [älmäN] 24; ~ **measles** rubéole *f* [rēbä·ôl] 170

get avoir [ävô·är] 18; ~ **in**, ~ **aboard** monter (en voiture) [môNtä (äN vô·ätēr)] 67; ~ **out**, ~ **off** descendre [desäNd(ər)] 117, 67; ~ **together again** se revoir [sə rəvô·är] 17

gin gin *m* [dzēn] 112

ginger gingembre *m* [zheN-zhäNb(ər)] 101

girdle ceinture *f* [seNtēr] 134

girl fille *f* [fē'ē] 35

give donner [dônä] 20

gladioli glaïeuls *m/pl* [gläyäl] 130

gland glande *f* [gläNd] 167

glass verre *m* [vär] 96; **water** ~ verre *m* à eau [vär ä ō] 97; **wine** ~ verre *m* à vin [vär ä veN] 97

glasses (*spectacles*) lunettes *f/pl* [lēnet] 138

glazier vitrier *m* [vētrēyä] 37

glossy (*adj.*) brillant [brēyäN] 132; (*noun*) illustré [ēlēstrā] 182

gloves gants *m/pl* [gäN] 134

glue colle *f* [kôl] 138

glycerine glycérine *f* [glēsärēn] 161

go aller [älä] 19

goal but *m* [bē(t)] 187; **kick a** ~ marquer un but [märkä eN bē(t)] 190

goalie gardien *m* de but [gärdyeN də bē(t)] 190

God Dieu *m* [dyä] 125

gold (*noun*) or *m* [ôr] 133; (*adj.*) doré [dôrā] 194; ~ **plated** doré [dô-rā] 133

golf golf *m* [gôlf] 188

good bien [byeN] 21

good-bye! au revoir! [ō revô·är] 17

goods marchandises *f/pl* [märshäNdēz] 70

goose oie *f* [ô·ä] 105; ~ **liver pâté** pâté *m* de foie gras [pätä də fô·ä grä] 102

gooseberries groseilles *f/pl* à maquereau [grôzä'ē ä mäkərō] 110

Gospel Evangile *m* [äväNzhēl] 125

Gothic gothique [gōtēk] 125

government office administration *f* [ädmēnēsträsyôN] 121

grammar school école *f* primaire [äkôl prēmär] 38

grand piano piano *m* à queue [pē·änō ä kä] 177

grandchild petit-fils *m* [pətē-fēs] 35

granddaughter petite-fille *f* [pətēt-fē'ē] 35

grandfather grand-père *m* [gräN-pär] 35

grandmother grand-mère *f* [gräN-mär] 35

grandparents grands-parents *m/pl* [gräN-päräN] 35

grandson petit-fils *m* [pətē-fēs] 35

grapefruit pamplemousse *f* [päN-pləmōōs] 110; ~ **juice** jus *m* de pamplemousse [zhē də päNpləmōōs] 112

grapes raisins *m/pl* [räzeN] 110

grateful reconnaissant [rekônäsäN] 21

grave tombe *f* [tôNb] 121

gravy jus *m* de rôti [zhē de rôtē] 101

gray gris [grē] 194; **ash ~** gris cendré [grē säNdrā] 194; **dark ~** gris foncé [grē fôNsā] 194; **pale ~** gris clair [grē klär] 194

grease graisse *f* [gres] 53

greasy gras [grä] 158

great grand [gräN] 22

green vert [vär] 194; **dark ~** vert foncé [vär fôNsā] 194; **light ~** vert clair [vär klär] 194

grill room grill-room *m* [grēl-rōōm] 91

grilled grillé [grēyā] 100

grocery store magasin *m* d'alimentation [mägäzeN dälēmäNtäsyôN] 94

group fare ticket billet *m* de groupe [bēyä də grōōp] 62

grown up adulte [ädēlt] 34

guard garder [gärdā] 44

guarded gardé [gärdā] 44

guest house pension *f* [päNsyôN] 91

guide guide *m* [gēd] 121

guilt culpabilité *f* [kēlpäbēlētā] 154

gums gencive *f* [zhäNsēv] 174

gym shoes chaussures *f/pl* de gymnastique [shôsēr də zhēmnästēk] 139

gymnast gymnaste *m* [zhēmnäst] 188

gymnastics gymnastique *f* [zhēmnästēk] 188; **~ with apparatus** gymnastique *f* aux agrès [zhēmnästēk ōzägrā] 188

gynecologist gynécologue *m* [zhēnäkōlôg] 162

H

haberdashery mercerie *f* [mārserē] 128

haddock aiglefin *m* [āgləfeN] 104

hail grêle *f* [grāl] 27

hair cheveux *m/pl* [shevā] 155; **~ conditioner** sèche-cheveux *m* [sāsh-shevā] 141; **~ drier** séchoir *m* [sāshô·är] 141; **~ loss** chute *f* des cheveux [shēt dā shevā] 158; **~ net** filet *m* [fēlā] 141; **~ spray** vaporisateur *m* [väpôrēzätār] 141; **~ style** coiffure *f* [kô·äfēr] 158; **~ tonic** lotion *f* capillaire [lôsyôN käpēlār] 141

hairbrush brosse *f* à cheveux [brôs ä shevā] 141

haircut coupe *f* de cheveux [kōōp də shevā] 157

hair-do coiffure *f* [kô·äfēr] 158

hairdresser coiffeur *m* [kô·äfār] 158

hairpiece perruque *f* [perēk] 156

hairpin épingle *f* à cheveux [āpeNg'əl ä shevā] 141

half demi [dəmē] 30

half fare demi-place *f* [dəmē-pläs] 59

half time mi-temps *m* [mē-täN] 188

hall hall *m* d'hôtel [äl dôtel] 91

ham jambon *m* [zhäNbôN] 102

hammer marteau *m* [märtō] 57

hammock hamac *m* [ämäk] 144

hand main *f* [meN] 167; *(on clock)* aiguille *f* [āg'ē'ē] 143; **~ brake** frein *m* à main [freN ä meN] 51; **~ luggage** bagage *m* à main [bägäzh ä meN] 63

handbag sac *m* à main [säk ä meN] 144

handball handball *m* [äNdbôl] 188

handicrafts objets *m/pl* artisanaux [ôbzhä ärtēzänō] 144

handkerchief mouchoir *m* [mōōshô·är] 134

handle poignée *f* [pô·änyā] 53

happen se passer [sə päsā] 18

harbor port [pôr] 72; **~ police sta-**

tion police *f* du port [pôlēs dē pôr] 73

hard dur [dēr] 100

hare lièvre *m* [lē·āv(ər)] 106

hat chapeau *m* [shāpō] 134; **straw ~** chapeau *m* de paille [shāpō də pä'ē] 134

have avoir [ävô·är] 18; **we're going to ~** nous aurons [nōōzôrôN] 25; **~ to** devoir [dəvô·är] 41

hay fever rhume *m* des foins [rēm dā fô·eN] 170

hazel nuts noisette *f/pl* [nô·äzet] 110

head tête *f* [tät] 167; **~ clerk** chef *m* de réception [shef də rāsepsyôN] 91

headlight phare *m* [fär] 53

head-on collision collision *f* de face [kôlēzyôN də fäs] 49

health resort station *f* climatique [stäsyôN klēmätēk] 175

heart attack crise *f* cardiaque [krēz kärdē·äk] 170

heart problems troubles *m/pl* cardiaques [trōōb'əl kärdē·äk] 170

heartburn aigreurs *f/pl* [āgrär] 170

hearts *(cards)* cœur *m* [kār] 181

heat canicule *f* [känēkēl] 27; chaleur *f* [shälär] 163

heating *(system)* chauffage *m* [shôfäzh] 54; **central ~** chauffage *m* central [shôfäzh säNträl] 90

heel talon *m* [tälôN] 139

height taille *f* [tä'ē] 79

helicopter hélicoptère *m* [ālēkôptär] 71

hello! salut! [sälē] 12; *(on answering phone)* allô! [älô] 12

helm gouvernail *m* [gōōvernä'ē] 76

helmsman pilote *m* [pēlôt] 76

help *(noun)* aide *f* [ād] 20; *(verb)* aider [ādā] 66; **mary I ~ you?** que désirez-vous? [ke dāzērā-vōō] 18

hemorrhage hémorragie *f* [āmôrä-

zhē] 170

hemorrhoids hémorroïdes *f/pl* [āmôrô·ēd] 170

herbs fines herbes *f/pl* [fēnzärb] 101

here ici [ēsē] 14

herring hareng *m* [äräN] 104

hi! salut! [sälē] 12

high haut [ō] 139; **~ mass** grand-messe *f* [grāN mes] 123; **~ pressure** *(system)* anticyclone *m* [äN-tēsēklôn] 27; **~ school** *(academic)* académie *f* [äkädāmē] 38; *(general)* lycée *m* [lēsā]; collège *m* [kôläzh] 38; **~ test** super *m* [sē-pär] 45

high-rise building building *m* [bēl-dēng]; tour *f* [tōōr] 121

highway autoroute *f* [ôtōrōōt] 42; **~ patrol** police *f* routière [pôlēs rōōtyär] 42

hiking path sentier *m* de randonnée [säNtyā də räNdônā] 121

hill colline *f* [kôlēn] 121

hip hanche *f* [äNsh] 167

history histoire *f* [ēstô·är] 39

hitch-hike faire de l'auto-stop [fär də lôtôstôp] 43

hoarseness enrouement *m* [äNrōō-māN] 170

hockey hockey *m* [ôkā] 188

hold up agression *f* [ägresyôN] 153

honey miel *m* [myel] 98

hood capot *m* [käpô] 54

hooks and eyes crochets *m/pl* [krô-shā] 136

horizontal bar barre *f* fixe [bär fēks] 188

horn avertisseur *m* sonore [ävertē-sär sônôr] 54

horse cheval *m* [shəväl] 189; **~ cart** roulotte *f* [rōōlôt] 41; **~ race** course *f* de chevaux [kōōrs də shəvô] 189

horseradish raifort *m* [rāfôr] 101

hospital hôpital m [ôpētäl] 49

hostel: ~ **father** père m aubergiste [pär ōbärzhēst] 95; ~ **mother** mère f aubergiste [mär ōbärzhēst] 95; ~ **parents** parents m/pl aubergistes [päräN ōbärzhēst] 95

hot chaud [shō] 25; (spicy) épicé [āpēsā]; piquant [pēkäN] 100; ~ **chocolate** chocolat m [shōkōlä] 98; ~ **spring** source f chaude [sōōrs shōd] 175

hotel hôtel m [ōtēl] 81; **beach** ~ hôtel m de la plage [ōtēl də lä pläzh] 91; ~ **restaurant** restaurant m d'hôtel [restōräN dōtēl] 91

hour heure f [är] 31; **every** ~ toutes les heures [tōōt läzär] 31; **half** ~ demi-heure [dəmē-är] 87; **quarter** ~ quart m d'heure [kär där] 87

hourly toutes les heures [tōōt läzär] 31

house maison f [māzōN] 91; ~ **key** clé f de la maison [klā dəlä māzōN] 91; ~ **number** numéro m de la maison [nēmārō dəlä māzōN] 121

how comment [kômäN] 18; ~ **are you?** ça va? [sä vä] 12

hub moyeu m [mô·äyə] 54; ~ **cap** enjoliveur m [äNzhōlēvär] 54

hundred cent [säN] 151

hundredweight quintal m [keNtäl] 193

hunting chasse f [shäs] 189; ~ **license** permis m de chasse [permē də shäs] 189

hurt (adj.) blessé [blesā] 49

husband mari m [märē] 13

hydrogen peroxide eau f oxigénée [ō ōksēzhānā] 161

hypertension hypertension f [ēpärtäNsyôN] 170

I

ice glace f [gläs] 27

ice cream glace f [gläs] 109; ~ **parlor** pâtisser glacier m [pätēsyā gläsyā] 113; **assorted** ~ glace f panachée [gläs pänäshä] 113; **chocolate** ~ glace f au chocolat [gläs ō shōkōlä] 113; **strawberry** ~ glace f à la fraise [gläs älä fräz] 113; **vanilla** ~ glace f à la vanille [gläs älä vänē'ē] 113

ice skating rink pâtinoire f [pätēnō·är] 180

icy road verglas m [verglä] 27

identity card carte f d'identité [kärt dēdäNtētä] 79

ignition allumage m [älēmäzh] 54; ~ **cable** fil m d'allumage [fēl dälēmäzh] 54; ~ **key** clé f de contact [klä də kôNtäkt] 54; ~ **lock** serrure f de contact [serēr də kôNtäkt] 54; ~ **system** installation f de l'allumage [eNstäläsyôN də lälēmäzh] 54

illness maladie f [mälädē] 170

inch pouce m [pōōs] 193

incisor incisive f [eNsēzēv] 174

included compris [kôNprē] 83

including inclus [eNklē] 41

indicator light lampe-témoin f [läNp-tāmô·eN] 53

indigestion embarras m gastrique [äNbärä gästrēk] 170

inflammation inflammation f [eNflämäsyôN] 170

influenza grippe f [grēp] 170

information renseignements m/pl [räNsen(yə)mäN] 65; information f [enfôrmäsyôN] 71; ~ **office** bureau m de renseignements [bērō də räNsen(yə)mäN] 60

infusion infusion f [eNfēzyôN] 172

inhale faire des inhalations f [fär däzēnäläsyôN] 175

injection piqûre f [pēkĕr] 172

injured blessé [blesä] 48

injury blessure f [blesĕr] 49

ink encre f [äNk(ər)] 138

inn auberge f [ōbārzh] 81

inner tube chambre f à air [shäNb(ər) ä är] 46

innocent innocent [ēnôsäN] 154

inquiry renseignement m [räNsen-(yə)mäN] 92

insect repelent remède m contre les piqûres d'insectes [remäd kôNt(ər) lä pēkĕr deNsekt] 161

inside (à) l'intérieur m [(ä) leNtä-rē·är] 47

in-sole semelle f intérieure [semel eNtärē·är] 139

insomnia insomnie f [eNsômnē] 170

inspection light lampe-témoin f [läNp-tämô·eN] 57

insulation isolement m [ēzôlmäN] 54

insurance assurance f [äsēräNs] 49; ~ **certificate** carte f d'assurance [kärt däsēräNs] 79

insured assuré; [äsērä] 49

intensive care unit service m de réanimation [servĕs də rä·änēmä-syôN] 172

intermission entracte m [äNträkt] 177

internal interne [eNtärn] 159

interpreter interprète m/f [eNter-prät] 37

interrupt interrompre [eNte-rôNp(ər)] 61

interrupter interrupteur m [eNterĕp-tär] 54

intersection croisement m [krô·äz-mäN] 42

intestinal catarrh entérite f [äNtärēt] 170

intestine intestin m [eNtesteN] 167

invitation invitation f [eNvētäsyôN] 16

invite inviter [eNvētä] 183

iodine teinture f d'iode [teNtĕr dyôd] 161

iron *(verb)* repasser [repäsä] 95

Islam islamisme m [ēslämĕsm] 125

island île f [ēl] 76

J

jack valet m; cric m [välä; krēk] 181; 47

jacket veste f; veston m [vest; ve-stôN] 134

jackknife couteau m de poche [kōōtō də pôsh] 144

jam confiture f [kôNfētēr] 98

January janvier [zhäNvyä] 33

jar verre m [vär] 126

jaundice jaunisse f [zhōnēs] 170

jaw mâchoire f [mäshô·är] 167

jelly gélatine f; aspic m; gelée f [zhälätēn; äspek; zhelä] 101

jellyfish méduse f [mädĕz] 186

jersey jersey m [zhersä] 137

jet turbo-réacteur m [tĕrbō rä·äktär] 71; ~ **plane** avion m à réaction [ävyôN ä rä·äksyôN] 71

jetty môle m [môl] 76

Jew juif [zhé·ĕf] 124

jewelry parure f; bijoux m/pl [pärĕr; bēzhōō] 133, 153; **costume** ~ bijoux fantaisie [bēzhōō fäNtäzē] 133

Jewish juif [zhé·ĕf] 125

joint articulation f [ärtēkĕläsyôN] 167

journalist journaliste m [zhōōrnä-lēst] 37

journey voyage m [vô·äyäzh] 43

judge juge m [zhēzh] 37

judo judo m [zhédō] 188

juice jus m [zhē] 98; **grapefruit** ~

jus de pamplemousse [zhē də päNpləmōōs] 112

juicy juteux [zhĕtä] 100

July juillet [zhē·ēyä] 33

June juin [zhē·eN] 33

K

key clé *f* [klā] 153

kidnapping enlèvement *m* [äNlävmäN] 153

kidney rein *m* [reN] 167; **~ stones** calculs *m/pl* rénaux [kälkäl ränō] 170

kidneys rognons *m/pl* [rônyôN] 107

kilometer kilomètre *m* [kēlōmät(ər)] 193

kind; what ~ of quel, ~le, ~ls, ~les [kel] 18

king roi *m* [rô·ä] 181

kiss *(noun)* baiser *m* [bāzā] 184; **kiss** *(verb)* embrasser [äNbräsā] 184

kitchen cuisine *f* [kē·ēzēn] 92

kitchenette coin *m* cuisine [kô·eN kē·ēzēn] 92

knee genou *m* [zhenōō] 167; **~ socks** mi-bas *m/pl* [mē-bä] 134

kneecap rotule *f* [rôtēl] 167

knife couteau *m* [kōōtō] 97; **pocket ~** couteau de poche [kōōtō də pôsh] 144

knight *(cards)* cavalier *m* [kävälyā] 181

knocks *(moteur)* cogne [kôn(yə)] 54

knot nœud *m* [nā] 76

L

ladies dames *f/pl;* mesdames [däm; mädäm] 65, 13; **~ 'room** toilettes *f/pl* pour dames [tô·älät pōōr däm] 92

lake lac *m* [läk] 76

lamb agneau *m* [änyō] 105

lamp lampe *f* [läNp] 54; **reading ~** lampe *f* de chevet [läNp də shevä] 92

land *(noun)* terre *f;* pays *m* [tär; pä·ē] 76; **land** *(verb)* aborder, accoster [äbôrdā, äkôstä] 76; **land** *(plane)* atterrir [äterēr] 70

landing atterrissage *m* [äterēsäzh] 71; **~ gear** train *m* d'atterrissage [treN däterēsäzh] 71; **~ place** endroit *m* de débarquement [äNdrô·ä də däbärkmäN] 76; **~ stage** débarcadère *m* [däbärkädär] 76

landscape paysage *m* [pā·ēzäzh] 121

lane chaussée *f;* ruelle *f* [shôsä; rē·el] 42; 121

lap rug couverture *f* de laine [kōōvertēr də lān] 76

lard saindoux *m* [seNdōō] 101

larynx larynx *m* [läreNks] 167

last dernier [dernyā] 59; **~ stop** terminus *m* [termēnēs] 121

late tard [tär] 17; **to be ~** *(train, bus)* avoir du retard [ävô·är dē retär] 61

later plus tard [plē tär] 32

launder (faire) laver [(fär) lävā] 87

laundromat laverie *f* automatique [lävrē ōtômätēk] 129

laundry linge *m* [leNzh] 92

laundry *(shop)* blanchisserie *f* [bläNshēsərē] 129

lavender lavande *f* [läväNd] 194

law droit *m* [drô·ä] 39

lawyer avocat *m* [ävōkä] 37

laxative purgatif *m* [pērgätēf] 161

leak *(verb)* goutter [gōōtä] 52

lean maigre [māg(ər)] 100

leash laisse *f* [läs] 144

leather cuir *m* [kē·ēr] 126; **~ coat** manteau *m* de cuir [mäNtō də kē·ēr] 134; **~ jacket** blouson *m* en cuir [blōōzôN äN kē-ēr] 134

leave partir; laisser [pärtēr; läsā] 34; 44

lecture cours m [kōōr] 38

left à gauche [ä gōsh] 116

leg jambe f; gigot m [zhäNb; zhēgō] 167; 106

legitimate theatre théâtre m [tā·ät(ər)] 177

lemon citron m [sētrôN] 101

lemonade limonade f [lēmônäd] 112

lend prêter [prätā] 48

lengthen rallonger [rälôNzhā] 137

lens (opt.) verre m [vär] 138

lens (photogr.) objectif m [ôbzhek-tēf] 132

letter lettre f [let(ər)] 34; **local ~** lettre f locale [let(ər) lôkäl] 145; **registered ~** lettre f recommandée [let(ər) rekômäNdā] 145

letter abroad lettre f pour l'étranger [let(ər) pōōr läträNzhā] 145

leukemia leucémie f [lāsāmē] 170

librarian bibliothécaire m [bēblē-ô-tākār] 37

library bibliothèque f [bēblē-ôtāk] 121

libretto livret m [lēvrā] 177

license plate plaque f d'immatriculation [pläk dēmätrēkēläsyôN] 54

life: ~ belt bouée f de sauvetage [bōō·ā də sôvtäzh] 76; **~ jacket** gilet m de sauvetage [zhēlā də sôvtäzh] 71

lifeboat canot m de sauvetage [kä-nō də sôvtäzh] 75

lifeguard maître-nageur m [mät(ər) näzhār] 185

light, pale clair [klär] 127

light (noun) lumière f [lēmyär] 88; **~ bulb** ampoule f électrique [äN-pōōl älektrēk] 92

lighter briquet m [brēkā] 140; **~ fluid** essence f à briquet [esäNs ä

brēkā] 140

lighthouse phare m [fär] 76

lighting system éclairage m [āklā-räzh] 54

lightning éclair m [āklār] 27

lights éclairage m [āklāräzh] 92

like: I'd ~ je voudrais [zhə vōōdrā] 73

lilacs lilas m [lēlä] 130

limbs membres m/pl [mäNb(ər)] 167

linen toile f [tô·äl] 137

liniment liniment m; friction f [lēnē-mäN; frēksyôN] 161

lining doublure f [dōōblēr] 136

lip lèvre f [lāv(ər)] 167

lipstick rouge m à lèvres [rōōzh ä läv(ər)] 141

liqueur liqueur f [lēkār] 112

liter litre m [lēt(ər)] 45

little: a ~ un peu [eN pā] 24

live vivre; habiter [vēv(ər); äbētā] 119; 14

liver foie m [fô·ä] 106; **~ problem** maladie f du foie [mälädē dē fô·ä] 170

living room séjour m [sāzhōōr] 93

loafers mocassins m/pl [môkäseN] 139

loan prêter [prätā] 57

lobby vestibule m; hall m [vestēbāl; ōl] 92

lobster homard m [ômär] 104; **spiny ~** langouste f [läNgōōst] 105

local call communication f urbaine [kômēnēkäsyôN ērben] 149

located: is ~ se trouve [sə trōōv] 19

lock (noun) serrure f [serēr] 92

lock up fermer à clé [fermā ä klā] 92

locker room vestiaire m [vestyär] 186

lockjaw constriction des mâchoires [kôNstrēksyôN dā mäshō·är] 171

locksmith serrurier m [serēryā] 37

long long [lôN] 133; **~ wave** grandes ondes *f/pl* [gräNdzôNd] 182

look after prendre soin de [präNd(ər) sô·eN də] 48

look for chercher [shershā] 18

loosen desserrer [deserā] 55

lost perdu [perdē] 153; **~ and found office** bureau *m* des objets trouvés [bērō dāzôbzhā trōōvā] 121

loss perte *f* [pert] 153

lounge salle *f* de séjour [säl də sāzhōōr] 74

love *(noun)* amour *m* [ämōōr] 184

love *(verb)* aimer [āmā] 184

lovely charmant [shärmäN] 16

low bas, -se [bä, bäs] 169; **~ pressure** *(system)* basses pressions *f/pl* [bäs presyôN] 27

lubricant lubrifiant *m* [lēbrēfyäN] 54

lubrication lubrification *f* [lēbrēfēkäsyôN] 46

luck: Good ~ Bonne chance [bôn shäNs] 23

luggage bagages *m/pl* [bägäzh] 59; **~ car** fourgon *m* [fōōrgôN] 64; **~ locker** consigne *f* automatique [kôNsen(yə) ōtōmätēk] 63; **~ rack** filet *m* [fēlā] 67

lumbago lumbago *m* [lôNbägō] 171

lunch déjeuner *m* [dāzhānā] 92

lung poumon *m* [pōōmôN] 167

M

mackerel maquereau *m* [mäkərō] 104

madam madame [mädäm] 13

magazine revue *f* [rəvē] 182; **fashion ~** journal *m* de modes [zhōōrnäl də môd] 182

maid femme *f* de chambre [fäm də shäNb(ər)] 87

maiden name nom *m* de jeune fille [nôN də zhän fē'ē] 79

mail *(verb)* expédier [ekspādē·ā] 34

mail *(noun)* courrier *m* [kōōryā] 85; **~ box** boîte *f* aux lettres [bô·ät ō let(ər)] 145; **~man** facteur *m* [fäktär] 37

main road route *f* principale [rōōt preNsēpäl] 43; **~ station** gare *f* centrale [gär säNträl] 60; **~ street** rue *f* principale [rē preNsēpäl] 43

major matière *f* principale [mätyär preNsēpäl] 38

male organ verge *f* [värzh] 167

malt liquor bière *f* de malt [byär də mält] 111

manager gérant *m* [zhäräN] 23

manicure manucure *f* [mänēkēr] 156;

many: how ~ combien de [kôNbyeN də] 18

map carte *f*; plan *m* [kärt; pläN] 40, 130; **road ~** carte *f* routière [kärt rōōtyär] 130

march mars [märs] 33

marital status situation *f* de famille [sētē·äsyôN də fämē'ē] 79

mark signe *m* [sēn(yə)] 79

markmanship tir *m* [tēr] 189

maroon rouge foncé [rōōzh fôNsä] 194

marriage mariage *m* [märē·äzh] 22

married marié [märē·ā] 79

mascara rimmel *m* [rēmel] 141

mass messe *f* [mes] 125; **high ~** grand-messe *f* [gräNmes] 125

massage *(noun)* massage *m* [mäsäzh] 175

massage *(verb)* masser [mäsā] 175

mast mât *m* [mä] 76

mat dessous *m* de plat [desōō də plä] 144

matches allumettes *f/pl* [älēmet] 140

material tissu *m* [tēsē] 137

mathematics mathématiques *f/pl* [mätämätēk] 39

mattress matelas *m* [mätlä] 90

maxillary sinus sinus *m* [sēnēs] 167

maximum speed vitesse *f* maximum [vētes mäksēmôm] 42

May mai [mä] 33

maybe peut-être [pätät(ər)] 21

meal repas *m* [repä] 86

mean: means veut dire [vä dēr] 18

meanwhile entre-temps [äNtrətäN] 32

measles rougeole *f* [rōōzhôl] 171

meat viande *f* [vē·äNd] 105

mechanic mécanicien *m* [mākänē-syeN] 37

mechanical engineering construction *f* mécanique [kôNstrēksyôN mäkänēk] 39

medical director médecin *m* chef [mädəsēN shef] 172

medicinal spring source *f* médicinale [sōōrs mädēsēnäl] 175

medicine remède *m* [remäd] 161

medicine *(discipl.)* médecine *f* [mädəsēn] 39

medium *(done)* à point [ä pô·eN] 100

meet *(again)* se revoir [sə revô·är] 183

melon melon *m* [məlôN] 110

membership card carte *f* de membre [kärt də mäNb(ər)] 95

memorial monument *m* commémoratif [mônēmäN kômemôrätēf] 119

men's room toilettes *f/pl* pour messieurs [tô·älet pōōr mesyä] 92

menstruation règles *f/pl* [räg'əl] 167

mention: don't ~ it il n'y a pas de quoi [ēlnyä pä də kô·ä] 21

meringue méringue *f* [märeNg] 113

metabolism métabolisme *m* [mätäbōlēsm] 167

metalworker métallurgiste *m* [mätälērzhēst] 37

meter mètre *m* [mät(ər)] 192

Methodist méthodiste *m* [mätôdēst] 124

middle milieu *m* [mēlēyä] 65; **~ ear inflammation** otite *f* [ōtēt] 171

midnight minuit *f* [mēnē·ē] 31

midwife sage-femme *f* [säzh-fäm] 37

mile lieue *f* [lēyä] 193; **nautical ~** mille *m* marin [mēl märeN] 193

mileage indicator compteur *m* kilométrique [kôNtär kēlōmätrēk] 54

military base base *f* militaire [bäz mēlētär] 121

milk lait *m* [lä] 114

millimeter millimètre *m* [mēlēmät(ər)] 193

mine à moi [ä mô·ä] 80

miner mineur *m* [mēnär] 37

minerals minéraux *m/pl* [mēnärō] 175

miniature golf mini-golf *m* [mēnē-gôlf] 180

ministry ministère *m* [mēnēstär] 121

minute minute *f* [mēnēt] 30

mirroir miroir *m* [mērô·är] 92

missing: is ~ il manque [ēl mäNk] 63

Miss mademoiselle *f* [mädəmô·äzel] 13

mist brouillard *m* [brōōyär] 27

molar molaire *f* [môlär] 174

mole môle *m* [môl] 76

moment instant *m* [eNstäN] 87; **at the ~** actuellement [äktē·elmäN] 32

monastery couvent *m* [kōōväN] 124

Monday lundi [leNdē] 33

money de l'argent *m* [də lärzhäN] 151; **~ exchange** bureau *m* de change [bērō də shäNzh] 60; **~ order** mandat-carte *m* [mäNdä kärt] 146

month mois *m* [mô·ä] 32

monument monument *m* [mônēmäN] 119

moon lune f [lēn] 27

moped cyclomoteur m [sēklōmôtär] 41

morning matin m [mäteN] 31; **good ~** bonjour [bôNzhōōr] 12; **this ~** ce matin [sə mäteN] 31

mortal danger danger m de mort [däNzhä də môr] 191

mortgage hypothèque f [ēpôtäk] 152

mosaic mosaïque f [môzä·ēk] 125

Moslem musulman [mēzēlmäN] 124

mosque mosquée f [môskä] 125

motel motel m [môtel] 81

mother mère f [mär] 35; **~-in-law** belle-mère f [bel-mär] 35

motion pictures cinéma m [sēnämä] 121

motor moteur m [môtär] 54; **~ oil** huile f de moteur [ē·ēl də môtär] 46; **~ scooter** scooter m [skōōtär] 41

motorail service train m auto-couchettes [treN ôtō-kōōshet] 60

motorboat bateau m à moteur [bätō ä môtär] 75

motorcycle moto f [môtō] 41

mountain montagne f [môNtän(yə)] 122; **~ range** chaîne f de montagnes [shen də môNtän(yə)] 122; **~ climber** alpiniste m [älpēnēst] 189; **~ climbing** alpinisme m [älpēnēsm] 189

mousse mousse f [mōōs] 109

moustache moustaches f/pl [mōōstäsh] 157

mouth bouche f [bōōsh] 168

mouthwash eau f dentifrice [ō däNtēfrēs] 161

move (verb) bouger [bōōzhā] 164; **~ in** emménager [äNmänäzhā] 92; **~ out** déménager [dāmänäzhā] 92

move (games) coup m [kōō] 181

movie film m [fēlm] 179

movies cinéma m [sēnämä] 179

Mr. monsieur [məsyā] 12

Mrs. madame [mädäm] 12

much: too ~ trop [trō] 127; **how ~** combien de [kôNbyeN də] 127

mucous membrane muqueuse f [mēkāz] 168

mud boue f minérale [bōō mēnäräl] 175; **~ pack** enveloppement de boue [äNvelôpmäN də bōō] 175

muggy lourd [lōōr] 25

mumps oreillons m/pl [ôräyôN] 171

murder meurtre m [märt(ər)] 153

Muscatel muscat m [mēskä] 111

muscle muscle m [mēsk'əl] 168

museum musée m [mēzä] 116

mushrooms champignons m/pl [shäNpēnyôN] 101

music musique f [mēzēk] 178

musician musicien m [mēzēsyeN] 178

mussels moules f/pl [mōōl] 104

mustard moutarde f [mōōtärd] 101; **~ jar** moutardier m [mōōtärdyä] 97

mutton mouton m [mōōtôN] 105

my ma, mon, mes [mä, môN, mä] 48

N

nail ongle m [ôNg'əl] 156; **~ file** lime f à ongles [lēm ä ôNg'əl] 141; **~ polish** vernis m à ongles [vernē ä ôNg'əl] 141; **~ polish remover** dissolvant m [dēsôlväN] 141; **~ scissors** ciseaux m/pl à ongles [sēzō ä ôNg'əl] 141

name nom m (de famille) [nôN (də fämē'ē)] 14 (79); **first ~** prénom m [pränôN] 79

napkin serviette f [servyet] 97

narcotics stupéfiants m/pl [stēpä-fē·äN] 154

narrow étroit [ätrô·ä] 127

national park parc m national [pärk näsyônäl] 121

nationality nationalité [näsyônälētä] 79; **~ plate** plaque f de nationalité [pläk də näsyônälētä] 79

nausea nausée f/pl [nōzā] 171; **nauseated: I feel ~** j'ai mal au cœur [zhā mäl ō kär] 164

nave nef f [nef] 125

nearby près d'ici [prā dēsē] 44

nearest prochain [prôsheN] 19

near-sighted myope [mē·ôp] 138

neck cou m [kōō] 168; **back of the ~** nuque f [nēk] 168; **nape of the ~** nuque f [nēk] 168

necklace chaîne f [shän] 133

need (Verb) avoir besoin de [avô·är bezô·eN də] 18

needle aiguille f [āgē·ē] 136; **sewing ~** aiguille f à coudre [āgē·ē ä kōōd(ər)] 136

negative négatif m [nägätēf] 131

nephew neveu m [nevä] 35

nephritis néphrite f [nāfrēt] 171

nerve(s) nerf(s) m/pl [när] 168

neuralgia névralgie f [nāvrälzhē] 171

neurologist neurologue m [närōlôg] 162

neutral (gear) point m mort [pô·eN môr] 53

never jamais [zhämä] 21

new nouveau, **~ elle** [nōōvō, nōōvel] 50

news informations f/pl [eNfôrmä-syôN] 182; **~ dealer** marchand m de journaux [märshäN də zhōōr-nō] 129

newspaper journal m [zhōōrnäl] 86

next prochain [prôsheN] 32

nice agréable [ägrä·äb'əl] 184

niece nièce f [nē·äs] 35

night nuit f [nē·ē] 82; **all ~** toute la nuit [tōōt lä nē·ē] 44; **at ~** la nuit [lä nē·ē] 31; **Good ~** Bonne nuit [bônē·ē] 17; **~ club** boîte f de nuit [bô·ät də nē·ē] 180; **~ duty** service m de nuit [servēs də nē·ē] 159; **~ rate** tarif m de nuit [tärēf də nē·ē] 148; **~ shirt; nightie** chemise f de nuit [shemēz də nē·ē] 134

night's lodging nuitée f [nē·ētā] 92

nine neuf [näf] 28

ninepins jeu m de quille [zhä də kē·ē] 189

no non [nôN] 21; **~ admittance** entrée interdite [äNtrā eNterdēt] 191

nobody personne [persôn] 49

non-swimmer non-nageur m [nôN-näzhär] 186

noodles nouilles f/pl [nōō·ē] 103

noon midi m [mēdē] 31; **this ~** ce midi [sə mēdē] 32

nose né m [nā] 168

nosebleed saignements m/pl du nez [sān(yə)mäN dē nā] 171

notary notaire m [nôtär] 37

nothing rien m [rē·eN] 21

novel roman m [rômäN] 130; **detective ~** roman m policier [rômäN pôlēsyā] 130

November novembre [nôväNb(ər)] 33

now maintenant [meNt(ə)näN] 32; **~ and then** de temps à autre [də täNzä ōt(ər)] 32

nude nu [nē] 185; **~ beach** plage f de nudistes [pläzh də nēdēst] 186

number numéro m [nēmärō] 64

nurse m/f infirmier, -ère [eNfērmyä, -är] 37; **night ~** infirmière f de nuit [eNfērmyär də nē·ē] 172

nursery chambre f d'enfants [shäNb(ər) däNfäN] 93

nutmeg muscade *f* [mĕskăd] 101

nuts noix *f/pl* [nô·ä] 110

nylon nylon *m* [nĕlôN] 137

O

oarsman rameur *m* [rämŭr] 189

observatory observatoire *m* [observätô·är] 121

occupation profession *f* [prôfesyôN] 79

occupied occupé [ôkĕpā] 66

ocean océan *m* [ôsā·äN] 77

October octobre [oktôb(ər)] 33

offer offrir [ôfrēr] 16

office bureau *m* [bĕrō] 74

office hours *(med.)* consultations *f/pl* [kôNsĕltäsyôN] 162

officer officier *m* [ôfēsyā] 74; **deck ~** premier officier [prəmyā ôfēsyā] 74

off-side hors-jeu [ôr-zhä] 190

often: how ~ combien de fois [kôNbyeN də fô·ä] 72

oil huile *f* [ē·ēl] 45; **~ change** vidange *f* d'huile [vēdäNzh dē·ēl] 46; **~ level** niveau *m* d'huile [nēvô dē·ēl] 46; **~ filter** filtre *m* à huile [fēlt(ər) ä ē·ēl] 54; **~ pump** pompe *f* à huile [pôNp ä ē·ēl] 54

ointment pommade *f* [pômäd] 161; **boric acid ~** acide *m* borique [äsēd bôrēk] 160; **burn ~** pommade *f* contre les brulûres [pômäd kôNt(ər) lā brĕlŭr] 160

old: I'm... years ~ j'ai... ans [zhā... äN] 34

older plus âgé [plēzäzhā] 34

olives olives *f/pl* [ôlēv] 102

one un, une [eN, ēn] 78; **~ way street** sens *m* unique [säNs ĕnēk] 58; **~ way ticket** (billet) aller [(bēyā) älā] 62

onion oignon *m* [ônyôN] 101

open *(adj.)* ouvert [ōōvär] 44

open *(verb)* ouvrir [ōōvrēr] 118; **Do not ~** Ne pas ouvrir [nə päzōōvrēr] 191; **~ market** marché *m* [märshā] 122

opera opéra *m* [ôpärä] 178; **~ glasses** jumelles *f/pl* de théâtre [zhĕmel də tā·ät(ər)] 178

operate on opérer [ôpārā] 172

operating room salle *f* d'opération [säl dôpäräsäysyôN] 172

operation opération *f* [ôpäräsyôN] 172

operator téléphoniste *m/f* [tālāfônēst] 150

operetta opérette *f* [ôpäret] 178

ophthalmologist oculiste *m* [ôkēlēst] 162

optician opticien *m* [ôptēsyeN] 37

oral surgeon chirurgien *m* dentiste [shērērzhē·eN däNtēst] 41

orange orange *f* [ôräNzh] 110; **~ juice** jus *m* d'orange [zhē dôräNzh] 112; **~ stick** cure-ongles *m* [kĕr-ôNg'əl] 141

orangeade orangeade *f* [ôräNzhäd] 112

orchestra orchestre *m* [ôrkest(ər)] 178; **~ seats** fauteuils *m/pl* d'orchestre [fôtä·ē dôrkest(ər)] 178

orchid orchidée *f* [ôrkĕdā] 130

order *(verb)* commander [kômäNdā] 115; **out of ~** ...ne marche pas [nə märsh pä] 23

organ orgue *m* [ôrg] 125

orthodontist (orthodonto-)stomatologiste *m* [(ôrtôdôNtō-)stōmätōlōzhēst] 174

orthopedist orthopédiste *m* [ôrtōpädēst] 162

otolaryngolist O.R.L. *m* [ō-är-el] 162

ouverture ouverture *f* [ōōvärtĕr] 178

overpass pont *m* [pôN] 65

oysters huîtres *f/pl* [ē·ēt(ər)] 102

P

pack; packet (petit) paquet *m* [(pətē) päkā] 126

package colis *m* [kôlē] 150

pad bloc *m* [blôk] 138; **scratch ~** bloc-notes *m* [blôk nôt] 138; **sketch ~** bloc à dessin [blôk ä deseN] 138

pail seau *m* [sō] 92

pain mal *m*; douleurs *f/pl* [mäl; dōōlär] 163, 171; **~ killer** remède *m* contre la douleur [rəmäd kôNt(ər) lä dōōlär] 173; **~ pills** comprimés *m/pl* contre la douleur [kôNprēmā kôNt(ər) lä dōōlär] 161

paint (verb) peindre [peNd(ər)] 119; **~ job** laque *m/f* [läk] 54

painter peintre *m* [peNt(ər)] 37

painting (noun) peinture *f* [peNtēr] 39

pair paire *f* [pär] 126

pajamas pyjama *m* [pēzhämä] 134

palace palais *m* [pälā] 119

palate palais *m* [pälā] 168

pale, light clair [klär] 127

pancreas pancréas *m* [päNkrā·äs] 168

panties slip *m* [slēp] 134

pants pantalon *m* [päNtälôN] 134; **~ suit** costume *m* [kôstēm] 134

paper papier *m* [päpyā] 132; **~-back** livre *m* de poche [lēv(ər) də pôsh] 130; **~ napkins** serviettes *f/pl* en papier [servyet äN päpyä] 144

papers papiers *m/pl* [päpyä] 78

paprika paprika *m* [päprēkä] 101

parallel bars barres *f/pl* parallèles [bär pärälāl] 188

paralysis paralysie *f* [pärälēzē] 171

parcel colis *m* [kôlē] 145; **small ~** petit colis [pətē kôlē] 150

pardon: Beg your ~ pardon [pärdôN] 20; 22

parents parents *m/pl* [päräN] 35

park (verb) stationner [stäsyônā] 43

park (noun) parc *m* [pärk] 122

parka anorak *m* [änôräk] 134

parking: no ~ stationnement *m* interdit [stäsyônmäN eNterdē] 42; **~ disc** disque *m* bleu [dēsk blā] 42; **~ lights** feux *m/pl* de position [fā də pôzēsyôN] 53; **~ lot** parking *m* [pärkēng] 42; **~ meter** parcomètre *m* [pärkômāt(ər)] 42; **~ space** box *m* [bôks] 44

parsley persil *m* [persēl] 101

part (stage) rôle *m* [rōl] 178

part raie *f* [rā] 157

part of town quartier *m* [kärtyā] 122

partridge perdrix *f* [perdrē] 105

party fête *f* [fāt] 183; **~ games** jeux *m/pl* de société [zhā də sôsē·ātā] 182

pass (mountain) col *m* [kôl] 42

pass (verb) passer [päsā] 99

pass (on the road) dépasser; doubler [dāpäsā; dōōblä] 43

passenger passager *m* [päsäzhā] 77; **~ car** voiture *f* particulière [vô·ätēr pärtēkēlyär] 40

passing: no ~ interdiction *f* de dépasser [eNterdēksyôN də dāpäsā] 42; **~ out** évanouissement *m* [āvänōō·ēsmäN] 171

passport passeport *m* [päspôr] 78; **~ control** contrôle *m* des passeports [kôNtrôl dā päspôr] 79

pastime passe-temps *m* [pästäN] 182

pastor curé *m*; pasteur *m* [kērā; pästär] 125

pastry chef pâtissier *m* [pätēsyā] 37

patch réparer [räpärā] 46

path chemin *m*; route *f* [shmeN; rōōt] 122; 19

patient malade *m* [mäläd] 172

patio cour *f* intérieure [kōōr eNtārē·är] 92

patterned imprimé [eNprēmā] 137

pawn *(chess)* pion *m* [pyôN] 181

pay *(verb)* payer [pāyā] 41; **I'd like to ~** l'addition, s.v.p. [lädēsyôN sēl vōō plā] 115; **~ out** payer; verser [pāyā; versā] 152

payment paiement *m* [pāmäN] 152

peas petits pois *m/pl* [pətē pô·ä] 108

peach pêche *f* [pāsh] 110

peanuts cacahouètes *f/pl* [kä-kä·ōō·et] 110

pear poire *f* [pô·är] 110

pearles perles *f/pl* [pärl] 133

pedal pédale *f* [pādäl] 54

pedestrian piéton *m* [pyätôN] 122; **~ crossing** passage *m* clouté [pä-säzh klōōtā] 122

pediatrician pédiatre *m* [pādē·ät(ər)] 162

pedicure pédicure *f* [pādēkēr] 156

pelvis bassin *m;* bas-ventre *m* [bä-seN; bäväNt(ər)] 168

pen: fountain ~ stylo *m* [stēlō] 138; **ballpoint ~** stylo *m* à bille [stēlō ä bē'ē] 138

penalty kick penalty *m* [pēnältē] 190

pencil crayon *m* [krāyôN] 138

pendant pendant *m* [päNdäN] 133

penis pénis *m* [pānēs] 168

pension pension *f* [päNsyôN] 81

people personnes *f/pl* [persôn] 41

pepper poivre *m* [pô·äv(ər)] 97; **~ mill** moulin *m* à poivre [mōōleN ä pô·äv(ər)] 97; **~ shaker** poivrier *m* [pô·ävrēyā] 97

peppermint menthe *f* [mäNt] 161

peppers poivrons *m/pl* [pô·ävrôN] 108

peptic ulcer ulcère *m* d'estomac [ēl-sär destōmä] 171

perch perche *f* [pärsh] 104

performance représentation *f* [re-präzäNtäsyôN] 176

perfume parfum *m* [pärfeN] 141

perhaps peut-être [pətät(ər)] 21

period époque *f* [āpôk] 119

permanent set permanente *f* [per-mänäN] 155

personal personnel [persônel] 80

petticoat jupon *m* [zhēpôN] 134

pharmacist pharmacien *m* [färmä-syeN] 37

pharmacy pharmacie *f* [färmäsē] 159; 39

pheasant faisan *m* [fāzäN] 105

phone *(verb)* téléphoner à [tālāfônä ä] 78

phone *(noun)* téléphone *m* [tālāfôn] 147; **~ book** annuaire *m* [änē·är] 147; **~ booth** cabine *f* téléphonique [käbēn tālāfônēk] 147; **~ call** coup *m* de téléphone [kōō də tālāfôn] 147; **pay ~** taxiphone *m* [täksēfôn] 148

photo shop magasin *m* de photo [mägäzeN də fôtō] 131

photographer photographe *m* [fôtō-gräf] 74

physics physique *f* [fēzēk] 39

pianist pianiste *m/f* [pē·änēst] 178

piano recital récital *m* de piano [rā-sētäl də pē·änō] 178

pick up venir chercher [vənēr shershā] 41

picture tableau *m;* image *f* [täblō; ēmäzh] 119; 144

picture film *m* [fēlm] 179

piece bout *m;* morceau *m* [bōō; môrsō] 57; 126

pier jetée *f* [zhetā] 77

pike-perch sandre *f* [säNd(ər)] 104

piles hémorroïdes *f/pl* [āmôrō·ēd] 171

pill pilule *f;* comprimé *m* [pēlēl; kôNprēmā] 161

pillar pilier *m* [pēlyā] 125

pillow oreiller *m* [ôrāyā] 87; **~-case**

taie f d'oreiller [tä dôräyā] 90
pilot commandant m de bord [kô-mäNdäN də bôr] 71
pin épingle f [āpeNg'əl] 136; **bobby pins** pinces f/pl à cheveux [peNs ä shevä] 140
pin up (hair) relever [rəlevā] 155
pincers tenailles f/pl [tenä'ē] 57
pinch serrer [serā] 139
pineapple ananas m [änänä] 110;
ping-pong: play ~ jouer au ping-pong [zhōō·ā ō pēngpôNg] 180
pink rose [rôz] 194
pinkie auriculaire m [ôrēkēlār] 167
pipe tuyau m [tē·ēyō] 54
pipe (tobacco) pipe f [pēp] 140; **~ cleaner** cure-pipe m [kér-pēp] 140
piston piston m [pēstôN] 54; **~ ring** segment m de piston [segmäN də pēstôN] 54
pitcher pichet m [pēchä] 97; **cream ~** pot m à lait [pôtä lä] 97
pity: what a ~ (quel) dommage [(käl) dômäzh] 22
place place f [pläs] 66; **~ of birth** lieu m de naissance [lēyə də nesäNs] 79; **~ of residence** domicile m [dômēsēl] 79
plaice plie f [plē] 104
plane avion m; appareil m [ävyôN; äpärä·ē] 68
plate plaque f [pläk] 174
plate assiette f [äsyet] 97; **bread ~** petite assiette f [pətēt äsyet] 97; **soup ~** assiette f à soupe [äsyet ä sōōp] 97
platform quai m; voie f [kä; vô·ä] 60
play (verb) jouer [zhōō·ā] 182
play (noun) pièce f (de théâtre) [pyäs (də tā·ät(ər))] 178
player joueur m [zhōō·ār] 190
playground terrain m de jeux [tereN dä zhä] 95
playing cards cartes f/pl à jouer

[kärt ä zhōō·ā] 144
playroom nurserie f [närsrē] 77
please s'il vous plaît [sēl vōō plä] 20
pleasure: with ~ avec plaisir [ävek plāzēr] 21
plenty assez [äsā] 127
pleurisy pleurésie f [plārāzē] 171
pliers pinces f/pl [peNs] 57
plug fiche f; prise f [fēsh; prēz] 92
plum prune f [prēn] 110
plumber plombier m [plôNbyā] 37
pneumonia pneumonie f [pnämōnē] 171
point point m [pô·eN] 188
poisoning empoisonnement m [äNpô·äzônmäN] 171
police police f [pôlēs] 49; **~ car** voiture f de police [vô·ätēr də pôlēs] 154; **~-man** agent m de police [äzhäN də pôlēs] 122; **~ station** commissariat m de police [kômēsärē·ä də pôlēs] 116
polish (verb) faire briller [fār brēyā] 156
political science sciences f/pl politiques [sē·äNs pôlētēk] 39
pool hall billard m [bēyär] 180
pork porc m [pôr] 105
port (land) port m [pôr] 77
port (side) bâbord m [bäbôr] 77; **~ fees** taxe f portuaire [täks pôrtē·ār] 77
portal portail m [pôrtä'ē] 125
porter porteur m [pôrtär] 64
portion plat m [plä] 115
possible possible [pôsēb'əl] 22
post office bureau m de poste [bērō də pôst] 116; **office box** boîte f postale [bô·ät pôstäl] 150
postage port m [pôr] 150
postal: ~ clerk employé m des postes [äNplô·äyā dā pôst] 150; **~ savings book** livret m de caisse d'épargne postale [lēvrä də kes

dāpärn(ə) pôstäl] 150; **~ transfer** mandat-poste *m* [mäNdä pôst] 146

postcard carte *f* postale [kärt pôstäl] 85; **picture ~** carte *f* postale illustrée [kärt pôstäl ēlēstrā] 150

postman facteur *m* [fäktăr] 150

pot pot *m* [pō] 92; **coffee ~** cafetière *f* [käfetyär] 97; **tea ~** théière *f* [tā·ēyär] 97

potatoes pommes *f/pl* de terre [pôm də tär] 108; **baked ~** pommes *f* de terre rôties au four [~ rôtē ō fōōr] 109; **boiled ~** pommes *f* nature [pôm nätēr] 109; **fried ~** pommes *f* sautées [pôm sōtā] 109; **mashed ~** pommes *f* mousseline [pôm mōōslēn] 109

pound livre *f* [lēv(ər)] 199

pouder poudre *f* [pōōd(ər)] 141; **~ puff** houppette *f* [ōōpet] 141

power station centrale *f* électrique [säNträl ālektrēk] 122; **~ steering** direction *f* assistée [dēreksyôN äsēstā] 54

practice entrainement *m* [äNtrānmäN] 188

prawns crevettes *f/pl* [krevet] 104

preach faire le sermon [fär lə sermóN] 123

precipitation chute *f* de pluie [shēt də plē·ē] 27

pregnancy grossesse *f* [grōses] 168

premium super [sēpär] 45

prepaid reply réponse *f* payée [rāpôNs pāyā] 147

prescribed prescrit [preskrē] 159

prescription ordonnnance *f* [ôrdônäNs] 159

present cadeau *m* [kädō] 80

press *(verb)* repasser [rəpäsā] 137

previously avant [äväN] 32

price prix *m* [prē] 92

priest prêtre *m* [prät(ər)] 123

print *(photo)* épreuve *f* [āprœv] 131

printed matter imprimé *m* [eNprēmā] 145

priority road route *f* à priorité [rōōt ä prē·ôrētā] 58

prison prison *f* [prēzôN] 154

probably probablement [prôbäb'əlmäN] 21

procession procession *f* [prôsesyôN] 125

producer producteur *m* [prôdēktär] 178

production production *f* [prôdēksyôN] 178

program programme *m* [prôgräm] 178

pronounce prononcer [prônôNsā] 24

prophylactics préservatifs *m/pl* [prāzervätēf] 141

Protestant protestant *m* [prôtestäN] 124

psychiatrist psychiatre *m* [psēkyät(ər)] 162

psychologist psychologue *m* [psēkôlôg] 162

psychology psychologie *f* [psēkôlozhē] 39

public: ~ garden parc *m* [pärk] 122; **~ notices** avis *m* au public [ävē ō pēblēk] 191; **~ rest room** toilettes *f/pl* publiques [tô·älet pēblēk] 122

pull *(tooth)* aracher [äräshā] 173

pulpit chaire *f* [shär] 125

pump room buvette *f* [bēvet] 175

pumpkin courge *f* [kōōrzh] 108

puncture trou *m* [trōō] 47

pupil élève *m* [ālāv] 37

purple pourpre *f* [pōōrp(ər)] 194

purse porte-monnaie *m* [pôrtmônā] 144

purser commissaire *m* [kômēsär] 74

push pousser [pōōsā] 191

Q

quai quai *m* [kā] 77

quail caille *f* [kä'ĕ] 105

quarter quart *m* [kär] 30

queen *(chess)* reine *f* [rān] 181

question: out of the ~ pas question [pä kestyôN] 21

quickly immédiatement [ēmädē·ät·mäN] 48

R

rabbi rabbin *m* [räbeN] 125

rabbit lapin *m* [läpeN] 105

race course *f* [kōōrs] 187; **~ car driver** coureur *m* automobile [kōōrâr ôtōmôbēl] 187

racing: ~ boat bateau *m* de course [bätō də kōōrs] 187; **~ car** voiture *f* de course [vô·ätẽr də kōōrs] 187

radiation therapy traitement *m* par les rayons [trätmäN pär lā rāyôN] 175

radiator radiateur *m* [rädē·ätẽr] 53; **~ grill** volet *m* du radiateur [vôlä dẽ rädē·ätẽr] 54

radio radio *f* [rädē·ō] 180; **~ play** pièce *f* radiophonique [pyäs rädē·ōfônēk] 182; **~ room** cabine *f* radio [käben rädē·ō] 74

rag chiffon *m* [shēfôN] 57

rail car automotrice *f* [ôtōmôtrēs] 60

railroad chemin *m* de fer [shəmeN də fâr] 67; **~ crossing** passage *m* à niveau [päsäzh ä nēvō] 42; **~ man** cheminot *m* [shəmēnō] 37; **~ station** gare *f* [gär] 67

rain *(noun)* pluie *f* [plē·ē] 25; **it's raining** il pleut [ēl plâ] 25

raincoat imperméable *m* [eNpermä·äb'əl] 134

raisins raisins *m/pl* secs [räzeN sek] 101

ranch wagon voiture *m* familiale [vô·ätẽr fämēlyäl] 40

rare *(meat)* saignant [senyäN] 100

rash éruption *f* [ārẽpsyôN] 171

raspberries framboises *f/pl* [fräNbô·äz] 110

rather: I'd ~ j'aimerais mieux [zhāmerâ myâ] 20

raw cru [krē] 100

razor rasoir *m* (mécanique) [räzō·är (mēkänēk)] 141; **safety ~** rasoir *m* de sûreté [räzō·är də sẽrtā] 141; **~ blades** lames *f/pl* de rasoir [läm də räzō·är] 141; **~ cut** coupe *f* au rasoir [kōōp ō räzō·är] 157

reading room salle *f* de lecture [säl də lektẽr] 74

ready prêt, -e [prā, prāt] 50

real estate agency agence *f* immobilière [äzhäNs ēmôbēlyär] 129

rear: at the ~ à l'arrière [ä läryär] 65; **~ end collision** téléscopage *m* [tālăskôpäzh] 49; **~ lights** feux *m/pl* arrières [fâ äryär] 53; **~ motor** moteur *m* à l'arrière [môtär ä l'äryär] 54; **~ view mirror** rétroviseur *m* [rātrōvēzär] 55

receipt quittance *f* [kētäNs] 150

recently l'autre jour [lōt(ər) zhōōr] 32

reception desk réception *f* [räsepsyôN] 92

recommend recommander [rekōmäNdā] 81

record disque *m* [dēsk] 130; **~ player** électrophone *m*; platine *f* [ălektrôfôn; plätēn] 182

recording tape bande *f* magnétique [bäNd mänyätēk] 182

recreation room salle *f* commune [säl kômẽn] 95

red rouge [rōōzh] 194; **~ cabbage** chou *m* rouge [shōō rōōzh] 108; **~ currants** groseilles *f/pl* [grōzā'ē] 110

reduced réduit [rādé·ē] 62; ~ **rate** réduction f [rādēksyŌN] 83

referee arbitre m [ärbēt(ər)] 189

refill remplir [räNplēr] 140

refreshments buvette f; bar m [bēvet; bär] 191

refrigerator réfrigérateur m [rāfrēzhārātär] 92

regards bon souvenir m [bŌN sōovenēr] 16

registered letter lettre f recommandée [let(ər) rekômäNdā] 16

registration immatriculation f [ēmätrēkēlāsyŌN] 43; ~ **form** fiche f d'hôtel [fēsh dôtel] 84

regret (noun) regret m [rəgrā] 22

regular (essence f) ordinaire f [(esäNs) ôrdēnār] 45

religion religion f [relēzhē·ŌN] 125

religious religieux [relēzhē·ā] 125

remedy remède m [rəmad] 70

renew renouveler [renŌovlā] 79

rent (noun) loyer m [lô·äyā] 92

rent (verb) louer [lōo·ā] 41

repair (verb) réparer [rāpärā] 46

repair (noun) réparation f [rāpäräsyŌN] 55; ~ **shop** atelier m de réparation [ätelyā də rāpäräsyŌN] 49

replace remplacer [räNpläsā] 138

reply (noun) réponse f [rāpôNs] 147

report déposer une plainte [dāpôzā ēn pleNt] 153

reservation réservation f [rāzervāsyŌN] 71

reserve réserver; retenir [rāzervā; retenēr] 62, 82; ~ **tank** bidon m de réserve [bēdôN də rāzerv] 45; ~ **wheel** roue f de secours [rōo də sekōor] 47

respiration respiration f [respēräsyŌN] 168

rest room toilettes f/pl [tô·älet] 60

result résultat m [rāzēltä] 188

retailer commerçant m [kômersäN] 37

retiree retraité m [retrātā] 37

retread rechaper [reshäpā] 46

return flight vol m de retour [vôl də retōōr] 71; ~ **postage** port m de retour [pôr də retōōr] 150

reverse gear marche f arrière [märsh äryār] 53

rheumatism rhumatisme m [rēmätēsm] 171

rhubarb rhubarbe f [rēbärb] 110

rib côte f [kōt] 168

ribbon ruban m [rēbäN] 136

rice riz m [rē] 109

ride (verb) rouler; monter à cheval [rōolā; môNtā ä shəväl] 66; 189

rider cavalier m [kävälyā] 189

riding équitation f [ākētäsyŌN] 189; ~ **stable** école f d'équitation [ākôl dākētäsyŌN] 180

rifle range (stand m de) tir m [(stäNd də) tēr] 188

right! c'est ça! [sā sä] 21

right à droite [ä drô·ät] 40; ~ **away** tout de suite [tōotsé·ēt] 96; ~ **of way** priorité f [prē·ôrētā] 43

ring bague f [bäg] 133; **wedding ~** alliance f [älyäNs] 133

rinse rinçage m [reNsäzh] 155

rise (verb) monter [môNtā] 25

river fleuve m [flāv] 70

road route f [rōot] 19; ~ **conditions** état m des routes [ätä dā rōot] 25; ~ **sign** panneau m de signalisation [pänō də sēnyälēzäsyŌN] 43

roast rôti m [rôtē] 107; ~ **chestnuts** marrons m/pl [märôN] 110

role rôle m [rôl] 178; **leading ~** premier rôle m [premyā rôl] 178

roll petit pain m [pətē peN] 98

roll rouleau m [rōolō] 126

Romanesque roman [rômäN] 125

roof capote f [käpôt] 55

room chambre f; [shäNb(ər) 82; **single** ~ chambre f pour une personne [shäNb(ər) pŌŌr ēn persôn] 82; **double** ~ chambre f à deux lits [shäNb(ər) ä dä lē] 82; **quiet** ~ chambre f calme [shäNb(ər) kälm] 82

root racine f [räsēn] 174; ~ **canal work** traitement m de la racine [trätmäN dəlä räsēn] 174

rope cordage m [kôrdäzh] 77

rose rose f [rōz] 130

rosemary romarin m [rōmäreN] 101

rough sea mer f agitée [mär äzhētä] 77

round rond [rôN] 156; ~ **trip** aller et retour [älä ä retŌŌr] 62; ~ **trip ticket** billet m circulaire [bēyä sērkēlär] 73

route route f; ligne f [rŌŌt; lēn(yə] 43; 59

row balcon m [bälkôN] 176

rowing aviron m [ävērôN] 189

rubber boots bottes f/pl de caoutchouc [bôt də kä·ōtshŌŌk] 139

ruby rubis m [rēbē] 133

rucksack sac m à dos [säk ä dō] 144

rudder rame f [räm] 77

ruin ruine f [rē·ēn] 122

rum rhum m [rôm] 112

run down (battery) est vide [ä vēd] 51

S

sacristan sacristain m [säkrēsteN] 125

sacristy sacristie f [säkrēstē] 125

saddle selle f [sel] 107

safety pin épingle f de sûreté [äpeNg'əl də sērtä] 136

sail (noun) voile f [vô·äl] 77

sail (verb) faire de la voile [fär dəlä vô·äl] 189; ~**-boat** bateau m à voiles [bätō ä vô·äl] 75

sailing voile f; yachting m [vô·äl; yōtēng] 189; ~ **school** école f de yachting [äkôl də yōtēng] 180

sailor matelot m [mätlō] 77

salesperson vendeur m; vendeuse f [väNdär; väNdäz] 37

saline content teneur f en sel [tenär äN sel] 186

salmon saumon m [sômôN] 104

salt sel m [sel] 97; ~ **shaker** salière f [sälyär] 97

salted, salty salé [sälä] 100

salve pommade f [pômäd] 161

sandals sandales f/pl [säNdäl] 139

sandpaper papier m verré [päpyä verä] 57

sanitary napkins serviettes f/pl hygiéniques [servyet ēzhē·änēk] 141

sapphire saphir m [säfēr] 133

Saturday samedi [sämdē] 33

sauce sauce f; jus m [sôs, zhē] 101

saucer soucoupe f [sŌŌkŌŌp] 97

sauerkraut choucroute f [shŌŌkrŌŌt] 108

sauna sauna m [sōnä] 175

sausage saucisse f [sôsēs] 98

savings book livret m d'épargne [lēvrä däpärn(yə)] 152

say dire [dēr] 24; ~ **what?** pardon? [pärdôN] 24

scalp massage massage m [mäsäzh] 157

scarf écharpe f [äshärp] 134

scarlet fever scarlatine f [skärlätēn] 171

scenery décors m/pl [däkôr] 178

scheduled flight vol m régulier [vôl rägēlyä] 71

scholar savant m [säväN] 37

school école f [äkôl] 38

sciatica sciatique f [sē·ätēk] 171

scientist savant m [säväN] 37

scissors ciseaux *m/pl* [sēzō] 136

screen écran *m* [ākräN] 179; **~ play** scénario *m* [sānārē·ō] 179

screw vis *f* [vēs] 55; **~ -driver** tournevis *m* [tōōrnvēs] 57

scuba diving plongée *f* sous-marine [plôNzhā sōōmärēn] 186; **~ equipment** équipement *m* de plongée sous-marine [äkēpmäN də plôNzhā sōōmärēn] 186

scull rame *f* [räm] 189

sculptor sculpteur *m* [skēltār] 37

sea mer *f* [mär] 77; **~ -sickness** mal *m* de mer [mäl də mär] 75

season saison *f* [sāzôN] 93

seasoned assaisonné [äsäzōnē] 100

seasoning épice *f* [āpēs] 101

seat siège *m* [syäzh] 55; **~ belt** ceinture *f* de sécurité [seNtēr də sākērētā] 55; **~ reservation** réservation *f* de place [rāzervāsyôN də pläs] 62; **have a ~** prenez place [prenā pläs] 16

second seconde *f* [segôNd] 32; **~ class** seconde *f* [segôNd] 62

secretary secrétaire *m/f* [sekrätār] 37

security valeur *f* [välär] 152

see voir; visiter [vô·är; vēzētā] 118; **~ you soon!** A bientôt! [ä byeNtō] 17

self-service libre service *m* [lēb(ər) servēs] 129

send envoyer [äNvô·äyā] 147

send *(luggage)* faire enregistrer [fār äNrezhēstrā] 63

sender expéditeur *m* [äkspādētär] 150

separately séparément [sāpärāmäN] 115

September septembre [septäNb(ər)] 33

serious grave [gräv] 165

service charge service *m* [servēs] 93; **~ station** station *f* service [stäsyôN servēs] 48

services service *m* religieux [servēs relēzhē·ā] 123

serving dish plat *m* [plä] 97

set designer décorateur *m* [dākôrätär] 178

setting lotion fixateur *m;* laque *f* [fēksätär; läk] 156

settings décors *m/pl* [dākôr] 178

seven sept [set] 28

sew (re)coudre [(rə)kōōd(ər)] 137

shame: What a ~ quel dommage [kel dômäzh] 22

shampoo shampooing *m* [shäNpô·eN] 141

shape forme *f* [fôrm] 127

shave of stock coupon *m* d'action [kōōpôN däksyôN] 152

sharp *(time)* précis [prāsē] 30

shave raser [räzā] 154

shaving: ~brush blaireau *m* [blārō] 141; **~ cream** crème *f* à raser [krām ä räzā] 142; **~ foam** mousse *f* à raser [mōōs ä räzā] 142; **~ soap** savon *m* à barbe [sävôN ä bärb] 142

shells, shellfish coquillages *m/pl* [kōkēyäzh] 186; 104

shin tibia *m* [tēbē·ä] 168

shining: is ~ brille [brē'ē] 26

ship bateau *m* [bätō] 72; **passenger ~** transatlantique *m* [träNsätläNtēk] 77; **~ -board party** fête *f* à bord [fāt ä bôr] 77

shipping: ~ agency agence *f* maritime [äzhäNs märētēm] 77; **~ company** compagnie *f* de navigation [kôNpänyē də nävēgäsyôN] 77

ship's doctor médecin *m* de bord [mādəseN də bôr] 77

shirt chemise *f* [shemēz] 135

shock choc *m* nerveux [shôk nervā] 171; **~ absorber** amortisseur *m* [ämôrtēsā̃r] 85

shoe chaussure f [shôsẽ̃r] 139; ~ **horn** chausse-pied m [shôs-pyä̃] 139; ~ **laces** lacets m/pl [läsä] 139; ~**-maker** cordonnier m [kôrdõnyä̃] 37

shoot tirer [tẽrä] 188

shop magasin m [mägäzeN] 122; **antique** ~ magasin m d'antiquités [mägäzeN däNtēkētä] 128; **barber** ~ coiffeur m [kô·äfẽ̃r] 128; **butcher** ~ boucherie f [bōōsherē] 128; **china** ~ magasin m de porcelaine [mägäzeN də pôrsəlen] 128; **cobbler** ~ cordonnerie f [kôrdônərē] 128; **dressmaker's** ~ tailleur m pour dames [täyä̃r pōōr däm] 128; **flower** ~ magasin m de fleurs [mägäzeN də flär] 128; **photo** ~ photographe m [fōtōgräf] 129; **tailor** ~ tailleur m [täyär] 129; **watchmaker's** ~ horlogerie f [ôrlôzhərē] 129; **wine** ~ marchand m de vin [märshäN də veN] 129

shopping mall centre m commercial [säNt(ər) kômersyäl] 122

shore rivage m [rēväzh] 77

short [kôr] 133; ~ **circuit** court-circuit m [kōōr-sẽrkē·ē] 55; ~**-sleeved** à manches f courtes [ä mäNsh kōōrt] 135; ~ **subject** court métrage m [kōōr mäträzh] 179; ~ **wave** onde f courte [ôNd kōōrt] 175

shorten raccourcir [räkōōrsẽ̃r] 137

shortly *(time)* peu; sous peu [pä; sōō pä] 31

shorts short m [shôrt] 135

shoulder épaule f [āpôl] 107

show montrer [môNträ] 83

shower *(rain)* averse f [ävers] 27

shrimps crevettes f/pl [krevet] 102

shuffle battre [bät(ər)] 181

shut fermer [fermä] 88

shutter obturateur m [ôbtẽrätã̃r] 132; ~ **release** déclencheur m [däkläNshä̃r] 132; **automatic** ~ déclencheur m automatique [däkläNshä̃r ôtōmätēk] 132

sick malade [mäläd] 12; **I feel** ~ j'ai mal au cœur [zhā mäl ō kä̃r] 70

side côté m [kôtä] 176; ~ **burns** favoris m/pl [fävôrē] 158; ~ **road** rue f secondaire [rē segôNdä̃r] 122; ~ **walk** trottoir m [trôtô·är] 43; ~ **wind** vent m latéral [väN lätäräl] 43

sights curiosités f/pl [kẽrē·ōzētä] 117

sightseeing visite f [vēzēt] 122

sign *(verb)* signer [sēnyä] 146; ~ **up** s'inscrire [seNskrẽr] 85

signature signature f [sēnyätẽr] 79

silk soie f naturelle [sô·ä nätẽrel] 137; **artificial** ~ soie f artificielle [sô·ä ärtēfēsē·el] 137; ~**thread** fil m (à coudre) [fēl ä kōōd(ər)] 136

silver argent m [ärzhäN] 133

silver *(adj.)* ~ **plated** argenté [ärzhäNtä]133, 194; ~**-ware** argenterie f [ärzhäNtərē] 97

since depuis [depē·ē] 32

sincere sincère [seNsär] 23

sinew tendon m [täNdôN] 168

singer chanteur m; cantatrice f [shäNtär; käNtätrēs] 178

singing chant m [shäN] 178

single célibataire [sälēbätä̃r] 79

sink lavabo m [läväbô] 93

sir monsieur m [məsyä] 13

sister sœur f [sär] 35; ~**-in-law** belle-sœur f [bel-sär] 35

size *(shoes)* pointure f [pô·eNtẽr] 139

skate patiner [pätēnä] 188

skater patineur m [pätēnä̃r] 188

skates patins *m/pl* [päteN] 188

ski *(noun)* ski *m* [skē] 189

ski *(verb)* faire du ski [fär dē skē] 189; ~ **binding** fixation *f* [fēksä-syôN] 189; ~ **jump** tremplin *m* (de saut) [träNpleN (də sō)] 189; ~ **lift** téléski *m* [tāläskē] 189; ~ **pants** pantalon *m* de ski [päNtälôN də skē] 135

skiing ski *m* [skē] 189

skin peau *f* [pō] 168; ~ **desease** maladie *f* de la peau [mälädē də lä pō] 171; ~ **lesion** égratignures *f/pl* [āgrätēnyēr] 171

skirt jupe *f* [zhēp] 135

skull crâne *m* [krän] 168

sky ciel *m* [syel] 26

slack peu serré [pẽ serā] 51

slacks pantalon *m* [päNtälôN] 135

sled luge *f* [lēzh] 144

sleep dormir [dôrmēr] 12

sleeper wagon-lit *m* [wägôN lē] 60; ~ **reservation** réservation *f* de wagon-lit [rāzervāsyôN də wägôN lē] 62

sleeping: ~ **bag** sac *m* de couchage [säk də kōōshäzh] 95; ~ **car** wagon-lit *m* [wägôN lē] 60; ~ **pill** somnifère *m* [sômnēfär] 173

slice tranche *f* [träNsh] 98

slide diapositive *f* [dē·äpôzētēv] 132; ~ **frame** petit cadre *m* pour diapositives [pətē käd(ər) pōōr dē·äpôzētēv] 132

sliding roof toit *m* ouvrant [tô·ä ōōvräN] 53

slip *(verb)* glisser [glēsä] 53

slippers pantoufles *f/pl* [päNtōōf'əl] 139

slippery road route *f* glissante [rōōt glēsäNt] 43

slow(ly) lentement [läNtəmäN] 24

slow *(clock)* retarder [retärdā] 31; ~ **down** ralentir [räläNtēr] 51

small petit [pətē] 127; ~**-pox** variole *f* [vär̃e·ôl] 78

smoke *(verb)* fumer [fēmä] 165

smoked fumé [fēmä] 100

smoking: no ~ non-fumeurs [nôN fēmär] 66

smuggling contrebande *f* [kôNtrə-bäNd] 154

snails escargots *m/pl* [eskärgō] 102

snapshot instantané *m* [eNstäNtä-nā] 132

sneakers chaussures *f/pl* de gymnastique [shōsẽr də zhēmnästēk] 139

snow *(noun)* neige *f* [nāzh] 27; ~ **chains** chaînes *f/pl* antidérapantes [shän äNtedäräpäNt] 52

snowing: it's ~ il neige [ēl nāzh] 27

soap savon *m* [sävôN] 78

soccer football *m;* [fōōtbôl] 189; ~ **field** terrain *m* de football [tereN də fōōtbôl] 186; ~ **game** match *m* de football [mätsh də fōōtbôl] 187; **play** ~ jouer au football [zhōō·ä ō fōōtbôl] 189

sociology sociologie *f* [sôsē·ôlôzhē] 39

socket prise *f* [prēz] 93; ~ **wrench** clé *f* anglaise [klā äNglāz] 57

socks chaussettes *f/pl* [shôset] 135

soft tendre [täNd(ər)] 100; ~ **drink** boisson *f* non-alcoolisée [bô·ä-sôN nôn-älkôlēzā] 112

solder souder [sōōdā] 55

sole semelle *f;* plante *f* du pied [semel; pläNt dē pyä] 139, 168; **leather** ~ semelle *f* de cuir [semel də kẽ·ēr] 139; **rubber** ~ semelle *f* de caoutchouc [semel də kä·ōtshōō] 139

sole *(fish)* sole *f* [sôl] 104

solid colar uni [ēnē] 137

somebody quelqu'un [kelkeN] 41

something quelque chose [kelkə-shôz] 183

.**sometimes** quelquefois [kelkəfô·ä] 32

son fils m [fēs] 14

song chanson f [shäNsôN] 178; **folk ~** chanson f populaire [shäNsôN pôpēlär] 178; **~ recital** récital m de chant [rāsētäl də shäN] 178

soon bientôt [byeNtô] 32

sore throat mal m de gorge [mäl də gôrzh] 171

sorry: I'm ~ Je regrette [zhə rəgret] 22; **I'm extremely ~** Je regrette infiniment [zhə rəgret eNfēnēmäN] 22

soup potage m [pôtäzh] 103

sour aigre [āg(ər)] 115

souvenir souvenir m [so͞ovənēr] 80

spa station f balnéaire [stäsyôN bäl-nä·är] 175

space place f [pläs] 44

spades pique m [pēk] 181

spare: ~ part pièce f de rechange [pyäs də reshäNzh] 55; **~ wheel** roue f de secours [ro͞o də səko͞or] 55

spark plug bougie f d'allumage [bo͞ozhē dälēmäzh] 55

speak to parler à [pärlā ä] 15

special spécial [spāsyäl] 46; **~ delivery** exprès [eksprā] 150; **~ issue stamp** timbre m d'émission spéciale [teNb(ər) dāmēsyôN spā-syäl] 150

specialist spécialiste m [spāsyälēst] 163

spectacles lunettes f/pl [lēnet] 138

speed limit limitation f de vitesse [lēmētäsyôN də vētes] 43

speedometer tachymètre m [täkē-mät(ər)] 55

spell épeler [āpəlā] 24

spice épice f [āpēs] 101

spinach épinards m/pl [āpēnär] 108

spinal cord moelle f épinière [mô·äl āpēnyär] 168

spine colonne f vertébrale [kôlôn vertābräl] 168

spleen rate f [rät] 168

spoke rayon m [rāyôN] 55

sponge éponge f [āpôNzh] 142

spoon cuiller f [kē·ēyär] 97; **tea-~** petite cuiller f [pətēt kē·ēyär] 97

sport shirt chemise f de sport [she-mēz də spôr] 135

sports sport m [spôr] 189; **~ event** manifestation f sportive [mänē-festäsyôN spôrtēv] 186; **~ fan** passionné m de sport [päsyônā də spôr] 190; **~-wear** vêtements m/pl de sport [vätmäN də spôr] 135

spot remover détachant m [dātä-shäN] 144

sprain se fouler qch. [sə fo͞olā] 164

sprain (noun) foulure f [fo͞olēr] 171

spring (techn. noun) ressort m [re-sôr] 55

spring (season) printemps m [preN-täN] 33

square place f; case f [pläs; cäz] 122; 181

square meter mètre m carré [mät(ər) kärā] 193

squash courge f [ko͞orzh] 108

stadium stade m [städ] 122

stage scène f [sän] 178; **~ director** metteur m en scène [metär äN sän] 178

stain tache f [täsh] 137

staircase escalier m [eskälyā] 93

stairwell cage f d'escalier [käzh deskälyā] 93

stake mise f [mēz] 181

stall (verb) caler [kälā] 54

stamp (noun) timbre-poste m [teNb(ər)-pôst] 150

stamp *(verb)* affranchier [äfränshēr] 150; ~ machine machine f à affranchir [mäshēn ä äfränshēr] 150

standard (oil) normale f [nôrmäl] 46

star étoile f [ātō·äl] 27; ~-board tribord m [trēbôr] 77

start commencer [kômäNsā] 176

starter démarreur m [dāmärär] 55

station gare f; arrêt m [gär; ärā] 67; 66

station *(broadc.)* station f [stäsyôN] 180; ~ master chef m de gare [shef dǝ gär] 67; ~ wagon voiture m familiale [vô·ätēr fämēlyäl] 40

statue statue f [stätē] 119

stay rester [restā] 78

steak bifteck m; entrecôte f [bēftek; äNt(ǝr)kôt] 106

steal, stolen voler, volé [vôlā, vôlā] 153

steamed étuvé [ātēvā] 100

steamer paquebot m [päkbô] 77

steep downgrade pente f [päNt] 43

steep upgrade côte f [kōt] 43

steering conduite f [kôNdē·ēt] 56; ~ wheel volant m [vôläN] 56

stern poupe f [pōōp] 77

stew pot-au-feu m [pôtôfā] 107

steward steward m [stōō·ärt] 77

stewed braisé [brāzā] 100

still encore [äNkôr] 31

stitch in the side point m de côté [pô·eN dǝ kôtā] 171

stock action f [äksyôN] 152

stockings bas m/pl [bä] 135

stole étole f [ātôl] 135

stomach pains maux m/pl d'estomac [mō destômä] 171

stop *(noun)* arrêt m [ärā] 59

stop *(verb)* s'arrêter [särātā] 66

stopover escale f [eskäl] 68

stopped up bouché [bōōshā] 88

stopping: no ~ arrêt interdit [ärā

eNterdē] 42

store magasin m [mägäzeN] 122; department ~ grand magasin m [gräN mägäzeN] 128; drug ~ droguerie f; pharmacie f [drôgerē; färmäsē] 128; grocery ~ épicerie f [āpēsǝrē] 128; liquor ~ vins et spiritueux m/pl [veN ā spērētē·ā] 129; stationery ~ papeterie f [päpätǝrē] 129; toy ~ magasin m de jouets [mägäzeN dǝ zhōō·ä] 129; ~ keeper propriétaire m de magasin [prôprē·ātär dǝ mägäzeN] 37

storm tempête f [täNpāt] 27

stove fourneau m [fōōrnō] 93

straight ahead tout droit [tōō drô·ä] 40

straighten out redresser [redrasā] 56

strait détroit m [dātrô·ä] 77

strand mèche f [māsh] 158

strawberries fraises f/pl [frāz] 110

street rue f [rē] 116

strict sévère [sāvār] 165

string ficelle f [fēsel] 57

stroke apoplexie f [äpôpleksē] 171

student étudiant m [ātēdyäN] 37

study *(verb)* étudier [ātēdyā] 38

stuff marchandise f [märshäNdēz] 127

stuffed farci [färsē] 100; ~ animal animal m en peluche [änēmäl äN pelēsh] 144

stuffing farce f [färs] 100

styptic pencil bâton m hémostatique [bätôN āmôstätēk] 161

subject matière f [mätyär] 39

subtitled sous-titré [sōō-tētrā] 179

suburb banlieue f [bäNlēyǝ] 123

suburban train train m de banlieue [treN dǝ bäNlēyǝ] 123

subway métro m [mātrō] 123

suddenly brusquement [brēskǝmäN] 54

248   **Dictionary**

suède daim *m* [deN] 139; ~ **coat** manteau *m* de chamois [mäNtô də shämô·ä] 135; ~ **jacket** blouson *m* de chamois [blōōzôN də shämô·ä] 135

sugar sucre *m* [sēk(ər)] 114; ~ **cube** ~ sucre *m* en morceaux [sēk(ər) äN môrsō] 114; ~ **bowl** sucrier *m* [sēkrēyā] 97

suit costume *m;* tailleur *m* [kôstēm; täyär] 135

suitcase valise *f* [välēz] 63

summer été *m* [ātā] 33; ~ **dress** robe *f* d'été [rôb dātā] 135

sun soleil *m* [sôlä·ē] 27; ~ **tan cream** crème *f* solaire [krām sôlär] 142; ~ **tan lotion** lotion *f* solaire [lôsyôN sôlär] 142

sunburn coup *m* de soleil [kōō də sôlä·ē] 171

sundae coupe *f* glacée [kōōp gläsā] 114

Sunday dimanche *m* [dēmäNsh] 33

sunglasses lunettes *f/pl* de soleil [lēnet də sôlä·ē] 138

sunlamp rayons *m/pl* ultraviolets [räyôN ēlträvē·ôlā] 175

sunrise lever *m* du soleil [levä dē sôlä·ē] 27

sunset coucher *m* du soleil [kōōshä dē sôlä·ē] 27

sunstroke insolation *f* [eNsôläsyôN] 171

super market supermarché *m* [sēpermärshā] 129

supplemental fare supplément *m* [sēplämäN] 62

suppository suppositoire *m* [sēpôzētô·är] 161

suppuration suppuration *f* [sēpērāsyôN] 171

surcharge: seasonal ~ taxe *f* saisonnière [täks säzônyär] 83

surgeon chirurgien *m* [shērēr-zhē·eN] 163

surgery: plastic ~ chirurgie *f* plastique [shērērzhē plästēk] 163

surroundings environs *m/pl* [äNvērôN] 123

suspenders jarretelles *f/pl* [zhärtel] 135

sweater pull(over) *m* [pēl(ôver)] 135

sweets bonbons *m/pl* [bôNbôN] 114

swelling enflure *f* [äNflēr] 171

swim nager; se baigner [näzhā; sə bänyā] 185

swimmer nageur [näzhär] 186

swimming natation *f* [nätäsyôN] 190; ~ **pier** passerelle *f* [päsərel] 186; ~ **area,** ~ **pool** piscine *f* [pēsēn] 122

swimsuit maillot *m* de bain [mäyô də beN] 135

Swiss Francs francs *m/pl* suisses [fräN sē·ēs] 152

switch *(noun)* commutateur *m* [kômētätär] 56

swollen enflé [äNflā] 164

sympathy sympathie *f* [seNpätē] 23

symphony concert concert *m* symphonique [kôNser seNfônēk] 178

synthetic thread fil *m* polyester [fēl pôlyester] 136

system time table indicateur *m;* Chaix *m* [eNdēkätär; shäks] 67

T

table table *f* [täb'əl] 93; ~ **tennis** ping-pong *m* [pēng-pôNg] 182

tablecloth nappe *f* [näp] 93

tablet comprimé *m* [kôNprēmā] 161

tailor tailleur *m* [täyär] 37

take prendre [präNd(ər)] 83; ~ **out** sortir [sôrtēr] 44; ~ **to** accompagner [äkôNpänyā] 17

taken réservé; pris [rāzervā; prē] 96

take-off départ *m* [dâpär] 71

talcum powder poudre *f* de talc [pōod(ər)] də tälk] 161

tampons tampons *m/pl* [täNpôN] 142

tangerine mandarine *f* [mäNdärēn] 110

tape ruban *m* [rēbäN] 136; **~ measure** centimètre *m* [säNtēmät(ər)] 136; **~ recorder** magnétophone *m* [mänyätôfôN] 182

target cible *f* [sēb¹əl] 189

tart tarte *f* [tärt] 114; **fruit ~** tarte *f* aux fruits [tärt ō frē·ē] 114

tartar tartre *m* [tärt(ər)] 174

taxi stand station *f* de taxis [stäsyôN də täksē] 116

tea thé *m* [tā] 98; **~ with lemon** thé *m* au citron [tā ō sētrôN] 98; **~ with milk** thé *m* au lait [tā ō lā] 98

teacher instituteur *m* [eNstētétär] 37

technical college école *f* supérieure technique [äkôl sēpâryär teknēk] 39

technician technicien *m* [teknē-syeN] 38

telegram télégramme *m* [tālāgräm] 147; **~ form** formule *f* de télégramme [fôrmēl də tālāgräm] 147

telegraphic télégraphique [tālāgrä-fēk] 152

telephone téléphone *m* [tālāfôN] 93; **pushbutton ~** téléphone *m* à touches [tālāfôN ä tōōsh] 150

television télévision ·*f* [tālāvēzyôN] 180; **~ play** jeu *m* télévisé [zhā tā-lāvēzā] 182

tell dire [dēr] 20

teller caissier *m* [kesyā] 152

temperature température *f* [täNpä-rätēr] 27; **~ chart** courbe *f* de température [kōōrb də täNpärä-tēr] 172

temple tempe *f; temple *m* [täNp;

tāNp¹əl] 168; 123

temporarily momentanément [mô-mäNtänämäN] 32

temporary provisoire [prôvēzô·är] 173

tender tendre [täNd(ər)] 100

tenderloin filet *m* [fēlā] 106

tendon tendon *m* [täNdôN] 168; **pulled ~** déchirement *m* des ten-dons [dāshērmäN dā täNdôN] 171

tennis tennis *m* [tenēs] 190; **play ~** jouer au tennis [zhōō·ā ō tenēs] 190; **~ ball** balle *f* de tennis [bäl də tenēs] 190; **~ court** court *m* de tennis [kōōr də tenēs] 190

tent tente *f* [täNt] 95

terrific! extra! [eksträ] 21

tetanus tétanos *m* [tātänôs] 172

thanks, thankyou merci [mersē] 21; **~ a lot** merci beaucoup [mersē bōkōō] 21; **~ very much** merci bien [mersē byeN] 21

thaw dégel *m* [dāzhel] 27; **it's thaw-ing** il dégèle [ēl dāzhel] 27

theatre théâtre *m* [tā·ät(ər)] 178; **~ schedule** affiche *f* de théâtre [äfēsh də tā·ät(ər)] 178

theft vol *m* [vôl] 153

there là [lä] 40

thermos bottle thermos *f* [termôs] 144

thermostat thermostat *m* [termôstä] 56

thief voleur *m* [vôlär] 154

thigh cuisse *f* [kē·ēs] 167

thimble dé *m* [dā] 136

third troisième [trô·äzyäm] 29

thorax thorax *m* [tôräks] 168

thread fil *m* (à coudre) [fēl ä kōōd(ər)] 136; **screw ~** filet *m* [fē-lā] 56

thriller roman *m* policier [rômäN pô-lesyā] 130

throat gorge *f* [gôrzh] 168

through car voiture f directe [vô·ä·tẽr dẽrekt] 61

throughway passage m [päsäzh] 123

throw up vomir [vōmẽr] 163

throw-in touche f [tōōsh] 190

thumb pouce m [pōōs] 167

thunder tonnerre m [tônär] 27

thunderstorm orage m [ôräzh] 27

Thursday jeudi m [zhẽdē] 33

thyme thym m [teN] 101

ticket ticket m; billet m [tēkā, bēyā] 59; **one-way ~** billet m aller [bēyā älä] 62; **round trip ~** (billet m) aller et retour [bēyā älä ä ratōōr] 62; **transfer ~** billet m de correspondance [bēyā da kôrespôNdäNs] 117; **~ sales** vente f de billets [väNt da bēyā] 178

tie cravate f [kräwät] 135

tight serré; étroit [serā; ātrô·ä] 51; 133

tighten serrer [serā] 55

tights collants m/pl [kôläN] 135

time temps m; heure f [täN; är] 15; 30; **what ~?** quand? [käN] 15; **any ~** à tout moment [ä tōō mô·mäN] 32; **on ~** à temps [ä täN] 32; **~ table** horaire m [ôrär] 60

tincture teinture f [teNtẽr] 161

tint colorer [kôlôrā] 158

tire pneu m [pnä] 47; **~ change** changement m de pneu [shäNzh·mäN da pnä] 47; **~ pressure** pression f des pneus [presyôN dā pnä] 47

tissues mouchoirs m/pl en papier [mōōshô·är äN päpyā] 142

to let à louer [ä lōō·ā] 191

toast toast m [tôst] 98

tobacco tabac m [täbä] 140

toboggan, ~ing luge f [lēzh] 190

today aujourd'hui [ōzhōōrdē·ē] 31

toe orteil m [ôrtä·ē] 168

toilet W.C. m [dōōblavä-sā] 82; **~ articles** articles m/pl de toilette [ärtēk'al da tô·älet] 142; **~ kit** nécessaire m de toilette [nāsesär da tô·älet] 142; **~ paper** papier m hygiénique [päpyā ēzhē·änēk] 142

tomato juice jus m de tomate [zhē da tômät] 112

tomb tombe f [tôNb] 123

tomorrow demain [dameN] 17; **the day after ~** après-demain [äprä-dameN] 31; **~ morning** demain matin [dameN mäteN] 31

tongue langue f [läNg] 168

tonic fortifiant m [fôrtēfyäN] 161; **~ water** eau f tonique [ō tônēk] 112

tonight cette nuit; ce soir [set nē·ē; sa sô·är] 31; 176

tonsilitis angine f [äNzhēn] 172

tonsils amygdales f/pl [ämēgdäl] 168

too aussi; trop [ôsē; trō] 47; 51

tool outil m [ōōtē] 57; **~ box, ~ kit** coffre m à outils [kôfrä ōōtē] 57

tooth dent f [däN] 168; **~ brush** brosse f à dents [brôs ä däN] 142; **~ paste** dentifrice m [däNtēfrēs] 142; **~ wisdom** dent f de sagesse [däN da säzhes] 174

toothache mal m aux dents [mäl ō däN] 174

toothpick cure-dent m [kẽr-däN] 97

top (car) capote f [käpôt] 56

topless sans soutien-gorge m [säN sōōtyeN-gôrzh] 185

touch: do not ~ prière de ne pas toucher [prē·är da na pä tōōshā] 191

tough coriace [kôryäs] 115

toupé postiche m [pôstēsh] 158

tour: guided ~ visite f guidée [vēzēt gēdā] 118; **~ guide's office** guide m [gēd] 74

tow remorquer [remôrkā] 48; **~ line**

câble *m* de remorquage [käb'əl də remôrkäzh] 49; ~ **truck** dépanneuse *f* [däpänäz] 49

towel serviette *f* [servyet] 142; **bath** ~ serviette *f* de bain [servyet də beN] 142

tower tour *f* [tōōr] 123

towing service service *m* de dépannage [servēs də däpänäzh] 49

town ville *f* [vēl] 40; **old** ~ vieille ville *f* [vyä·ē vēl] 121

toy jouet *m* [zhōō·ā] 144

track voie *f* [vô·ä] 67; ~ **and field** athlétisme *m* [ätlātēsm] 190; ~ **suit** survêtement *m* [sērvätmäN] 135

traffic circulation *f* [sērkēläsyôN] 43; ~ **light** feux *m/pl* [fä] 43; ~ **regulations** code *m* de la route [kôd də lä rōōt] 43

tragedy tragédie *f* [träzhädē] 178

trailer remorque *f* [remôrk] 41; caravane *f* [kärävän] 94

train train *m* [treN] 61

trainee apprenti *m* [äpräNtē] 38

tranquilizer calmant *m* [kälmäN] 161

transfer ticket *m* de correspondance [tēkā də kôrespôNdäNs] 59

transfer *(bank)* virement *m* [vērmäN] 152

translate traduire [trädē·ēr] 24

translation traduction *f* [trädēksyôN] 130

translator traducteur *m* [trädēktär] 38

transmission boîte *f* de vitesses [bô·ät də vētes] 56

travel agency agence *f* de voyage [äzhäNs də vô·äyäzh] 82

traveling voyager [vô·äyäzhā] 78; ~ **group** groupe *m* de voyage [grōōp də vô·äyäzh] 78

tray plateau *m* [plätō] 97

trick levée *f* [levā] 181

trim couper les pointes [kōōpā lā pô·eNt] 155

trip voyage *m* [vô·äyäzh] 43; **Have a good** ~ **!** Bon voyage! [bôN vô·äyäzh] 17

tripes tripes *f/pl* [trēp] 107

tripod pied *m* [pyä] 132

trotting race course *f* de trot attelé [kōōrs də trō ätlā] 189

troubles efforts *m/pl* [efôr] 21

trousers pantalon *m* [päNtälôN] 135

trout truite *f* [trē·et] 104

truck camion *m* [kämyôN] 41; ~ **driver** camionneur *m* [kämyônär] 38

trump atout *m* [ätōō] 181

trunk coffre *m* [kôf(ər)] 56

tube chambre *f* à air [shäNbrä är] 56

tube tube *m* [tēb] 126

tubeless sans chambre (à air); tubeless *m* [säN shäNb(ər) (ä är); tēbles] 47

tuberculosis tuberculose *f* [tēbärkēlōz] 172

Tuesday mardi *m* [märdē] 33

tug remorqueur *m* [remôrkär] 77

tulip tulipe *f* [tēlēp] 130

tumor tumeur *f* [tēmär] 172

tuna fish thon *m* [tôN] 104

turbot turbot *m* [tērbō] 104

turkey dinde *f* [deNd] 105

turn (re)tourner [(re)tōōrnā] 43

turn *(the car)* faire demi-tour [fär demē tōōr] 43; ~ **off** *(a road)* bifurquer [bēfērkā] 43; ~ **off** *(lights)* éteindre [āteNd(ər)] 182; ~ **on** allumer [älēmā] 182

tweezers pincettes *f/pl* [peNset] 142

two-piece deux-pièces *m* [dä-pyäs] 135

two-stroke motor moteur *m* (à) deux temps [môtär (ä) dá täN] 54

typewriter machine *f* à écrire [mäshēn ä äkrēr] 138; ~ **paper** papier *m* machine [päpyā mäshēn] 138

typhoid fever typhus *m* [tēfḗs] 172

U

ulcer ulcère *m* [élsār] 172
ultrasonics écographie *f* [ākôgrăfḗ] 175
umbrella parapluie *m* [părăplḗ-ē] 144
umpire arbitre *m* [ärbēt(ər)] 190
uncle oncle *m* [ôNk'əl] 35
under age mineur [mēnār] 34
underpants caleçon *m* [kälsôN] 135
underpass passage *m* souterrain [päsäzh sōōtereN] 65
undershirt *(men's)* gilet *m* du corps [zhēlä dē kôr] 135; *(women's)* chemise *f* [shəmēz] 135
understand comprendre [kôNpräNd(ər)] 185
undertow courant *m* [kōōräN] 185
underwear sous-vêtements *m/pl* [sōō-vātmäN] 135
undisturbed sans être dérangé [säNzät(ər) däräNzhā] 183
university université *f* [ēnēversētā] 38
unlock ouvrir [ōōvrēr] 92
unstamped non-affranchi [nôN äfräNshē] 150
until jusqu'à [zhēskä] 32
urine urine *f* [ērēn] 168
urinalysis analyse *f* d'urine [änälēz dērēn] 165
urologist urologue *m* [ērōlôg] 163
us nous [nōō] 87
usher ouvreuse *f* [ōōvrāz] 179
uterus utérus *m* [ētärēs] 168

V

vacant libre [lēb(ər)] 66
vaccinate vacciner [väksēnā] 164

vaccination vaccination *f* [väksēnä-syôN] 78
valerian drops gouttes *f/pl* de valé-riennes [gōōt də vălărē·en] 161
valid valable [väläb'əl] 62
valley vallée *f* [vălā] 123
valuables objets *m/pl* de valeur [ôb-zhā də välār] 84
value declaration valeur *f* déclarée [välār dāklärā] 150
valve soupape *f* [sōōpäp] 47
vanilla vanille *f* [vänē'ē] 101
vase vase *m* [väz] 130
veal veau *m* [vō] 105; **~ stew** blan-quette *f* de veau [bläNket də vō] 106
vegetable légumes *m/pl* [lägēm] 108; **~ market** marchand *m* de lé-gumes [märshäN də lāgēm] 129
vehicle véhicule *m* [vāhēkēl] 41
vein veine *f* [vān] 168
velvet velours *m* [vəlōōr] 137
veneral disease maladie *f* véné-rienne [mälädē vänärē·en] 172
venison chevreuil *m* [shevrā'ē] 105
ventilation aération *f* [ä·äräsyôN] 93
verdict jugement *m* [zhēzhmäN] 154
very beaucoup [bōkōō] 21
vest gilet *m* [zhēlä] 135
victory victoire *f* [vēktô·är] 188
video cassette cassette *f* vidéo [kä-set vēdā·ō] 144
view finder viseur *m* [vēzār] 132
village village *m* [vēläzh] 123
vinegar vinaigre *m* [vēnāg(ər)] 101
violets violettes *f/pl* [vē·ôlet] 130
violin recital récital *m* de violon [rā-sētäl də vē·ôlôN] 178
visit visiter [vēzētā] 78
visiting hours heures *f/pl* de visite [ār də vēzēt] 173
vitamin pills comprimés *m/pl* de vi-tamines [kôNprēmā də vētämēn] 161

vocational school centre *m* de formation professionnelle [säNt(ər) də fôrmäsyôN prôfesyônel] 39

voltage voltage *m* [vôltäzh] 75

volume volume *m* [vôlēm] 130

vomiting vomissement *m* [vômēsmäN] 172

voyage voyage *m* en bateau [vô·äyäzh äN bätô] 77

W

wafers gaufres *f/pl* [gôf(ər)] 114

wait attendre [ätäNd(ər)] 87

waiter serveur *m;* garçon *m* [servär; gärsôN] 38; 96

waiting room salle *f* d'attente [säl dätäNt] 69

waitress serveuse *f* [servâz] 38

wake réveiller [rāvāyā] 86

walking shoes souliers *m/pl* de marche [sōōlyä də märsh] 139

wall mur *m* [mēr] 93

wallet portefeuille *m* [pôrtfä'ē] 144

want, I ~ je veux [zhə vâ] 21

ward service *m* [servēs] 173

warm chaud [shō] 67

warning triangle triangle *m* avertisseur [trē·äNg'əl ävertēsär] 56

warship bâtiment *m* de guerre [bätēmäN də gär] 77

wash nettoyer; laver [netô·äyä; lävä] 47, 95; **~ cloth** gant *m* de toilette [gäN də tô·älet] 142; **~ room** lavabo *m* [läväbô] 94

washing line corde *f* à linge [kôrd ä leNzh] 144

watch montre *f* [môNt(ər)] 142; **pocket ~** montre *f* de poche [môNt(ər) də pôsh]; **wrist ~** montre-bracelet *f* [môNt(ər)-bräslä] 143; **~ band** bracelet *m* (pour montre) [bräslä pōōr môNt(ər)] 143

watchmaker horloger *m* [ôrlôzhā] 38

water eau *f* [ō] 45; **cooling ~** eau *f* du radiateur *f* [ō dē räde·ätär] 45; **soda ~** soda *m;* eau *f* de Seltz [sôdä; ō də sels] 112; **mineral ~** eau *f* minérale [ō mēnäräl] 112; **carbonated ~** eau *f* gazeuse [ō gäzäz] 112; **non-carbonated ~** eau *f* non-gazeuse [ō nôN-gäzäz] 112; **~ glass** verre *m* à eau [ver ä ō] 93; **with running ~** avec eau courante [ävek ō kōōräNt] 82; **~ skiing** ski *m* nautique [skē nôtēk] 185

waterfall cascade *f* [käskäd] 123

wave vague *f* [väg] 77

way, the right ~ la bonne direction [lä bôn dēreksyôN] 40; **by ~ of** passer par [päsä pär] 61; **no ~!** en aucun cas! [äNôkeN kä] 21

weather temps *m* [täN] 25; **~ prediction** prévisions *f/pl* météorologiques [prāvēzyôN mātā·ôrôlōzhēk] 27; **~report** météo *f* [mātä·ō] 25

wedding mariage *m* [märē·äzh] 123

Wednesday mercredi [märkrədē] 33

week semaine *f* [smen] 31

weekend week-end *m* [ōō·ēkend] 32

weekly toutes les semaines [tōōt lä smen] 32

welcome bienvenu, -e [byeNvenē] 12; **You're ~** Je vous en prie [zhə vōōzäN prē] 21

well bien [byeN] 12; **Get ~ soon!** Bon rétablissement! [bôN rätäblēs·mäN] 20; **~ done** bien cuit [byeN kōō·ē] 100

wet mouillé [mōōyä] 155

what? quoi? [kô·ä] 18; **~ for?** pourquoi? [pōōrkô·ä] 18 wheel roue f [rōō] 47

when? quand? [käN] 18

where? où? [ōō] 18; ~ from? d'où? [dōō] 18; ~ to? où? [ōō] 18; ~ is there…? où y a-t-il…? [ōō yätēl] 19

which? quel (-le)? [kel] 18

white blanc, blanche [bläN, bläNsh] 194

who? qui? [kē] 18

wholesaler grossiste m [grōsēst] 38

whom? qui? [kē] 18; to ~? à qui? [ä kē] 18; with ~ avec qui? [ävek kē] 18

whose is that? à qui est-ce? [ä kē es] 19

why? pourquoi? [pōōrkô·ä] 18

wide large [lärzh] 127

widowed veuf, veuve [vǎf, vǎv] 79

wife femme f [fäm] 13

wig perruque f [perěk] 156

win gagner [gänyā] 188

wind vent m [väN] 27

windbreaker anorak m [änôräk] 135

winding road route f en lacets [rōōt äN läsä] 43

window fenêtre f [fenät(ər)] 65; ~ seat coin-fenêtre m [kô·eN-fe-nät(ər)] 67

windshield pare-brise m [pär-brēz] 47; ~ wiper essuie-glace m [esē·ē-gläs] 55; ~ washer lave-vitre m [läv-vēt(ər)] 56

windy: it's ~ il fait du vent [ēl fä dē väN] 25

wine vin m [veN] 101; ~ list carte f des vins [kärt dā veN] 96; red ~ vin m rouge [veN rōōzh] 111; white ~ vin m blanc [veN bläN] 111

wing aile f [āl] 71

winter hiver m [ēvär] 33

wire fil m métallique [fēl mätälēk] 57

wire télégramme m [tālägräm] 147

wish (verb) souhaiter [sōō·etā] 20;

best wishes félicitations [fālēsē-täsyôN] 23

wisp mèche f [māsh] 158

withdraw résilier [rāzēlyā] 152

within dans [däN] 32

witness témoin m [tāmô·eN] 49

wood carving sculpture f en bois [skēltēr äN bô·ä] 144

wool laine f [len] 136

word mot m [mō] 24

work (verb) travailler; marcher [trä-väyā; märshā] 15; 23

work (noun) œuvre f [ǎv(ər)] 178

worker ouvrier m [ōōvrēyā] 38

working: not ~ right pas en bon état [päzäN bôN ätā] 50

worsted laine f peignée [len penyā] 137

wound plaie f [plā] 172; ~ salve pommade f cicatrisante [pômäd sēkätrēzäNt] 161

wrapping paper papier m d'emballage [päpyä däNbäläzh] 138

wrench clé f anglaise [klā äNglāz] 57

wrestle lutter [lētā] 190

wrestler lutteur m [lētār] 190

wrestling lutte f [lēt] 190

wrist poignet m [pô·änyā] 168

write down écrire [ākrēr] 24

writer écrivain m [ākrēveN] 38

writing paper papier m à lettre [pä-pyä ä let(ər)] 138

wrong faux, fausse [fō, fōs] 148

X

x-ray (noun) radiographie f [rädē·ō-gräfē] 173

x-ray (verb) radiographier [rädē·ō-gräfyā] 173

Y

yard un mètre (0,914 m) [eN mät(ər)] 126

year année f; an m [änā; äN] 32

yellow jaune [zhōn] 194

yes oui [ōō·ē] 21

yesterday hier [ē·är] 31

you vous; tu [vōō; tē] 12

young jeune [zhän] 34

younger plus jeune [plē zhän] 34

your votre; vos; ton, ta, tes [vôt(ər), vō; tôN, tä, tā] 12

youth group groupe m de jeunes [grōōp də zhän] 95

youth hostel auberge f de jeunesse [ōbärzh də zhänes] 95; ~ **card** carte f d'A.J. [kärt dä·zhē] 95

Z

zebra crossing passage m clouté [päsäzh klōōtā] 43

zero zéro [zārō] 28

zipper fermeture f éclair [fermetēr āklär] 136

zoo zoo m [zō] 119

zoology zoologie f [zō·ōlōzhē] 39

FRENCH WEIGHTS AND MEASURES

Linear Measures

km	kilomètre	=	1 000 m = 0.6214 mi.
m	mètre	=	1 m = 3.281 ft.
dm	décimètre	=	$^1/_{10}$ m = 3.937 ft.
cm	centimètre	=	$^1/_{100}$ m = 0.394 in.
mm	millimètre	=	$^1/_{1000}$ m = 0.039 in.
	mille marin	=	1 852 m = 6080 ft.

Square Measures

km²	kilomètre carré	=	1 000 000 m² = 0.3861 sq. mi.
m²	mètre carré	=	1 m² = 1.196 sq. yd.
dm²	décimètre carré	=	$^1/_{100}$ m² = 15.5 sq. in.
cm²	centimètre carré	=	$^1/_{10000}$ m² = 0.155 sq. in.
mm²	millimètre carré	=	$^1/_{1000000}$ m² = 0.002 sq. in.

Land Measures

ha	hectare	=	100 a or 10 000 m² = 2.471 acres
a	are	=	100 m² = 119.599 sq. yd.

Cubic Measures

m³	mètre cube	=	1 m³ = 35.32 cu. ft.
dm³	décimètre cube	=	$^1/_{1000}$ m³ = 61.023 cu. in.
cm³	centimètre cube	=	$^1/_{1000000}$ m³ = 0.061 cu. in.
mm³	millimètre cube	=	$^1/_{1000000000}$ m³ = 0.00006 cu. in.

Measures of Capacity

hl	hectolitre	=	100 l = 22.01 gals.
l	litre	=	1 l = 1.76 pt.
dl	décilitre	=	$^1/_{10}$ l = 0.176 pt.
cl	centilitre	=	$^1/_{100}$ l = 0.018 pt.
st	stère	=	1 m³ = 35.32 cu. ft. (of wood)

Weights

t	tonne	=	1 t or 1 000 kg = 19.68 cwt.
q	quintal	=	$^1/_{10}$ t or 100 kg = 1.968 cwt.
kg	kilogramme	=	1 000 g = 2.205 lb.
g	gramme	=	1 g = 15.432 gr.
mg	milligramme	=	$^1/_{1000}$ g = 0.015 gr.